Advance Praise for

THE WILL TO ARISE

"For those who are fascinated by that exciting phenomenon, the evolving Church in Africa (particularly South Africa), *The Will to Arise* will prove a very helpful guide."

Archbishop Desmond Tutu, Nobel Peace Prize Laureate

"Caleb Oluremi Oladipo's theological reflection on the demolition of apartheid documents how the contextualized Christian faith worked with non-Christian faiths in South Africa to bring about this demise. In his view, this colossal achievement bears testimony to the unintended spiritual, moral, and political time bomb impregnated in the gospel seed, planted by the missionaries, waiting to be detonated by historical events.

In the process of his reflection, Oladipo not only revives the controversial delicate act of theological balancing between exclusivism and inclusivism, but also raises questions on the appropriateness of the traditional concept of Christian conversion vis-à-vis what he calls 'transformation' or 'cross-fertilization.' These are foods for thought for theologians to chew on."

Reverend Professor Osadolor Imasogie,
President Emeritus, Nigerian Baptist Theological Seminary

"Although meant for the serious Christian theologian, educator, and practitioner, this book is surely a must for all the peoples of Africa and its Diaspora, and those everywhere who are privileged to be their neighbors. Forceful and nuanced, informed and informing, this book is a wake-up call to those who slumber at the portals of a world that has come of age again—a new world of floating pluralities, including religious ones. The challenge and clarion call of this book is to dream new dreams that take the African reality in that new world seriously."

Chirevo Victor Kwenda,
Department of Religious Studies, University of Cape Town

THE WILL TO ARISE

PETER LANG
New York • Washington, D.C./Baltimore • Bern
Frankfurt am Main • Berlin • Brussels • Vienna • Oxford

CALEB OLUREMI OLADIPO

THE WILL TO ARISE

Theological and Political Themes in African Christianity and the Renewal of Faith and Identity

PETER LANG
New York • Washington, D.C./Baltimore • Bern
Frankfurt am Main • Berlin • Brussels • Vienna • Oxford

Library of Congress Cataloging-in-Publication Data

Oladipo, Caleb Oluremi.
The will to arise: theological and political themes in African
Christianity and the renewal of faith and identity / Caleb Oladipo.
p. cm.
Includes bibliographical references and index.
1. Christianity and politics—South Africa—History.
2. South Africa—Church history. I. Title.
BR1450.O43   276.8—dc22   2005023207
ISBN 0-8204-6389-2

Bibliographic information published by **Die Deutsche Bibliothek**.
Die Deutsche Bibliothek lists this publication in the "Deutsche
Nationalbibliografie"; detailed bibliographic data is available
on the Internet at http://dnb.ddb.de/.

Cover design by Joni Holst

The paper in this book meets the guidelines for permanence and durability
of the Committee on Production Guidelines for Book Longevity
of the Council of Library Resources.

Affectionately dedicated to

Gbenga

Ení r'áya rere fé
Ó r'ójú rere l'ódò Olórun
(Proverbs 31:10-21)

Many women have done excellently,
But you surpass them all
(Proverbs 31:29)

and to

Christopher Taiwo
A true global citizen and a constant reminder
of the confluence of faith and knowledge

Caroline Kehinde
A remarkable human being and a bridge
of intergenerational faith and identity

Clement Olu-Ayo
An independent thinker and active gatekeeper
of our shared faith and African roots

In honor of my two fathers

Benjamin A. Oladipo

and

Josiah A. Oladipo

Two brothers who taught me the ABC's of Christian
theology

� TABLE OF CONTENTS

PREFACE

One of the most urgent matters in the life of the Church and religious communities worldwide today is addressing what religions are doing to the followers. Religions are reducing the devotees to communities that seek and abuse worldly powers. Even the Church with an honorable historical identity as a reconciling community, is not entirely blameless. The Church is also becoming a religious community that is tainted with worldly powers.

In South Africa, for example, the Church was in captivity under apartheid, and the unjust social structures were reinforced and legitimated under the banner of Christianity. One should be concerned, therefore, about what Christian leaders have done and continue to do to the Christian faith. I have stressed this point in view of the exaggerated image of a Christian West ever seeking to expand Christian dominion over unsuspecting "pagan" world of Africa. Not all what happened in South Africa was God-honoring. At the same time, the constructive roles of mission in Africa cannot be ignored.

What is clear is that the Christian faith has renewed its destiny in South Africa, providing an opportunity for a society fractured by the racist ideology of apartheid to come together. In this sense, the Christian faith has become a cementing factor in the post-apartheid era. The question raised in this book is fundamental. "What can Christians worldwide learn from the African Christian experience?"

The tremendous growth of the Church in Africa in the last century was astounding, and some scholars in the West have stated that Black Africa can no longer be conceived apart from Christianity.[1] One can also say, however, that Christianity in the world can no longer be conceived apart from the African experience. In 1900, for example, it was estimated that there were 8,756,000 million Christians in Africa or approximately 1.568 percent of the total population of Christians worldwide. In 2005, African Christians grew to 389,304,000 or approximately 18.5 percent of the total population of Christians in the world. With an increase of over 4,000 percent in the last century, and an annual growth rate of 2.48 percent, Africa is one of the fastest growing Christian continents in the world today.

Little in this world unfolds exactly as we have predicted, but my best prognosis for the rapid expansion of Christianity in Africa is that the faith will continue to have significant implications for the wider picture of Christianity worldwide, and this will enhance the international image of the African peoples. Africa will not only be one of the spiritual centers of Christianity by the middle of this century, but millions of Christians in the world will also begin to see themselves as belonging to the African Christian world. Thus, Africans in the Diaspora will be identified not only with the physical characteristics of Africa, but also, and for the first time, in connection with the manifested African Christian identity.

I have explored in the book the theological and political themes of Christianity in post-apartheid era with a broader appeal aimed at promoting faith and Christian identity in the Western world. It is firm in my mind that something genuinely transformational is slowly emerging and the old structures and centers of Christianity would embrace new identity with African particularities.

One of the first lessons I learned at the University of Cape Town in 2003 was that the temple of privileges for the few was becoming a shrine of equality for all. I met Zimbabweans and Nigerians serving as heads of department at major South African universities, working collegially with the descendants of the Dutch in South Africa. I also met Afrikaners serving as heads of the department at Technikons with Indians, Coloured (South African citizens classified under apartheid as of mixed blood types or races), and Zulus as colleagues. Any one who was in South Africa in March 1960 and witnessed the Sharpeville massacre on the 21st of that month, or read about the events of June 16, 1976 in Soweto, would know that South Africa of today is different. The country is quickly becoming a beacon of hope, of which all Africans should be proud. The roles that both Christian and non-Christian communities played in securing a new path without a civil war were enormous.

The history and destiny of South Africa would remember the Most Reverend Desmond Tutu, the retired Anglican Archbishop of Cape Town, for his unwavering dedication to his people, his steadfast faith in God, his courage in the midst of endless opposition, his tenderness in the ministry, his wisdom in difficult times, and his exuberant joy that signaled hope for all South Africans.

Some of my friends who witnessed the events in the twin decades of 1960s and '70s shed tears of thanksgiving in the decades that followed. They expressed their moments of unexpected joy and sorrow during the struggles that led to the end of apartheid in 1994. Their tears of joy saturated their personal stories during my interviews and meetings in South Africa. The South Africa of 2003 that I saw firsthand was better than the South Africa of the 1960s and '70s that I read about. As the wounds of the past continue to heal, both individually and collectively, and as those wounds are shared through the platform of discussions provided by religious communities, especially the Church, the South Africa of the future would be better than the South Africa of today.

My confidence for African unity was stronger when I met many Zulus who, naturally, addressed me in their mother tongues, although I am not a native South African. I was also impressed when an Afrikaner at the University of Cape Town corrected me by giving in full a West African name I shortened. All these are a mark of the anticipated unity and progress of the future.

On the way to the upper campus of the University of Cape Town from my Kopano residence, there is a tunnel with an inscription that reads: "until the philosophy which holds one race superior and another inferior is finally and permanently discredited and abandoned." At the Chancellor Oppenheimer Library were Indian, Coloured, Black, and White students, working together in an atmosphere of genuine intellectual freedom. Young boys and girls in their school uniforms walked to school every morning, Indian boys holding the hands of Coloured girls, and White boys holding the hands of Black girls as they crossed the busy streets of Cape Town together. South Africa was "free at last" from the shackles of apartheid and the affliction of contemptuous racial oppression. Everyone at the cafeteria and in the classrooms seemed to be saying without altering a word: "We can feel it now! The continent is truly our home!" It was also as if God was saying to South Africans: "All is now forgiven."

Although the focus of this book is the theological and political themes in post-apartheid Christianity, and the roles of the Church—Protestant and Roman Catholic, the Reformed tradition as well as the free and Evangelical Church—in rebuilding South African society, a comparative volume on the roles of the non-Christian communities in rebuilding post-apartheid South African society would also benefit interested readers.

The modern world witnessed the beginning of a global de-racialization of civil society and an unexpected result of political sagacity in 1994 when South Africans elected Nelson Mandela their first true democratic president after a long and sustained struggle for freedom for all South Africans. A cultivated legal mind, Mandela has a sense of culture and moral courage that transcended any political ambition or adventure. Courage disdained fame for

Mandela, but wins it. All South Africans are grateful to him today for craft-ing a new democratic dispensation with grace and magnanimity.

God can and will continue to bring good out of evil, and the Christian communities prayed and offered the world a rare gift of hope and a new be-ginning. Thus, out of the evil of apartheid, God used men and women, young and old, Christians and non-Christians, who were willing to give and spend their all, and make the best use of every opportunity. One of the greatest les-sons one must learn about the characters of Christianity in Africa today is in the number of elevated minds the Church has produced who are lifting up the continent, positing the spiritual authority of their fellow believers. Africa has always produced brilliant scholars and respected Church leaders from the days of antiquity. The modern era is not an exception, but the humiliation that Africans suffered because of slavery, colonialism, and apartheid, made it relatively difficult for contemporary religious communities to recognize Af-rican Christian scholars and take them seriously. This has started to change in post-apartheid era.

Religious leaders in Africa are now calling the West to transcend its modern history so that it does not rest its oars on its missionary-sending status. African Christians are bold in their opposition to certain practices of the Church in the West, a sign that the Church in Africa has graduated from infancy. Churchmen and Churchwomen all over Africa often take a strong stance against lifestyles they consider inconsistent with ancient values of Christianity. Perhaps, they do not see themselves as detached from the bibli-cal world, but as its extension. By elevating certain ancient values, such as a strong opposition against sodomy and an extensive use of the Bible, to guide Christian's daily living, the Church in Africa is now testing the youth of modernity. The Church in the Western world can no longer look at the Afri-can Church with an eye of the expansion of its religious and political values.

It is often easier to write about what the Church has failed to do in criti-cal times than to write about the positive contributions of the Church during moments of national and international crises. Those who belong to the Church tradition and who train ministers at seminaries and theological insti-tutions at these formative years of a young century, know how difficult it is to provide a list of the Church accomplishments to students—and those who would interpret mainstream Christianity for our time—and what the Church has done to combat injustice, oppression, poverty, racism, sexism, neo-colonialism, and the aggression of imperialism and military masculinity. Of-ten, younger generations are put off by these social evils. Yet one is aware of the silence of the Church during World War I, World War II, Nazism, apart-heid, and the Rwanda-Burundi genocide. In not too distant past, the world saw Bosnia, the Middle East, and the Kashmir as human lives were wasted.

Examples are many of orgiastic violence in virtually all the continents of the world.

Yet there are many reasons for a collective action—the location, the character, the scale of callousness, and the circumstances of brutality. These factors often coincide for a collective action of the Church, but the Church has consistently remained silent in the face of these societal evils. There are both ideological and theological excuses for the collective inaction of the Church in the past. This collective withdrawal only hardened apathy and callous indifference. Never has the Church become so reduced to the periphery despite the amount of resources we have to act in the name of God.

The new Church slowly emerging in Africa is different, and South Africa is leading the way with a new proclamation that the Church is indeed the light of the world.

Churches in South Africa are not completely disconnected with the Church denominations in the West. This is partly because the historical origins of the Church in South Africa can be traced to the Churches in European countries that sent missionaries to evangelize South Africans as early as 1488. Yet the South African Church today has branched off in substantial ways because the contexts are now different, and so is the proclamation of the Church.

When compared with the Church and denominational activities in the Western world, there are certain core differences and uniqueness one would need to associate with Christianity in South Africa; a thoughtful reflection upon the similarities and differences can help us to understand our mutual interdependence in the new Christian world order.

The Church in South Africa is intimately involved in the existential condition of the people she serves. Mutual caring among Christians characterizes the Pentecostal and Charismatic Churches in South Africa. This has pushed the mainline Churches almost to the periphery of the Christian denominational life. The apartheid years meant that Churches were against one another. There were Churches on the opposing sides of the struggle, and the wounds that Christians and non-Christians sustained in the struggle against apartheid were deep. The Church was not only against the Church, however, because there was also unresolved tension and animosity between Churches of different denominations and within a particular Christian denomination. The Church was also against the Church in biblical translation. Some Churches saw racial segregation as biblically sound, arguing that the story of God's creation in Genesis was about separation. The creation story is about sobriety and differentiation. The undifferentiated, they argued, was uncreated. In God's unity there is also differentiation and this suggests discrimination. Thus, separation has its usefulness in the creation story and a life without appropriate differentiation is not a life created by God. Naming represents bodies that God gives to the eternal realities when they were created. Like all physical bodies, they are ephemeral and will soon vanish away. What is more important is that in creation story one sees that physical bodies have fixed archetypes in God. The major difficulty in the categorization of separation in the creation story is that our interpretation cannot be God's interpretation because human beings do not fully know the names of the physical bodies as God intended and taught them to Adam. Perceiving Physical bodies as God sees them can only be achieved by loving the way God loves. Therefore, the names that apartheid invented, such as Blacks, Coloured, Indian or Afrikaners will ultimately perish hopelessly.

Other Churches, however, saw racial segregation as against biblical principles. Thus, while certain Church members saw racial segregation as pragmatically necessary, the majority saw it as unthinkable in the Christian context of brotherly love. How ordinary South African Christians dealt with this discomfort was significant in the process of healing and reconciliation.

Christians also gave indigenous definitions to their faith and crafted their vision for the future in ways that were consistent with African vitality and inner spiritual strength. There is no doubt that what keeps these ordinary South Africans awake at night and wakes them up early in the morning (without the aid of alarm clocks) is their sense of faith, hope, and courage; faith that God is just, hope that the future will be better than the past, and courage to see that things do not remain the way they have been.

While mainline Churches are still preoccupied with Christian doctrines, and what kind of spiritual formation the Church should adopt, Churches in South Africa are laying emphasis on what their religions say about the poor condition of the people. Therefore, they are more concerned about the lives of ordinary South Africans, and how to mend the lives that have been twisted by oppression and the injustice associated with apartheid.

South Africans have always been connected to the Church. But the apartheid years taught them not to trust human institutions, including "churchly" institutions. Christians in South Africa have been shaped and shaken by the boundaries such institutions have erected both for them and for those they love.

Thus, when young believers moved away from their patrimonial Church, it was not because of asylum or as a voluntary exile. It was not because of a lack of loyalty or because of disaffection for the Church. Quite the contrary, it was primarily because of their love for the universal, for the "big" picture, and for the total Gospel, which is radically transparent. They had a desire to experience the God who is incomprehensible, but who has embodied divinity in a particular person (Jesus of Nazareth), so that they may know the eternal one that is difficult for them to understand under the clouds of injustice of apartheid.

The mystery of the knowledge of God has always fascinated Christians worldwide. South African Christians are particularly interested to know how all these pieces of the Church of Jesus Christ fit together. How can Church members participate in politics meaningfully? Why do Church members preach love on the one hand, and encourage political policies that endorse oppression and hatred on the other?

Christians in South Africa have been involved in theological quests for a long time. But they have been naïve about the Church inner mechanics and, perhaps, ignorant of its internal polity. Thus, opportunistic politicians exploited the Dutch Reformed Church in South Africa to support apartheid on controversial theological grounds. But it is in the faces of human beings that South Africans encountered the God who was made known in the life of Jesus of Nazareth.

African Christians have persistently lifted others to the forefront, and they have consistently applauded the accomplishments of Europeans, affirming the dignity of humanity and nurturing God's endless creativity. Their humility, however, is not a self-deprecation. Christians in South Africa have been nose to nose with the framers of apartheid from the beginning. They knew that the integrity of their humanity in God's image was at stake. Like Jesus, South African Christians are often strong campaigners for human dignity. They are tough negotiators and tenacious leaders who are no novice in defending justice. Like Jesus who tackled the Pharisees, the Sadducees, and the Judges, so did South African Church leaders. They tackled the State-sponsored oppression, the secular establishment, and the status quo. South African Church leaders did this with unparalleled effectiveness in the decades of the 1980s and 1990s by speaking out publicly against racism, discrimination, and economic injustice all over the world, and challenging the legalistic rules of apartheid so that South Africa can be healed of its wounds.

The pages of this book would not show their faces or project their voices, but will tell about their collective stories and individual struggles. Several South Africans have been on the frontline, putting their lives in danger and assuming the roles of Christ.

In the process of fighting against injustice, they also discovered their authentic Africanness. Thus, South African Christians have the responsibility to posit the moral, spiritual and theological authority of their faith. This authority was acquired through the agony of half a century of oppression, and they are now calling contemporary believers to re-examine their own faith and Christian identity with honesty.

The lives of South African Christians have been and continue to be unsettling, uncomfortable, unsatisfying, demanding, restless, and, sometimes, humiliating. It would have been much easier for the brave men of South Africa to stay in their villages, rearing cattle, tending the garden, and planting onions and tomatoes; and for the courageous women to stay out of politics and be selling chickens and eggs to raise their beautiful children. But when all is said and done, South Africans have assumed, with gratitude, the pain that God must have suffered when the children created in God's image were brutally tortured and murdered by the state.

There is no doubt that South African Christian life has become a part of God's vision for the redemption of all humanity. Christians seem to recognize that the authentic Christian life does not depend on clinging to ideological differences.

The challenges to non-South African Christians are simply this: How many of us knew that the Church in South Africa was prepared in 1994 to pray for a miracle where it was least expected? How many of us knew that the Church in South Africa was capable of dealing with the crises at hand and so to represent the image of Christ so transparently to the world? How many can say with confidence that there would be no bloodshed in South Africa before the transition from apartheid to a full democracy? How many of us could have endured the pains South Africans suffered in order to proclaim that all South Africans were created in God's image? How many believed that their internal and external struggles would retrospectively show that God was not only alive but also active? How many of us knew that the Church in the Southern part of the African continent may not have sufficient theological training to carry them through the next day of academic debates, but they were determined to stand up for Christ and share their transparent spirituality with the world when it really mattered? How many Christians in the Western world today are willing to accept the leadership of their Christian brothers and sisters in Africa, and elsewhere, to proclaim the liberty year of the Lord? How many Churches in the Western world would not be resistant to African leadership?

In the seventeenth and eighteenth centuries, Africa was a fertile mission field. But Christians on the continent are now poised to sending missionaries to transform the West and to tell Christians about God's love for the world. How many of us would be willing to accept that the Church in the West has not only conquered but has also surrendered to the Church in the non-Western world? How many of us would accept that the West is also a mission field? If the Christian world map has been re-drawn to incorporate African Christians, how many are ready to accept the new Christian World map with Africans as leaders?

In the final analysis, how many Churches in the West are now ready to put the Gospel above politics so that the Church can regain its relevance in what matters in the world? And how many of us are prepared to accept non-white Christians to lead the way?

It was not the Church as an institution per se that bothered South Africans, for this was unavoidable. It was not even the labeling of fundamentalism or liberalism in the Western theological discuss that they found frustrating. What they found distasteful was the intellectual arrogance and the self-righteousness and the apparent self-sufficiency of the West in the years of the struggle against injustice. They knew that they would not be politically or economically free until they gained spiritual freedom.

The fundamentalist's claim to know exactly the changes in the society that mattered most to God, and where God stood on every ethical and social issue, is profoundly disturbing. It was as if those who formulated the policies of apartheid in South Africa were not making the same claim that God was on their side. Their rhetoric was nothing but a noisy gong that stood in the way of any serious and useful thought. Their theological thoughts often looked suspicious and more like a slogan for political action.

The liberals, on the other hand, added to the frustration of South African Christians during the years of struggle by thinking that God's kingdom ought to wait.

No one knew who God will count "in" or "out" and the liberal thinking that God values them against the fundamentalist, and that God's kingdom will not come if they said they were not ready, was seen to be profoundly ludicrous. They often denied the essential renewal that the Church desperately needed. Their intellectual curiosity has not only been misdirected, but has also become an excuse for a lack of justifiable action. These artificial categories (fundamentalism and liberalism) were alien to South African Christianity and they did not accurately describe many of the Church members in South Africa who were struggling for justice.

South African Christians know a lot about Jesus and they have a good idea of his ministry and message themes—faith, hope, and courage.

South African Christians also know that through Jesus God acted directly and decisively. His own mission, therefore, was all what mattered, and the most important thing that people could do that really counted was to follow him and live according to his teachings. Other matters were not as important, and he himself did not say that religious demands of his day were not valid. What reduced everything to the lowest edge for men and women, however, was that God loves them and that God acted decisively and definitely through Jesus of Nazareth to demonstrate his love for the world.

So South African Christians know who Jesus was, what he did, what he taught, and why he died. They also know, most importantly, that he inspired his followers who were so loyal to him that they were prepared to die than deny him. It is they who changed the course of history by proclaiming the credibility of his life and message. This is what modern South African Christians are trying to practice—the love of God through Jesus Christ.

In my view, the Church in South Africa is now trying to reconstruct the historical burden of the past as a way of liberating the Church. Through faith and fear, and despite what the Church has suffered under apartheid, the Church still has more to give. Although the most obvious corporate victory in South Africa is the dismantling of apartheid, our collective responsibilities to rebuild the country have only begun.

The Church in South Africa also takes seriously the foundation of the Church—Jesus Christ. Therefore, the African Church has an unbelievable capacity for renewal. To quote Leander Keck: "It would be gross faithlessness to assume that the Christian faith, itself repeatedly renewed by the gospel, now lacks the capacity to renew the churches—as if our situation were more effective in draining off the vitality of the faith than that of our predecessors."[2]

Perhaps, the African Church of the future would have to redefine its identity. This would require ecclesiastical boldness because new paths always create tension among Christians, for it is so difficult to abandon the doctrinal certainties of the past. One of the ways to do this would be to replace the face of a white Jesus on the cross, which Emperor Constantine popularized in 321 C.E. when he declared Sunday a weekly holiday,[3] with an empty tomb with a rainbow. This would partly help the Church of this generation to regain its confidence.

South African Christians would readily understand this new imaginary symbol since they have suffered much in the past under the white rule that tainted them as evil because they looked different. Perhaps this change will not be complete in this generation or in our lifetime, nor will it be complete in this millennium. This change, however, has already begun in Africa, Asia, and South America.

Notes

[1] See Barrett, David B. and Todd M. Johnson, "Annual Statistical Table on Global Mission: 2004" in *International Bulletin of Missionary Research,* 28: (2001): 24–25.

[2] Leander E. Keck, *The Church Confident: Christianity can repent, but it must not Whimper* (Nashville, Tennessee: Abingdon Press, 1993), 19.

[3] M. Thomas Thangaraj, *The Common Task: A Theology of Christian Mission* (Nashville, Tennessee: Abingdon Press, 1999), 107.

ACKNOWLEDGMENTS

The *Will to Arise* is much more than the work of its author. There are many scholars both in South Africa and in the United States whose contributions I cannot estimate, and without them the book would not have been completed.

I am indebted, first, to my students and colleagues at the Baptist Theological Seminary at Richmond for their encouragements during the early stages of my writings. In South Africa, my colleagues and friends at the University of Cape Town are numerous, and they assisted me to gather resource materials during the early stages. I enjoyed the support of the head of the department of Religious Studies, Chirevo V. Kwenda, and the faculty. John W. de Gruchy, James Cochrane, Brenda Cooper, and Harry Garuba were my closest friends and they have been important authorities in the research areas that interested me. They also welcomed me with South African hospitality and they were much better prepared than I was in the analysis of the Church in post-apartheid South Africa. Fortunately for me, many of my friends in South Africa have also written extensively on similar academic fields and they were of tremendous assistance in the research that stood behind this book.

Gary Ross, William Wagner, and Edgar Carolissen made their homes available for me, and I will always be grateful for their friendship.

I am grateful to *Worldmark Encyclopedia of Religious Practices* and its editorial staff for the permission to include in chapter three of this book, in revised form, portions of my entry: "*South Africa*" (2005); and I thank the editorial board of the *Journal of Church and State* for permission to include in chapter five a different form of my article *"Piety and Politics in African Christianity: The Roles of the Church and the Democratization Process"* which appeared in volume 45 number 2 (Spring 2003). I am also grateful to *Philosophia Africana* and its editors for permission to include in chapter six of this book, a portion of my article: *"An Epistemological Defense of Religious Tolerance: Faith, Citizenship, and Crises of Religious and Cultural Identities in Post-Western Missionary Africa,"* which appeared in Volume 8 number 1 (March 2005).

If readers knew my wife, they would see why I am indebted to her for our amazing three children. When I took a trip to the University of Cape Town in 2003, I knew that her dexterity in domestic matters was the source of my confidence about the home I was leaving behind. Although she assured me that our children would be of assistance to her in my absence, I knew that they were active teenagers and would keep her busy in my absence. Had it not been for her, the research that stood behind this book would not have been undertaken, and it is impossible for me to thank her enough for the selfless toil she has put into the smooth running of our home. They also know why it is appropriate to dedicate this book to her.

Richmond, Virginia
August 23, 2006.

ABBREVIATIONS AND ACRONYMS

AAC	All-African Convention (of 1935)
AIC	African Indigenous (or Initiated) Churches
AFM	Apostolic Faith Mission
AME	African Methodist Episcopal Church
ANC	African National Congress
APEC	African Protestant Episcopal Church
ATR	African Traditional Religions
AZAPO	Azanian People's Organization
BAD	Bantu Administration Department
BCM	Black Consciousness Movement
BCSA	Baptist Convention of South Africa
BK	Belydende Kring
BOSS	Bureau for State Security
BPC	Black People's Convention
BPSG	Black Priests' Solidarity Group
BUSA	Baptist Union of South Africa
CAIC	Council of African Instituted Churches
CALS	Center for Applied Legal Studies (University of Witwatersrand)
CCG	Conservative Christian Group
CCSA	Christian Council of South Africa (the precursor of SACC)
CELAM	Latin American Bishops' Conference (Consejo Episcopal Latino Americano in Bogotá, Colombia)
CESA	Church of England in South Africa
CI	Christian Institute

CIIR	Catholic Institute for International Relations, London.
CLSA	Christian League of Southern Africa.
CMS	Church Missionary Society
CNBB	National Council of Brazilian Bishops (*Conferência Nacional dos Bispos do Brasil*).
CODESA	Convention for a Democratic South Africa
COI	Call of Islam
COSATU	Congress of South African Trade Union
CP	Conservative Party
CPSA	Church of the Province of Southern Africa
DRC	Dutch Reformed Church (*Die Nederduitse Gereformeerde Kerk in Suid-Afrika*)
DRMC	Dutch Reformed Mission Church (*Sendingkerk*)
ECC	End Conscription Campaign
ELCSA	Evangelical Lutheran Church of Southern Africa
EMPSA	Ecumenical Monitoring Program in South Africa
FF	Frontline Fellowship
FRELIMO	Front for the Liberation of Mozambique
GDL	Gospel Defence League
GK	Gereformeerde Kerk
GMC	General Mission Council
GNU	Government of National Unity
ICT	Institute for Contextual Theology
IDASA	Institute for Democracy in South Africa
IEC	Independent Electoral Commission
IFCC	International Fellowship of Christian Churches
IFP	Inkatha Freedom Party (predominantly in KwaZulu Natal)
IMBISA	Inter-Territorial Meeting of Bishops of Southern Africa
IMF	International Monetary Fund
ISAL	Church and Society in Latin America (*Iglesia y Sociedad en America Latina*)
JMC	Joint Management Center
JUT	Jamiatul Ulama Transvaal
LIC	Low Intensity Conflict Strategy
LMS	London Missionary Society
LUCSA	Lutheran Communion in South Africa
MCSA	Methodist Church of Southern Africa
MDM	Mass Democratic Movement

MJC	Muslim Judicial Council
MK	(shorthand for) Umkhonto weSizwe (Spear of the Nation)
MPLA	Popular Movement for the Liberation of Angola
MYMSA	Muslim Youth Movement of South Africa
NCCR	National Coordinating Committee for Repatriation
NEC	National Executive Committee (of the SACC)
NGK	*Nederduits Gereformeerde Kerk* (Dutch Reformed Church)
NGKA	*Nederduits Gereformeerde Kerk* (Black DRC)
NGO	Non-Governmental Organization
NIC	National Intelligent Service
NIR	National Initiative for Reconciliation
NMS	National Management System
NP	National Party (Institutionalized apartheid system in 1948)
NPA	National Peace Accord
NRC	Native Representative Council
NSMS	National Security Management System
OAU	Organization of African Unity
PAC	Pan-Africanist Congress
PCR	Program to Combat Racism (of the World Council of Churches)
PCSA	Presbyterian Church of Southern Africa
RICSA	Research Institute on Christianity in South Africa
RWCG	Right-Wing Christian Group
RPC	Reformed Presbyterian Church (of South Africa)
SABC	South African Broadcasting Corporation
SACBC	Southern Africa Catholic Bishops' Conference
SACC	South African Council of Churches
SACPO	South African Colored People's Organization
SADF	South African Defense Force
SAIC	South African Indian Congress
SAHMS	South African Hindu Maha Sabha
SAIRR	South African Institute of Race Relations, (in Johannesburg).
SANC	South African Native Convention
SANNC	South African Native National Congress (later changed to ANC)
SAP	South African Police
SASO	South African Students Organization
SCA	Student Christian Association

SCM   Student Christian Movement
SDA   Seventh Day Adventist Church
SFT   Standing for the Truth (a joint SACC & SACBC campaign
               of 1988)
SPOBA   St. Peter's Old Boys Association.
SPROCAS   Study Project on Christianity in Apartheid Society
SPROCAS II   Special Program for Christian Action in Society
SSC   State Security Council
SWAPO   South West African People's Organization

TAC   Theological Advisory Commission (of the SACBC)
TEASA   The Evangelical Alliance of South Africa
TRC   Truth and Reconciliation Commission
UCCSA   United Congregational Church of Southern Africa
UCM   University Christian Movement
UDF   United Democratic Front
UMCSA   United Methodist Church of South Africa
URCSA   Uniting Reformed Church in Southern Africa
WARC   World Alliance of Reformed Churches
WB   World Bank
WCC   World Council of Churches (Geneva, Switzerland)
WCRP   World Conference on Religion and Peace
WHO   World Health Organization
WPCC   Western Province Council of Churches
ZANU   Zimbabwe African National Union
ZCC   Zion Christian Church (Zion City, Moria)

INTRODUCTION

The character of the Christian faith in modern South Africa is broad and comprehensive. South African Christians have themselves entered a time of transition and spiritual questioning unmatched in the history of Christianity in Africa.

One thing is also clear about Christians in the modern world—they are curious about the people of other cultures and they have an incessant desire to know them and their religious experience. The *Will to Arise* is written to satisfy their curiosity and provide a stimulus for understanding the cultures and faiths of the peoples of South Africa.

The world changed dramatically on September 11, 2001. In a single moment, the Western world realized the importance of understanding non-Western religions and cultures. The challenges of understanding people who do not share Westerners' political, economic, and religious values became clearer and more important than ever before. The event also made it clear that it is imperative for Christians worldwide to have a broad set of international skills and a cross-cultural understanding of their faith. In an age of interdependence, citizens of the world could no longer afford to be like a runner who restricted himself to the use of only one leg. He may learn to hop outstandingly well, but he would not be as swift and steady as a runner using both legs.

The *Will to Arise* aims at advancing the knowledge base and the character of African Christianity (especially South Africa) so that the human family can become swift and steady about their faith and theological identity.

The book is also a disciplined reflection on the Christian experience of the peoples of South Africa. It examines how their lives have been both enriched and transformed by apartheid and by the unique experiences of the struggle that dismantled it and reshaped Christian identity for all.

One of the recurring themes of the book is the character of African Christianity. Four factors have particularly shaped the history of Christian experience in modern Africa—the Western missionaries, the Africans' own unique worldview, the struggles for political independence and economic justice, and the new emerging non-denominational Church groups. These factors have created an atmosphere that makes it possible to look at the Christian faith with fresh eyes and concentration.

The book represents a response to some of the questions posed by college and seminary professors who are searching for answers to many questions they face in their classrooms about the character of African Christianity and its rapid growth and theological developments. The desire to write the book goes beyond that, however; it is to establish a baseline theory of African retentions of cultural elements through the Christian religion. Thus, non-specialist readers can access the African worldview and the inner strength and vitality of the peoples, and gain fresh insights into the verity of the Christian religion. The baseline theory of African Christianity I tried to affirm in the book will also foster the knowledge of African cultures that includes religions, arts, music, traditional political structures, and the concepts of immortality.

During the second half of the twentieth century, there was a resurgence of interest all over the world about Africa. The steady stream of scholarly materials and popular works on Africa during this period demonstrated that the Western and the non-Western worlds no longer regarded Africa as "a step child" in religious knowledge. The last decade of the twentieth century also demonstrated especially that Africa has become a laboratory of knowledge for scholars of religion, sociology, cultural anthropology, and psychology.

Before this period, many scholars saw Africa as vast, poor, and distant. In political and economic terms, the continent was terribly neglected except when its peoples provided raw materials for Western industries or when they became valuable markets for Western goods and services. This has hurt Africans and the rest of the world alike. Africa, however, has retained a central place in Western intellectual consciousness, and the steady body of knowledge acquired since the end of World War II showed that the peoples of Africa could not be neglected permanently.

The vast continent of Africa is unique, and so is the Christian character of its peoples. This is partly because human beings have been living in Africa longer than anywhere else in the world. Africa is also unique because of its creative struggles to overcome Western domination and ethnocentrism.

Africa's sense of disconnectedness (a result of internal political displacement and the struggle to overcome the vestiges of colonialism) has also provided a reason to study Africa's unique Christian character. But despite the numerous dangers and difficulties Africans are facing today, the continent can feel strangely like a motherland even to people of European and Asian descent.

For many American-Africans (or African-Americans if this means the people of African descent with more than a symbolic or filial relations to Africa), the connection to Africa is more immediate because of slavery and the sustained emotional attachment to Africa that was denied African-Americans for generations. The presence of African-Americans is a constant reminder to Americans of European and Asian descent that no matter why or how each person came to live in the Americas or Europe, the relationship with Africa carries the scars and wounds of the past. Therefore, the people of African descent everywhere will always be an important part of who we are, either collectively or individually. For this reason, it is important to study the theological categories of African Christianity and how adding an African indigenous definition to the Christian faith can bring illumination and a sense of renewal to Westerners' own faith in God.

It is my hope that the book will help scholars and non-specialist readers to respond creatively in a way that affirms new Christian developments in the "African" world. Embracing these new developments in the non-Western world can serve as a gateway to a spirit of tolerance of the global Christian transformation that is partly characterized by flexibility.

Chapter one is about the theological foundation of Christianity in South Africa. The subject matter is the religious factors in South Africa that created a situation of both privilege and of division. Deep ideological divisions existed between whites and blacks from the beginning, but the Church did not have the will to ameliorate the oppressive situation; the result of the Church's failure to protest and protect the weak was segregation by race. But the Church in later years possessed the courage to condemn apartheid, redefining Christianity as a religion of love and compassion, not of ideological segregation. From a theological stance, South African Christians redefined the original message of early European missionaries, which emphasized religious repentance (as preached in the New Testament by John the Baptist). Christian leaders in Africa, particularly in Southern Africa, started to emphasize the message of love and redemption (proclaimed by Jesus of Nazareth), using Christian vocabularies and African traditional religious idioms to do so.

In chapter two, the study focuses on the success of missionaries to South Africa. But missionaries were not as successful as scholars once perceived. This is partly because by adopting the Christian faith, Africans were encouraged to abandon their ancestral wisdom following their conversion to Christianity. The cost of adopting Christianity this way, as supposed to cross-fertilizing it with indigenous spirituality, is the gradual decay of ancestral mores. Thus, what was the missionary's success was in reality a form of cultural failure for the majority of South Africans. By abrogating the traditional religious identity of South Africans and supplanting it by Christianity, the Dutch Reformed Church (DRC) became an organ of the government, playing a pivotal role in the theological justification for apartheid. Thus, a twisted Calvinistic understanding of the DRC contributed to oppressing the majority of South Africans. This failure of the missionaries would not have occurred or so culturally and spiritually damaging to Africans if they had been players in shaping their spiritual direction from the beginning.

In chapter three, the focus is on the Africans' successful adoption of the Christian faith despite the fact that missionaries failed in their methods. The key issue in this Chapter is the creativity of South Africans and how they crafted an indigenous definition of the Christian religion. Therefore, the majority of South African believers today own their faith, and they have transformed Christianity to a powerful tool for unity and healing, rather than a weapon of segregation. The majority of South Africans are Christians, and more than 70 percent of the total population in South Africa belongs to one Christian denomination or another. Despite the missionary's failure, Christianity is a brilliant success in South Africa.

Chapter four builds upon chapter three, exploring modern developments of Christianity in South Africa. It shows that Christianity so crafted in indigenous language, is the faith of the black majority and it is rooted in African idioms and cultures. One of the most remarkable developments of the Christian faith that the chapter points out is that African Christian leaders were least expected by mission Churches to adopt the vocabularies of the Christian faith to secure civil liberty for all South Africans. The chapter also argues that this is one of the unintended consequences of missionary's activities in South Africa.

Chapter five deals with the challenges facing South African Christianity thus crafted in African idioms. Some of the factors contributing to these challenges have deep and external political roots, while others have internal sources. The chapter also deals with factors that will continue to promote Christian growth, such as the exuberant joy characteristic of many Africans, as well as factors that will continue to hinder its developments, such as ravaging diseases.

Religious tolerance in South Africa is the focus of chapter six. The chapter also traces the fundamental religious, ethical, and cultural life of South Africans and how this has been translated into the religious vitality of Africans everywhere. The chapter speaks more directly from the richness of the African religious ethos, relating this richness to the basic composition of African Christian communities in the Diaspora. The chapter further underscores Christian interdependency in the modern world and the need for mutual understanding of the common pain and joy that Christians share with non-Christians.

Chapter seven raises a fundamental question about life after death and articulates new directions for interpreting the resurrection of Jesus Christ. The focus of the chapter is on the existential aspects of the Resurrection and how it has been interpreted among African Christians as a sign of their own existential hope. Here, the book argues that "strangers" are often more effective in interpreting the essential categories of Christianity than those who profess to understand its tenets and doctrines from within. Thus, the discussion turns to Nelson Mandela, a statesman who has not publicly professed Christianity, yet has interpreted the Christian faith for the modern era by demonstrating forgiveness, love, and courage—some of the most important characteristics of the resurrected life one finds in Christianity.

The concluding chapter deals with a fundamental definition of religion in general and of Christianity in particular. The argument of the study falls within the domain of the intellectual culture of our age. Each era's significance is measured by how seriously it takes its own definition of the Christian faith, and each is challenged to renew the Christian identity without domesticating the texts with its own cultural particularity.

The book is a focused study on the character of contemporary South African Christianity, including instructive episodes from the apartheid years. It is a hard-hitting understanding of the Christian faith, positing the moral, spiritual, and theological authority of African Christians, acquired through struggles and agonies of half a century, boldly calling Christians today to re-examine contemporary characters of their faith.

Previous research on Christianity in Africa raised questions about its psychological dimension. This study raises fundamental questions about renewal and restoration of Christian dignity in post-apartheid era. In developing an indigenous definition of Christianity, what will the Church seek to change or modify? How, for example, have the religious organizations represented in this study attempted to rediscover and enliven the traditional religious elements of South Africa? How can they revive the rich indigenous cultures in the formation of their Christian identity? These are practical and underlying questions that the book addresses. Beyond these specific questions, however, is a more fundamental issue: recent polls in South Africa show that the mainline Churches are losing membership while the AICs are growing with amazing rapidity. Both Robert J. Schreiter and Philip Jenkins have claimed that Africa, with 852 million population now has over 382 million Christians, and it is one of the fastest growing Christian continents in the world today.

In a recent study, *The Next Christendom: The Coming of Global Christianity* (2002), Jenkins devoted his writings to Africa at many stages and claimed that the largest Christian communities today are to be found in Africa and South America. Kenyan scholar, John Mbiti, has also stated that Kinshasa, Addis Ababa, and Manila have replaced Geneva, Rome, Athens, Paris, and London as the new centers of the universal Church. Furthermore, recent studies have indicated that the AICs are among the most respected institutions in South Africa today. How, then, are some groups within the AICs seeking to build a more participatory and responsible society, and what are their prospects for achieving this goal?

The study further shows that African Christianity can be an important intellectual property for Christianity worldwide because South Africa has witnessed a series of important events in its history during the past few decades. In many ways, contemporary South African society is similar to certain aspects of African-American experience in the 1950s and 1960s. Serious Christian theology tends to develop out of human suffering and a vigorous religious, political, and cultural milieu. Collectively, these form the intellectual property of a society.

My driving concerns at the beginning of the book are twofold:

First, theology often depends on a constant agitation of undying human questions: Why is there suffering of the innocent if Christ overcame death by his resurrection? What is the meaning of conversion? Is it possible for a person to convert to Christianity or to another religion and totally depart from his or her religio-ancestral roots? What is the purpose of human existence? Why do the innocent die young? What is the cause of pain in life? What does the future hold for Christianity in a pluralistic age? Christians do not silence these queries but integrate the answers to their Christian awareness, giving a depth of meaning to a shared existential condition. In post-apartheid South Africa, these queries are addressed in an atmosphere of genuine intellectual boldness that gave birth to a moment of literary resurrection. This book offers some insights into the contemporary South African Christian intellectual property. The South African struggle against apartheid also resonates with the African-American push for justice during the Civil Rights movement of the 1950s and 1960s, and thus the literature of both movements dovetails.

Second, Africans have many things in common with African-Americans, including liturgical liveliness. These similarities of cultural patterning and similar political history could create a common ground for Christian identity.

Scholars and teachers of religion should not only honor what is known about Christianity, but also question it in light of their own Christian experience.

The book is not a "town hall" or a "clearing-house" of information for pastors and teachers who are interested in interdisciplinary knowledge and research that deal specifically with Church-State issues in Africa. Rather, it is about Christian identity formation intended for students and scholars who are facing serious questions about the character of African Christianity in post-apartheid and post-TRC era.

❀ Chapter One
THE ORIGINS OF THE CHURCH IN SOUTH AFRICA

All over the world, it is evident that the Church is experiencing unparalleled relative freedom, a condition quite unlike the first century, and certainly unlike the centuries that immediately followed. The post-apartheid era is in many ways a time of privilege for the Church in South Africa. More than any other period in modern history, this is the best time to be a part of the Church in South Africa.

Although this is an exciting time to be ministers of the gospel of healing and reconciliation, Christians are also living in a troubled world, and there are many challenges associated with the mission of the Church in South Africa and elsewhere. Is the Church prepared to meet these challenges? Christians are no longer poor and lacking resources but rich and influential. Yet, the Church has traditionally been a community of the marginalized and the poor. The Church that is in a troubled world is also the Church that is in a position to be an agent of healing. The Church is now both in crisis and in a position of a unique opportunity.

Protestant Churches in South Africa are no longer small, calling the poor to Church activities by shouting on mountaintops; they are large and numerous in the South African country sides, calling the rich to Church services by driving expensive cars to take believers to the sanctuaries. The Church is no longer illiterate but well advanced in knowledge. In the South Africa of the 1990s and 2000s, one can readily see the first fruits of the Western education that was offered by missionaries in the 1920 and '30s. The Church in South Africa is no longer subservient to state authority—it possesses authority by itself. It is essentially because of this privilege that the Church has to be an agent of healing the wounds of the society she serves.

In the past, the Church in South Africa was incapacitated by apartheid and by the fear of the brutality of state-sponsored oppression. The Church either withdrew from the world, or collaborated creatively with an unjust society. Today, however, the Church has the capacity to be the light of the world with a message of healing.

At the time the Church in South Africa possesses the capacity to serve, the Church elsewhere, within Africa as well as in the non-African world, surrendered to worldly authorities and to "worldly" powers with either timidity or innocence. The Protestant denominations have only grudgingly assisted in revealing past government-sponsored atrocities in Africa and in the United States—among them are the notorious question of slavery, the disenfranchisement of women, and the expropriation of Native American lands. The scars of these unjust practices would not go away.

After the dismantling of apartheid, the Church in South Africa seems to be careful not to stigmatize people who are different, realizing that the declaration of "otherness" is usually the first step toward the destruction of those who do not share traditional Christian beliefs and values. Such stigmatization was part of the ideology of apartheid and of oppression that many South Africans have now left behind. In religious language, these stigmas include "enemies of God" or "the anti-Christ" or "gentiles" or "heathens" or "liberals" or "fundamentalists" or "pagans." But in political language, they are words like "communists" or "terrorists" or "infidels." These are the terms that are often used to create hatred, which is then deployed to justify violently harming those that are outside a people's own religious and political groups. Most South Africans have graduated from the mentality of labeling "others" as enemies.

But if labeling is what created hatred in the modern world neither the Church in South Africa nor any other religious community is entirely blameless. In her modern history, the Church in the Western world sometimes has a puritan image of herself with the perception that both the religious values and governments of distant lands are irrelevant or illegitimate. She propels her own polity and life, on the other hand, not only to convert but also to create emissaries among her converts to build God's kingdom on earth.

This is essentially what is different in the new South African Church and civil society. Perhaps one of the greatest lessons that the South African Christian experience can teach others worldwide is that there are specific cultural and ideological values that intersect with Christian principles and that these values do not necessarily threaten the role of Christianity in public life. Thus, religious values can play more than just a symbolic role in public life, and there can be an aspect of spirituality in the political process.

It should not be surprising that a world that was created by the Church and shaped by its traditions yesterday is now being condemned wholesale.

Leander Keck wrote: "That non-Christians find the Christian faith objection-able is not new, for already the apostle Paul wrote about the *skandalon* of the cross. What is new is that the antipathy toward the Christian tradition and its culture now comes from Christian theologians themselves."[1] This is also why the Church in the Western world has no power to exercise a profound positive change in the world. The result of the Church's domination of the world with a religio-political vision rather than a clearer ministerial empha-sis is problematic in the experiences of modern devotees of religions and their conversion to Christianity.

A Conversion or a Transformation?

In an article entitled "The Missionary Position,"[2] David Frawley noted that conversion to Christianity always entails an implicit psychological vio-lence. However discreetly it is conducted, proselytization only has one aim: "to turn the minds and hearts of people away from their native religion to one that is generally unsympathetic and hostile to it."[3] Frawley continues by stating the following:

> Missionary activity and conversion, therefore, is not about freedom of religion. It is about the attempt of one religion to exterminate all [the] others. Such an exclusion attitude cannot promote tolerance or understanding or resolve communal tensions. The missionary wants to put an end to pluralism, choice and freedom of religion. He wants one religion, his own, for everyone and will sacrifice his life to that cause. True freedom of religion should involve freedom from conversion. The missionary is like a salesman targeting people in their homes or like an invader seeking to con-quer.[4]

The author himself is an American citizen who converted from Catholi-cism to Hinduism. His bold statements characterize what conversion has come to mean in a pluralistic age. Among the intellectuals, conversion has become irritating and offensive to a society endowed with the wisdom of re-ligious plurality. High value is placed on harmonious relationships among unequals, as if emphasis on conversion would jeopardize mutual understand-ing.

In an earlier and more provocative work by a native of India who is now a Professor of English and Comparative Literature at Columbia University in New York, Frawley's claim was not without a sympathetic antecedent. In his work, Gauri Viswanathan stated that conversion is profoundly threatening to dominant communities because it possesses the potential to destabilize the society.[5] Viswanathan's comments have a broader implication in the South

African context, implying that missionaries should recognize cultural boundaries.

Early missionaries to South Africa were not protected by the reinforcement that elements of the native African religions were in fact consistent with the Gospel. These missionaries' denial of religious freedom to South Africans was echoed by the apartheid government's denial of cultural and racial identity in subsequent years. But new evidence suggests that not all early missionaries ignored the territory of religious tolerance. Henry Venn's three-self formulae,[6] for example, clearly suggest that missionaries acknowledged the cultural boundaries of their converts in Africa. What was not recognized was that their converts also possessed the inner strength to Africanize the new faith just as much as the missionaries possessed the inner strength to Christianize them.

Scholars often pay little attention to Africans' contributions in the process of their "conversion" to Christianity. In his most celebrated work, *The Invention of Africa: Gnosis, Philosophy, and the Order of Knowledge* (1988), the Congolese Philosopher, V. Y. Mudimbe reinforced this view by suggesting that missionaries to Africa had ulterior motif. He stated: "One might consider that missionary speech is always predetermined, pre-regulated, let us say colonized."[7] He went further by stating that: "a person whose ideas and mission come from and are sustained by God is rightly entitled to the use of all possible means, even violence, to achieve his objectives. Consequently, 'African conversion' rather than being a positive outcome of a dialogue—unthinkable per se—came to be the sole position the African could take in order to survive as a human being."[8] In Mudimbe's assessment, Africans have been given no choice but to convert. By depriving Africans of any independent will or agency except to convert, missionaries paid little attention to the idiosyncratic, invisible strength of Africans in the process of conversion.

The view of conversion as a form of cultural violence espoused by David Frawley, Gauri Viswanathan, and V. Y. Mudimbe no longer speaks to the wellspring of African new experience of Christianity. Therefore, their interpretation does not represent the dominant view among ordinary African Christians. Jean and John Comaroff have given one of the most notable examples of a different interpretation of conversion. In their analysis of the nineteenth-century London Missionary Society (LMS) among the Tswana peoples of South Africa, they wrote that "the missionary encounter must be regarded as a two-sided historical process; as a dialectic that takes into account the social and cultural endowments of, and the consequences for, all the actors—missionaries no less than Africans."[9]

In light of this, one must ask further questions about conversion. What does it mean to be converted? How can one get into the mental framework of the one who is converted? Is conversion to Christianity a Colonization of the mind?[10]

As a noun, the word "conversion" occurs sparingly in the New Testament, perhaps only in Acts 15:3, when Paul and Barnabas reported to the Jewish believers in Phoenicia and Samaria "the *conversion* of the Gentiles." But the verb "convert" appeared more frequently in the New Testament because it was used more theologically (and spiritually) to mean a complete change of heart and mind toward God. In other words, the verb "convert" does not mean to change a religion. Addressed to Jews or Gentiles in the New Testament, to convert means to turn in repentance from sin toward God.[11] The point to be emphasized here is that the agent of conversion was not the missionary and the object of conversion was not the new believer. Religions are not in view in the process because conversion is an inward journey toward God.

Paul and Barnabas, therefore, reported to the Church in Antioch at the end of their first missionary journey that God "had opened a door of faith for the Gentiles."[12] A rebirth to faith in God cannot be occasioned or orchestrated by human agency because more is required. Hence, whatever validity sociologists or psychologists of religion may associate with the conversion of Africans to Christianity in the modern era, Christian theology cannot be content with any understanding of conversion to God as purely a matter of human agency, whether on the part of the missionary or on the part of the African converts. Every conversion to God is a "going home" experience since the believer is turning to God the creator.

Andrew F. Walls, one of the most influential scholars currently writing in the field of mission studies, has insisted that conversion in the New Testament is not primarily about a replacement of one religion by another but about the internal transformation and reorientation of humanity towards God.[13] In this sense, one should not see the South Africans' adoption of Christianity as a conversion but rather as a transformation. The emphasis in the New Testament as well as in contemporary South Africa, is predominantly on the convert's turning in repentance away from sin toward God. It is still the case whether it is the Zulu, or the Coloured, Indian, Afrikaner, Jew, Gentile, Muslim, Hindu, or Christians, who is doing the turning. Traditionally, however, only Christians acknowledge Jesus as the embodiment of God and as the Savior. The idea of conversion as a substitution of one "religion" for another is not the uppermost when one turns to God. Jews who turned to Christ in the New Testament continued to practice Judaism, worshiping Yahweh in the synagogue and offering animal sacrifices in ways and manners that were consistent with Judaism. Walls reiterated that "converts" in the New Testament were not to be made carbon copies of the Jewish believers, but were expected to express allegiance to Christ within their own particular cultural and religious context.[14] Therefore, it should not be surprising that in South Africa, one could find a Hindu "little Christ," a Muslim one, or a Zulu, Gentile, or Christian "little Christ." What is involved in conversion is the communication of a broader theological concept, not a narrower definition of a translation of religious framework. The field is what matters, not the narrow path that could lead astray. Thus, in South Africa many indigenous Christians have conjoined their particular story of redemption with the universal story of salvation. They have read their own stories into the pages of the Bible and have applied biblical narratives to their own existential situations. In this spiritual confluence, new identity is formed, as emerging and transformational characters are re-discovered. And part of the attraction to Christianity in South Africa is that the Christian faith offers hope for the future in the particularity of South Africans' existential condition. They rediscover the sense of *ubutu*[15] in Christianity. This could mean that South Africans have a loose religious filter, tolerating the currents of new religious sensibility. One can see this open ended-ness and unpredictable nature of South African Christianity as both creative and dangerous. It is creative because it offers new dimensions of Christian spirituality. But it is dangerous because it has no traditional regulatory body to measure its religious activities and teachings.

Perhaps this is a point of departure, and African Christians can enrich or correct the Christian doctrine by addressing the imbalances associated with the missionary's culturally conditioned understanding of the Christian faith. At the same time, African Christians have the capability to distort orthodoxy by filtering out emphases in Christianity they find less relevant to their own particular cultural and religious moment. But this would only mean that they have responded to what they have seen in the Gospel and not necessarily to what missionaries have taught them to see or hear in the Gospel. Ultimately, however, it is the appropriation of Christianity—not the rote memorization and mimicry of the biblical text or missionary programs—that demonstrates a true change of heart toward God.

South Africans perform religious rituals every day, and before the arrival of Christianity they engaged in many indigenous religious activities. Therefore, South Africans are truly *Homo religiosos*. Today, one can see Christian religious expressions in baptism, confirmation, initiation, pilgrimage, and worship services, to name a few. As South Africans engage one another socially and culturally, their religious expressions become increasingly complex, taking a form that is not seen in the Western Christian traditions. But their faith in God and their Christian awareness is not totally unaffected by the particularity of their specific culture. For a millennia perhaps, social and cultural intercourse have shaped historical Christianity in South Africa.

When the National Party (NP) came to power in 1948, racial segregation was formalized, and apartheid became the law of the land. It then became clear that an overreach of political authority would lead to tyranny in unexpected places. But elsewhere in Africa, radical religious and political freedom frequently resulted in licentiousness and disintegration of the civic society. In some nation states, this has led to an outright anarchy. Religious teachings or doctrines in post-apartheid era are now easier to share than to prove, as South Africans continue to leave behind the dark days of doctrinaire rigidity of the past.

In South Africa, as in many parts of the world, public certitude about religious teachings have often generated more heat than light. Even the epistemological criteria of right and wrong in living faiths are still soft and tender in the new South Africa of post-apartheid era. Inner certitude in living faith is possible without public propaganda or proselytization. In the modern history of South Africa, Christianity at its most profound level is both a burden and liberation. The faith that was once a burden for the majority of South Africans—because the apartheid leaders professed Christianity and used it as a weapon of oppression—is also a tool for liberation in the new dispensation.

But Christianity is more than a liberation tool; South Africans also see echoes of their ancestral religion in Christianity. The distinct lines that separated their religion from Christianity are now becoming blurry. What a beautiful overlap! Yet, it is absurd to maintain that South Africans see every religion in the same way. Plurality of ideas is always beneficial in constructive religious discussions, and there can be no religious truth untested in the laboratory of self–discovery.

The experiences of South African Christians about their faith are not all the same. Some have caused South Africans to wonder if God is still "up there." Others have made them laugh or cry. Perhaps, the term "Christianity" for them has become a complex religious term. Whereas, the term "religious" has become a useful adjective, which describes a unified effort to grasp the totality of their existence as a "rainbow people" of God.

What is a Christian South Africa?

Thus, one cannot define accurately what religion in South African context is, and likewise one cannot define what "Christianity" is. Human religious traditions are only the beginning point of understanding the divine. No religious tradition can completely fathom who God is, and religious expressions are not the end of human discovery of the divine, that can be translated or exported to other territories of beliefs.

Religions tell more about humanity than about God. Religion is an expression of faith into which each devotee is nurtured. It is the source of our relation to God. It is open not only to the priests but also to the laity. Like language, God is infinitely transparent to the educated and to the unschooled, to the wise and to the unlearned. Theological expression in all its rich varieties can be correct and be well formed, or incorrect and be ill–formed. No theology can give an exhaustive account of God. Furthermore, all our religious rituals can be classified as performances, and they cannot be easily harmonized into a single rigid structure. They are like grammatical rules. We cannot apply a single rule of interpretation to all aspects of our religion, language or the Scriptures. While the scripture may not contradict itself, it exists in a wide variety, and there is no one religious performance that can subsume all other performances. There will always be new possibilities, because God is inexhaustible.

But what does it mean for an ordinary South African to convert from his traditional religious worldview to Christianity or from an African Traditional Religion to Christianity?

Perhaps it is more appropriate to say that Africans were not converted from one theistic belief to another. What has taken place in the lives of ordinary South Africans can be more appropriately described as a "creative transformation," or a reorientation, but not a radical conversion from their traditional religions to Christianity.

From a practical standpoint, conversion from one religion to another often seems superficial. The new faith often fails to touch certain psychic factors of the old spiritual awareness. In a way, one can say that it is *transformation* within the old faith that has taken place for South Africans. South Africans could not possibly depart from their old religious roots, even when many have pretended to be successful in doing so. South Africans who feel at home with Christianity are those who have integrated their new faith with the old spiritual awareness with integrity. A non–superficial expansion of the Christian faith is impossible without authentic ingredients and values of native spirituality.

When Christian teachings interact with the indigenous religious paradigm, devoted followers have responded in several ways. It is often the case that most of these responses do not demonstrate faith, and three illustrations come to mind: (1) First, South African followers of African Traditional Religions who are confronted by Christianity have responded by retreating along their traditional lines or to the spirituality of the ancestors. This response, however, has not been considered by either the practitioners or the missionaries to be a demonstration of faith. (2) Second, followers of African Traditional Religions have also responded by arguing against Christianity and have even tried to show that the truth and goodness in the Christian faith are entirely false insofar as they differ from what is found in African Traditional Religions. This also does not express faith. (3) Third, the devotees of African Traditional Religions have opened up themselves to learn from Christianity. Impressed by what they learned from Christian teachings, and no longer impressed by their Traditional African Religions, they responded by "converting" to Christianity. But this response also showed a lack of faith. If in learning from Christianity, South Africans simply added new information to the old, leaving the old unchanged, and the new uninformed by the old, the experience would still not be a demonstration of faith.

Faith or authentic "conversion" is always transformational. This transformation experience is often a binding together of the old and the new. Thus, South Africans that have been open to Christianity, allowing it to transform their Traditional Religions and retaining the old psychic phenomenon of native traditions, have been truly converted to God. The new must be allowed to dwell richly in the old to fulfill and enliven the old. This is the way of creative religious transformation that now makes South Africans own their Christian faith.

Christians in the Western world can learn from the South African religious experience that those who do not direct their spiritual destiny by the genius of their own culture, their own language, and their own native religious thought–form and ancestral spirituality, will find it difficult to achieve the full length of their spiritual destiny—especially when the very ones who exercise the final judgment over what is to be institutionalized in religions are people of a different cultural, historical, and ancestral backgrounds.

Perhaps, another lesson that Christians in the Western world can learn from the South African religious experience is that there is no "conversion" as such but only a "transformation" or a "calling" for spiritual renewal. If transformation is a return to God, every experience of transformation is a "reversion." This calling or reversion is a transformation within the domain of the existing religion. Religious expression in the South African experience is a particular effort by South Africans to grasp the totality of their existence as a people. Ultimately, the word "conversion" is counterproductive, and we see this in the course of the Christian experience of Europeans themselves.

Conversion in the 19th-century Europe was less and less a religious act and more and more a secular one. It was an entrance ticket to the European culture and modern civilization of Europe. This pseudo-conversion was not new and probably started in England when Benjamin Disraeli, a Jew, was baptized into the Anglican Church on 31 July 1817 at age twelve. This conversion secured him a seat in the British Parliament when Jews were legally admitted in 1858. Benjamin Disraeli later became a British Prime Minister. Karl Heinrich Marx also converted to Christianity in 1824. Marx's grandfather had been a Jewish Rabbi in Trier until his death in 1789. As was the case with Disraeli, Marx's conversion to Christianity subsequently ensured him a position of intellectual significance in the Western world.[16] A German historian and a great friend of the Jews, Theodor Mommsen, pointed out about conversion from Judaism to Christianity in Germany that: "Christianity was not so much a name for a religion as the only word expressing the character of today's international civilization in which numerous millions all over the many-nationed globe feel themselves united."[17] What conversion to Christianity was in the 19th-century, the adoption of the English language has become in the 20th-century and will be in the 21st—it is not for the love of the language; rather, it is a skillful strategy to be a part of the modern civilization. The reasons were secular, and Christian baptisms are now partly the entrance-ticket to a new World culture.

Ironically, it is because of this privilege of conversion that the modern Church is different from the early Church. The Church of antiquity did not have the privilege that the modern Church has, but what a light to the nations it was. There is now both silver and gold within the walls of the Church. This makes it easier for non-Christians outside of Europe to want to be converted to Christianity of the Western sort. As a result of the wealth of the Church in the Western world, Christianity is not esteemed as a pillar of society, and certainly not an organ of compassion or the champion of the helpless in many underdeveloped regions of the modern world.

One wonders if the goal or purpose of the Church is still that of service and not of power.[18] The Church in the modern world will only rediscover herself as she loses herself in the service of others in the world, rather than seeking worldly powers. For the Church to rebel against the hostile society in which she has been implanted in our time—the society that gave the Church full citizenship (grudgingly if at all)—would be the beginning of salvation of the modern Church. This is partly because the Church is the only society that exists primarily to serve God and the world.

For one thing, Jesus stated: "the poor will always be with you." The rich hardly stay in the Church once they have made their million. At the time when there was bread, Jesus cautioned: "man shall not live by bread alone," but the Church must now ask what to do about those who do not have bread at all. Perhaps salvation for those people would be the redistribution of God's bounty in the world and of the earthly goods and power. It is a promising moment because the Church has the financial means and prestige to help the poor. Hence, this is also a promising moment in the life of the Church—to be the Church in the world. Thus, the Church is simultaneously at a moment of crisis and opportunity.

But how can the Church now change the world she has dominated, or the world that has dominated the Church? Two other questions are connected to this one: First, how would the Church that is liberated from the ghetto of hostility and secularization adjust to society? Second, how could the society adjust to a liberated Church? When the Church has tasted worldly powers, how can it avoid the deadly risk of poison associated with the world? How can the Church now claim that she is only in the world but not of the world? There is a worm in the apple, and the Church must ask: "Is the Church merely a detached messenger of the Good News and not also the message itself?" The true Church is neither exclusively the messenger nor the message. The true Church is both, but the Church has not always taken the responsibility as the embodiment of the message of salvation in the world seriously. The Church remains one of the major institutions in this time and age to serve the world, but at the same time she is now one of the only missing pages between the world of privilege and a world in need of salvation—between sickness and health, between life and destruction, and between war and shalom.

The Church on the Defensive

The Christian Church of the 21st-century does not need to take the same step as the Church in the first century. But the 21st-century Church does not need to be on the defensive. The Church today does not need to follow uncritically in the steps of the pillars of the Christian tradition of antiquity, but the Church cannot afford to depart from the proclamation that God loves the world. Tradition allows the Church to think on her own, just as the forebears thought and articulated the categories of the Christian faith on their own. There is nothing wrong in standing with them where the modern Church can. Current experiences, however, are different from theirs, and the modern Church in the West, and elsewhere, needs to differ from the older Church where she must.

Jaroslav Pelikan's epigram says it best with a rhythm: "Tradition is the living faith of the dead; traditionalism is the dead faith of the living."[19] Can it then be concluded that empty attachment to tradition is a sign of a lack of faith? A lack of reverence for the honored tradition is not good for the Church, and neither is the Church's disregard for human innovation and scientific progress good for the Christian proclamation. It is by embracing her time-honored traditions that the Church can speak prophetically and more eloquently in the world. At the same time, the Church should recognize that human progress could be indicative of the presence of God in new ways. Has God departed from the "traditional Church" and how does one know this? For one thing, one can sense this departure because "God has gone to where God is wanted." Religions often arise, flourish, or decline in close association with the paths of specific communities, and even a whole people, in their multiplicity. The Church has been growing rapidly for generations in the southern hemisphere, and Western scholars are now just noticing it and writing about "the next Christendom." For example, there is credible evidence of Christian witnesses in Africa during the European Medieval period. Christianity is as old as creation in Africa, and its adumbrated forms survived in African cultures and life-styles up till today.

When, in 1910, the representatives of Western Protestant missions gathered in the hall at the World Missionary Conference at Edinburgh to coordinate their strategy for evangelization of the world in their generation, they probably expected the greatest triumphs of conversion from India, Japan, North Korea, Hong Kong, and China. Human civilization was associated with this part of the world and the indigenous people only needed Christianity to enhance the quality of their lives. These pious European Church leaders least expected missionary success from the primitive and sparsely populated continent of Africa. Perhaps European Christians are also surprised today that Christianity has experienced such a burst and renewal in Africa, the "dark continent." One of the difficulties stems from divergent European view and the African worldviews.

In traditional African worldview, a dichotomy does not exist between the physical and the spiritual worlds. In the Western perception, however, God is in the realm of the *noumenal* (spiritual) world, but languages and experiences are confined to the phenomenal (physical) world. There is a chasm between the two worlds that cannot be bridged, and this makes human language replete of strength in its application to the *noumenal* world. Does that mean that Christians cannot say anything concrete about God any more?

Modern disciples of Immanuel Kant (1724–1804) have gone further by stating that language does not describe reality; it creates reality. Therefore, human language, it is argued, cannot tell us anything about God. Does that mean that we must do away with any hope of knowing God or be done with our capacity to know once and for all? In other words, should we draw a line under the Church's traditions and start history afresh? We cannot choose between these options in good faith because our "self-constructed" God still loves us, and it is through the feeling of God's love that our choices are to be measured. Hence, we should not startle even when we realize that the ladder of language is still too short to reach the full heights of the truth about God. Africans have hundreds of names to describe the one God they have always known before 1910, and their ancestors loved and worshiped God. The current resurgence and rapid expansion of Christianity in Africa should not surprise us at all. God has not only gone to Africa where God is needed, God has never departed from Africa, where humanity was created in the first place. Our highest religious experiences often elude human words even among Africans. The Names of God Litany of the Second National Meeting of the United Church of Christ Women expresses it best:

> O God, because you are the source of all life and love and being,
>   *We call you Creator;*
> Because we know the history of your presence among your covenanted people and honor their tradition,
>   *We call you Lord;*
> Because our savior, Jesus Christ, your obedient child, knew you intimately and spoke of you so,
>   *We call you Father;*
> Because you are present in the act of birth and because you shelter, nurture, and care for us,
>   *We call you Mother;*
> Because you hold us up and give us strength and courage when we are weak and in need,
>   *We call you Sustainer;*
> Because we have known you in our pain and suffering,
>   *We call you Comforter;*
> Because beyond pain lies your promise of all things made new,
>   *We call you Hope;*
> Because you are the means of liberation and the way to freedom,
>   *We call you Redeemer;*
> *Confident that you will hear, we call upon you with all the names that make you real to us, the names that create an image in our minds and hearts, an image that our soul can understand and touch. And yet, we know that you are more than all of these.*
>   *Blessing and power, glory and honor be unto you, our God. Amen.*[20]

The Enlightenment thinkers and their modern disciples should not shake us. This is because language, at best, is only a metaphor that denotes God but does not connote God. Language does not get to the deepest layer of our being, where God who created us is felt. The Christian faith, at its most basic level, can be defined as statues of religious feelings enlivened and regulated by biblical images that we may or may not completely understand. Therefore, the Church does not need to be on the defensive. Our option does not have to be an agnostic option, because we can assess that our languages are inadequate to speak for us about God.

If we can use our words to demonstrate God empirically for the world, we have already tainted the nature of God. But at the same time, the game is over if Christians cannot employ human language to speak about God metaphorically. This is because the God disclosed through Jesus Christ also wanted us to communicate the love of God for us and for the world, however imperfect our "babbling" might sound. Thus, language denotes but does not connote, and one can still speak of God without claiming to have defined God. One can approach God through the analogies of humanity, however imperfectly. Thus, most Africans simply refer to God as "the One above."

In her well-crafted book, *Metaphor and Religious Language* (1985) Janet Martin Soskice puts it best when she stated that we can speak of God without claiming to define God and we can do so by means of metaphor.[21] She then argues that human language about God is "referential without being tied to unrevisable description."[22] Our metaphorical language about God, therefore, "denominates rather than describes God."[23] We know what we are talking about, although we know we may distort the essence of God and make mistakes in talking substantially about God.

One analogy that comes to mind is the analogy of two lovers. If asked to state whether a husband loves his wife, the answer would most likely be in the affirmative. If asked to describe the "how," and the "why," or the "when" of his love for her, the husband could be right, but he could also distort the essence of the relationship. Language is imperfect, but it is not irrelevant or useless in articulating relationships. A husband, who wanted to surprise his wife and decided to show his love by cooking for her and her friends at a party, went to the market to buy what he will need for the cooking. At the end of the party, the wife's friends were analyzing the occasion and the amount of salt and peppers the husband used to cook the meals that impressed some of the attendees. Almost no one, however, could see the ineffable—the husband's love. The same could be said about God's relationship to the world—the analysis of what we can see, taste, feel, or hear cannot fully describe God's infinite love for the world.

Likewise, God is beyond theism and atheism, and a pillar of certainty does not support our language, nor is language diaphanous enough to pass through the door of God's internal love and mystery.

This is to say that human language is inadequate to convey the essence of God (Immanuel Kant), but language also suggests that God's self-disclosure can be real through human language. Our languages are inadequate, but they are not useless or irrelevant in talking about God. This is a supreme paradox in Christian theology, understood, however imperfectly, by many South African Christians.

There is a new energy in the African Church that is revitalizing the human language in communicating what is ineffable to the entire body of believers all over the world. Therefore, the Church is now on the road to recovery and renewal. This will result in a new manifestation of the Church as a divine and human institution that proves God's unfailing love to a watching and waiting world.

There are powerful and living forces in Africa and elsewhere that are not particularly recognized by the traditional academic communities. These forces nevertheless are asking for new structures, new language, new theologies, new symbols, and new vision to make the gospel speak anew to the world. For this, a new ecclesiastical vision is necessary. The vision, however, would not require systematic programs by academicians. The global reality requires grassroots participation that will take on the new challenges, raise criticisms, and make suggestions for a new model of the Church; it will also reflect on these suggestions in transparent and radical ways.

The Message of John: "Repent!"

The foundation of the Church is Jesus Christ. More than in any other living religion, Christianity centers on the life and ministry of one person— Jesus Christ. Scholars of the New Testament have maintained this assertion consistently. From theological point of view, however, John the Baptizer was indeed the founder of the Church. At least in South Africa, the Church adopted John the Baptizer's strategy for gathering believers, building a Church, and for planting a congregation. The Church has done this for at least 500 years in South Africa.

This strategy was to tell the people of South Africa that they were sinners. Therefore, they needed to repent. After their repentance, they were welcome into the Kingdom of God that was at hand.

In the New Testament, the word "repentance" occurs in Luke 14 times, in Acts 11 times, and in the book of Revelation 12 times. The word occurs elsewhere in the New Testament, giving us a total of approximately 62. Luke, however, uses the word more frequently than others. According to E. P. Sanders, "only Luke gives concrete stories about Jesus' calling on people to repent, and…only Luke thought that Jesus persuaded the wicked to repent and pay back their ill-gotten gains."[24] In one of the most dramatic moments of Church establishment in the New Testament, scholars observe that the main purpose of Jesus was not to condemn but to be compassionate. He knew human frailty, and he did not go around blaming and condemning people that they were morally and spiritually bankrupt. That was not his style of building God's kingdom and edifying the Church. Jesus grew up in Nazareth where he probably worked among the poor and the lowly. In E. P. Sanders' words, "he did not want to be a stern taskmaster or a censorious judge, who would only add to their burdens."[25]

This, however, was not the expectation of his people. They wanted a Messiah that would tell them to first clean up their mess and inadequacies before they could meet God. The ticket to God's kingdom became righteousness.

What was quite omitted here is that Jesus came to them to share with them the image of God that humanity could not attain. There was no point in trying to be what we could never be. In a sense, one can say that while John the Baptizer was preparing his people to meet God, Jesus was bringing God to the people.

Only Jesus, God's viceroy and the exact representation of God to humanity, is capable of being in the likeness of God. Hence Matthew asserted:

> Come to me, all who labor and are heavy laden, and I will give you rest. Take my yoke upon you, and learn from me; for I am gentle and lowly in heart, and you will find rest for your souls; for my yoke is easy and my burden is light. (Matt. 11:28–30).

John the Baptizer, on the other hand, required repentance. In Luke's gospel, the voice of John the Baptizer cried in the wilderness saying:

> Prepare the way of the Lord,
> make his paths straight.
> Every valley shall be filled,
> and every mountain and hill
> shall be made low,
> and every crooked shall be made
> straight,
> and the rough way made
> smooth;
> and all flesh shall see the salvation
> of God." (Luke 3:4b–6)

Luke further records:

> John said to the crowds that came out to be baptized by him, "You brood of vipers! Who warned you to flee from the wrath to come? Bear fruits worthy of repentance. Do not begin to say to yourselves, 'We have Abraham as our ancestor'; for I tell you, God is able from these stones to raise up children to Abraham. Even now the ax is lying at the root of the trees; every tree therefore that does not bear good fruit is cut down and thrown into the fire." (Luke 3:7–9).

From this warning of John, it is rather clear that, according to John's strategy, the strong line of building the Church and God's kingdom was to preach a message of repentance. That was his style, and it was effective in those days and time. It was easier for people to be told what to do in order to fit into God's kingdom. They asked: "what are the requirements for me to belong?" The question that was foremost in the minds of the disciples of John, therefore, was "how can I participate?" Underneath this question was a presupposition that our life and our ways were not good enough for God and that we must clean up, make sacrifices, pray for forgiveness, and turn around before we can enter into the Church.

John himself demonstrated this when he isolated himself in the wilderness. He would not drink or eat with the people publicly. About this ritual or religious isolation we read:

> For John the Baptist has come eating no bread and drinking no wine, and you say, 'He has a demon;' the son of Man has come eating and drinking, and you say, 'Look, a glutton and a drunkard, a friend of tax collectors and sinners!' (Luke 7:33f; cf. Matt. 11:18f.).

As if this were not enough, John fasted and required his disciples to fast in order to fulfill all the "repentance" requirements. In this way, he prepared his people to meet God. Jesus, although closely associated with the one who baptized him, did not follow this model of building God's kingdom. Hence, he did not fast regularly, and neither did he require his own disciples to fast. Some criticized him for this. When Jesus and his followers heard the criticism, it demanded an immediate response from Jesus: "Can the wedding guests fast as long as the bridegroom is with them?" (Mark 2:18–22). This response further proves the point that "Jesus was no Puritan."[26]

When John the Baptizer was imprisoned, he demanded proof that Jesus was truly the Messiah, the Son of God and God's spokesman. This was shortly after the beginning of the active ministry of Jesus. John sent some of his disciples to inquire: "Are you he who is to come, or shall we look for another?" This is to say to Jesus, "you are too regular an individual, too ordinary, too simple, too unspiritual, and too radical to be the Messiah I am preparing my disciples to expect; please confirm this to me." Realizing that this was an important moment of decision for John, the Messiah responded uncharacteristically by asking John's disciples to go back with a message:

> Go and tell John what you hear and see: the blind receive their sight and the lame walk, lepers are cleansed and the deaf hear, and the dead are raised up, and the poor have good news preached to them. And blessed is he who takes no offence at me. (Matthew11: 2–6).

In this passage, Jesus is recalling the prophetic voice of Isaiah in chapter 35, where a similar list is recorded. He is also claiming that Isaiah's prophecy is fulfilled in his own work and ministry, and this leads to one conclusion—Jesus is indeed "the one who is to come."

Perhaps one of the major differences between John and Jesus is in their fundamentally divergent views of the message they proclaimed. Using modern language, John would be seen as too "exclusive" and parochial in his religious view, whereas Jesus would be seen as more "inclusive" and, perhaps, liberal. Jesus, for example, treated with full seriousness the spiritual views of a Samaritan woman, and he concerned himself with a Roman soldier. Jesus told parables that showed a magnanimous spirit toward non-Jews, something John did not do. Jesus told parables in which, for example, a man devoted to another religion—a Samaritan—was the embodiment of true piety. By contrast, he was at odds with the Pharisees, whose vision and religious rigidity validated Judaism itself. His opposition to the Pharisees and Sadducees was directed not necessarily against their religion but against their legalistic traditions, which he saw as the enemy of true piety. Their doctrinaire and legalistic approach to religion was insensitive to true spirituality. Thus, and unlike John, Jesus gave an authentic measure of dignity and respect to sincere believers whose views differed from his own religious tradition. In *Pluralism: Challenge to World Religions* (1985), Harold Coward maintained that: "a basis exists for a Christian openness to other faiths."[27] Likewise, Krister Stendahl has argued that the openness of Jesus may be seen in the fact that he came preaching God and the Kingdom as recorded in Mark 1:14. Stendahl continued that in the early church, when the kingdom did not come, perception shifted to focusing on Jesus as the Lord. Thus, Jesus preached a theocentric message about God's kingdom, but his disciples and subsequent representatives of the Church preached a Christocentric message. There is little doubt that the connection between the theocentric message of Jesus and the Christocentric proclamation of his followers, is found in the vision of the subsequent believers and the early Church, who extended the message of Jesus to incorporate the doctrine of hypostatic unity.[28]

The Message of Jesus: "God loves you."

It is important to look briefly at the background of the message of Jesus. Why did he preach the way he did? What was his motivation? Did he get his ideas from the earlier prophets? Why did we depart from their fundamental message to humanity? The fundamental Jewish teaching that was so dear to Jesus was the principle of human life. This is the center of Jewish philosophy and the gift of Judaism to the world. Simply stated, it is believed that when it comes to human life, quantitative factors did not signify. This means that an individual, if innocent, might not be sacrificed for the lives of a group. It was an important principle of the Mishnah that each man is a symbol of all humanity, and whoever destroys one man destroys, in a sense, the principle of life, just as, if he saves one man, he rescues all humanity.[29] The major teachings of Judaism in their adumbrated forms are still found in Christianity, including the principle of life. Nothing captures the imagination of the anti-apartheid theologians in South Africa more than the dehumanization of the peoples created in God's image. In this sense, the South African understanding of humanity is consistent with Judaism and mirrors it.

The four gospels affirmed this fundamental principle of life, and the expression "the Jews" even appears five times in each of the gospels of Matthew and Luke, and six times in Mark and seventy-one in John. John used the term more not because he was hostile to "the Jews," but because he used the term "the Jews" in many more ways than the other three gospels. In its original form, John may have been the earliest of the gospels. He may have used the term "the Jews" to mean many different things—the Sadducees, the Pharisees, or both together, the Temple security personnel, the Jewish establishment, the Sanhedrine, the Jewish ruling class—but also, and more importantly, the Jewish people. The most common meaning of the term in Christian consciousness and in theological dictionary, however, is "the opponents of Jesus and his teachings."[30]

A breach with Judaism was inevitable in the course of Christian history. For example, according to Jewish thought, the Torah existed before creation. It was not just a book about God. It pre-existed creation in the same way God did. In fact, the Torah was used by God to create the world. It was the blueprint of creation.[31] It was, however, not only the instrument God used in creating the world, as though God read it aloud like a magician when God said "Let there be light," but also "it had lain in God's bosom for 974 generations before God used it to create the universe."[32] According to Paul Johnson, a Jewish writer even stated:

> Some sages believed it had been offered simultaneously to seventy different nations in seventy languages, but all had refused. Israel alone had accepted it. Hence it was in a peculiar sense not just the Law and religion but the wisdom of Israel and the key to the ruling of Jews. Philo called it the ideal law of the philosophers, as Moses was the ideal lawgiver."[33]

Consequently, God ordained the inspiration of the Torah and of the Hebrew Scriptures. This became the Christian "Old Testament" after Christians also decided that some of their literature (not all) was also scripture and inspired. This they called the "New Testament." Christians believed that Hebrew prophets had spoken about Jesus and that he fulfilled prophetic expectations. Therefore, Christians could read the Jewish prophets and find things that Jesus must have done.[34] The major point of departure for Christians, however, was in regard to what the Jews could accept and what Christians cannot. This made a complete breach with Judaism inevitable. The Jews could accept the decentralization of the Temple: many had long done so, and soon all had to follow. They could accept a different view of the Law. What they could not accept was the removal of the wall of absolute distinction they had always drawn between God, the creator, and human beings, the created. That was the essence of Jewish theology and the belief that separated them from the pagans and the Christians. By removing this wall of distinction, with the doctrine of the incarnation of Jesus Christ, the Christians took themselves irrecoverably out of the Judaic faith and fell into the pagan theological territory.[35]

Furthermore, the Jewish thought that sinfulness and virtue were collective as well as individual. The Bible showed repeatedly that a city, a community, or a nation earned both merit and retribution by its actions. The Torah bound the Jews together as one body and one soul.[36] Just as a man could benefit from the worth of his community, so he was obliged to contribute to it. This is quite similar to the South African concept of *ubuntu*. We might recall what the famous Jewish teacher, Hillel the Elder, laid down: "Separate not yourself from the community and trust not in yourself until the day of your death." A Jew, who was aloof from the community, whether for a saintly or a devilish intent, would have no share in the next world because of his anti-social behavior. The Jews held tenaciously to the holistic notion that one man's sin, however small, affects the entire world, and vice versa. Judaism, therefore, never allowed the principle of individual guilt and judgment to override completely the more primitive and purer principle of collective judgment. Running the two in tandem produced a sophisticated and enduring doctrine of collective and social responsibility. Perhaps this is one of the greatest Jewish contributions to human social and religious development. Unlike the Greeks, who introduced the concept of a universal culture, the Jews introduced the concept of collective responsibility that was later developed into a religion of ethical monotheism.

It is both logical and consistent with Jewish thought to propel a strict concept of justice out of this. Therefore, the Jews were the first to introduce the concept of repentance and atonement, which also became a primary Christian theme.[37] The Jewish Scripture is full of references to "the change of heart": "turn ye even to me with all your heart," "rend your hearts and not your garments," and "make ye a new heart."

What Jesus challenged in Judaism was that fundamental salvation is reached by good deeds, or by repentance, or by making religious sacrifices. Specifically, he opposed in principle, the election, the covenant, and the Law. "They were inoperative, superseded, finished."[38] In this regard, Paul the apostle was very close to Jesus. Both had their roots in Palestinian Judaism. What both were preaching was new, and it was essentially the same theology—grace—without denying the moral or ethical values of the Jewish faith. Jesus stripped the law of everything but its moral dimension and ethical elements. It was not that Jesus was lax. To the contrary, he was even stricter in certain respects. He would not, for example, admit divorce. But divorce was a subject that would later become, and remains till today, enormously important in Christian ethics and religious life. But just as he would not accept the Temple when it came between God and the human pursuit of holiness, so he dismissed the Law when it impeded, rather than assisted, the path to God. In this sense, Jesus is within Judaism while at the same time transcending it.

It is with confidence and enthusiasm that we should affirm, therefore, that the message of Jesus was: "God loves you." He did not conform to any of the existing patterns of making peace with God in the Jewish tradition. He was not a Jewish nationalist. Jesus was a Jewish Universalist. Like John the Baptizer, Jesus affirmed that the program of repentance and rebirth should be carried to the multitude. But it was not the mission of Jesus as the viceroy of God, to hide in the desert or in the caves. It was not his mission to sit in the seat of the mighty, like the Sanhedrin. Rather, it was his mission to preach to *all,* in a spirit of humility, that God loves them. This did not make sense to the people then, and makes little sense to many today. Jesus Christ knew the Jewish history very well. He knew that some of the most exalted leaders in the Jewish religious traditions were internationalists. King David, for example, was one of the earliest internationalists. On the other hand, King Saul and some of the earliest Israelite leaders had been narrowly re-gionalist. It was in Jesus' message that God is for *all* people and that God loves them all.

What we must emphasize is also his method and how people responded to him. When John preached his message of repentance, prostitutes repented in sackcloth and ashes. Thieves became sober, and armed robbers threw down their weapons. This did not happen when Jesus preached. John was ascetic, and people knew it. They loved John. He was a saintly figure, and people respected him for that.

Jesus, on the other hand, ate with sinners, drank with prostitutes, and befriended tax collectors. In one important respect, Jesus was different from both his contemporaries and those who preceded him in prophetic tradition. The prophets before him, for example, spoke on behalf of the poor and defended the widows and the orphans. The prophets before him also defended those who were oppressed and exploited by the wicked, the rich, and the powerful. Jesus went further, however, by proclaiming them blessed, and actually took a stand among the pariahs of this world as well as among those who were despised by the respectable. In this sense, Jesus was more radical, more human, more assertive and transparent about the human condition, and more "unbelievable." Therefore, people hated him. The righteous hated him because he was not pious enough. The sinners did not like him because he did not participate in their sinfulness. Among the Gentiles, he was a Jew; among the Jews, he was like the Gentiles. He broke all the social taboos of his time. He spoke with the Samaritan woman in public,[39] and allowed a woman with hemorrhage to approach him for healing—not in private, but in the midst of a pressing crowd.[40] The woman dared to approach Jesus for healing even though she was an outcast according to the Jewish purification law. Jesus did not invoke the Law but healed her and restored her fully to the community.[41] Jesus is a healer who touches individuals in all dimensions of suffering, including the suffering of spiritual pride as well as sloth. Furthermore, Jesus welcomed the company of women and felt at home in the house of Mary and Martha of Bethany.[42] He exorcised women[43] and healed their children even if they were not Jews.[44] Wealthy women accompanied him and provided financial assistance for his ministry.[45]

Perhaps, Jesus thought that John's call to repentance was a good idea but that it was not ultimately effective. In fact, it was a counterproductive approach, for people would repent, cry, get emotional, roll on the ground, wear sack clothes, and make John feel good. But they returned to their normal sinful routine and wicked ways when Sabbath was over. Thus, their repentance was superficial, and John's approach was only partially successful, if at that. The method of Jesus was different. He refused to repeat John's failure and tactics. On the contrary, Jesus was open to the people. He ate and drank with the wicked people that his society condemned as unfit for the Kingdom. Jesus simply told the wicked that God loved them and that the kingdom was at hand. Did Jesus hope that his hearers would change their ways? Probably he did, but may be he did not. The kingdom of God does not depend on man's decision to change his ways; it is totally and radically about God. Therefore, he did not tell the people that they should change now or be destroyed. That was up to God. The message of Jesus was purely descriptive. John's message was prescriptive. Jesus' message was not about destruction but about healing. It was not about doing, it was about being; it was not about hell, it was about heaven; it was not about the God who was, it was about the God who was to come; it was not about damnation, it was about redemption. The message of Jesus was simply, "God loves you."

While early missionaries presented South Africans with the message of John, South Africans seem to have adopted, instead, the message and method of Jesus in their new Christian identity.

The Efficacy of the Message of Jesus

Is the message of Jesus now in crisis? The modern culture is antagonistic to it, just as the people of his day failed to understand it. They preferred the message and the method of John the Baptizer. The failure to see the transforming effect of the message of Jesus has endangered modern Christian culture, which is now in need of radical redress.

Nothing illustrates this better than the missionary activities of the 19th-century in Africa. Missionaries had no doubt about the superiority of their message, which was encoded in European culture. Early missionaries to South Africa were ethnocentic. There is a narrow line between one's regard for one's own religion and civilization, and a total disregard for the values and achievements of others. Missionaries dismissed the African way of life as evidence of religious and cultural depravity—reasons for it to be replaced by "their gospel" and their civilization.[46] Charles Villa-Vicencio, an anti-apartheid theologian from Cape Town, put it this way: "Converting souls to Christ meant, for many missionaries, a complete rejection by blacks of the African worldview and a denial of traditional social custom."[47] The assumption was that Africans were not good enough and that they must "repent" and turn around from their traditional ways in order for them to be acceptable and fit into God's kingdom. Early missionaries echoed John the Baptizer for South Africans in quite astonishing ways. The missionary assumption was that African Traditional Religion was unacceptable in God's kingdom. They claimed that Africans were worshipers of idols. On closer examination, however, Africans, like most near Eastern religions of antiquity, did not regard idols of wood, stone, or bronze as gods in themselves. They saw the images as a practical means whereby the ordinary, simple worshipers could visualize the divinity and achieve spiritual communion with the God that is real. This put both Africans and missionaries into a crisis of definition—what is the message of Christ, and what are the methods of articulating the message to other people? Could missionary observers of African worldview and religious ethos make mistakes of interpretations as they observed African worshippers? Is Christ the sole image of God?

Like John the Baptizer, missionaries addressed the question of religion but not that of faith. Religious awareness is its own value and that is what it has always been. It does not necessarily make people good or bad, more realistic or pure, or more saintly or godly. In some cases, religion has made bad people worse. At its most basic level, religion addresses human being's finitude, his inadequacy, his failure, his suffering, and his constant struggle with his existence. Religion is both rational and logical. It deals with human capacity to organize and understand. From this point of view, missionaries believed that there is only one true religion—Christianity. This idea, now losing grounds in European religious consciousness itself, was the single most important propeller of missionaries to Africa. Jesus, however, did not assert that only one religion is real. He asserted that only one God is real—an idea that is rooted in Judaism.

Is religion, therefore, useless to Jesus? Perhaps religion is useful in the sense that it serves as a stimulus to resistance against evil, injustice and oppression. This is, perhaps, the most effective tool Christians used against apartheid in the political context of South Africa. When one promotes justice, therefore, one is saving lives created in God's image. Thus, religion can help the one resisting injustice to gain self-awareness on the path to reaching God's kingdom. One of the primary functions of religion is to provide a stimulus for resisting injustice so that one can be truly free in the world. Christians used their faith as a tool against injustice in South Africa and did so effectively.

Religion as only a ritual would not promote the unconditional ethos in harmony with God's will in the world. The idea that only one religion is true is now on shaky grounds even in Europe, the continent that sent the largest number of missionaries to Africa in the 19th century. In the last half of the twentieth century, many Churches in Europe were half-full. How did Europe get from the point of sending the largest number of missionaries, to becoming a continent that now welcomes them? Why is it that many devoted followers of Christ in the Anglican tradition no longer teach that only one religion is true? For different reasons, the view that only one God is real resonates deeply in the views of many Christians both in Europe and in Africa.

What unified Jews was not a common belief in one religion or a common ancestry. Rather, there was a common devotion to a particular local shrine.[48] Many scholars of repute in the nineteenth and the early twentieth centuries dismissed the notion of a common descent of the Jews from the stock of Jacob.[49] They preferred to see the tribal groups of distant and disparate origins organizing themselves as an amphictyony[50] around the Israelite shrines that were being established about this time. The gathering of neighbors to defend a common religious belief does not mean that a common blood was a necessary factor. Genesis 37:1 even describes Jacob as a stranger in connection with a particular religious identity.

Within the social milieu of ancient Israel, two religious concepts emerged as more predominant than others. First, there was monolatry, the worship of one God without precluding the existence of others. Secondly, many of the leading religious figures were henotheists—they believed in a sole God, attached to a particular people, but nonetheless recognized the attachment of other people to their own Gods. This is the formative period upon which many people built their religious identity, and it is likely that this idea had its root in Judaism and in the religions of the Canaanites.

Faith on the other hand, is a more comprehensive religious phenomenon. The fundamental distinction between religion and faith is more or less a normative theological difference. Religion is the perennial human tendency to subject the word of God to the conditions of human thinking and desire. But faith is the exercise of the freedom granted by God's grace to hear, interpret, and follow God's words. Faith sometimes (not all the time) distrusts religion and its basic claims to logic. In the modern era, there is no peaceful co-existence between religion and faith. There is rather a tension. This does not mean that religion must disappear. No! Rather, it means that religion has become homeless and is now too harmful to faith. Faith is a restructuring of one's religious life in a truthful way by accepting one's finitude and celebrating God's love for the world. Bert Hoedemaker puts it best: "Faith refers to a system in which all aspects of reality—the ends of the earth and the end of time—are drawn together into one perspective, a perspective to which believers respond with trust and loyalty, and in which they find their spiritual home."[51]

Therefore, the message of Jesus has not been efficacious. The fault is our own, but it is also inevitable. Human nature wants proof, logic, and requirements for belonging. We find it difficult to return to the community of faith without absolution. But are we not to surrender our logic and be dependent on the sovereignty of God? Is that not faith? A return to God will enable us to reject the monitoring of our finitude by the standard of religion and give a sense of a decisive new beginning with God.

The love of God is not new. It is so old that we seemed to have forgotten its power. Yet, just as it was once recorded in our memory, in Africa it is now being recorded again for us to see it anew. The very God who seemed to have lost control of our lives in our religious disarray is constantly in charge and ready to invert our condition. It is better for the Church, therefore, to rediscover God, who is free, sovereign, and willing to take responsibility for his "sovereignty." When this happens, our religious funeral would turn to a festival, regrets and sorrow will become doxology, and fear and despair will turn to amazing grace.

The efficacy of the message of Jesus of Nazareth for our time would ultimately depend on making the transition from a funeral to a festival in which children of God everywhere would sing a new song and discern the new situation, that God loves them eternally and unconditionally. The message of John the Baptizer was efficacious because he spoke and organized his disciples and the first Church on the basis of religious principle and human failure. Early missionaries did the same in South Africa. John the Baptizer spoke about religions and all that failed. Jesus, on the other hand, spoke about God's love, and all that will never fail. There was only a false hope in the message of the Baptizer—there was no future without repentance. But there was no future for sinners who have repented but failed to know that God loves them. Only those who know that God loves them are truly free. Jesus of Nazareth quoted the book of Deuteronomy and the Prophet Isaiah more than any other passage from the Hebrew Scriptures. We read in Isaiah:

> Ho, everyone who thirsts, come to the waters; and you that have no money, come, buy and eat! Come, buy wine and milk without money and without price.

> Why do you spend your money for that which is not bread, and your labor for
> that which does not satisfy? Listen carefully to me, and eat what is good, and de-
> light yourself in rich food. (Isaiah 55:1–2).

Isaiah recorded the goodness of God to a disposed people, and Jesus
echoes this in the gospels. God's goodness takes us from the bondage of religion to the liberation of faith, from penitence to doxology. Isaiah also
stated in an earlier passage:

> Even youths will faint and be weary, and the young will fall exhausted; but those
> who wait for the Lord shall renew their strength, they shall run and not be weary,
> they shall walk and not faint. (Isaiah 40:30–31).

There was little doubt in the mind of the Prophet that the key phrase in
his message was "those who wait for the Lord." Therefore, it is not because
of what we have done but because of the love of God. Commenting on
Isaiah's words, the distinguished Hebrew Bible scholar, Walter Brueggemann stated: "It is in receiving and not grasping, in inheriting and not pos-
sessing, in praising and not seizing. It is in knowing that initiative has passed
from our hands and we are safer for it."[52] Thus, African Christianity is partly
a critique of every human effort to follow logic and reorganize on his or her
own. The newness in South Africa that comes from knowing the love of God
as articulated by Jesus of Nazareth is the only serious source of Christian energy in the world. The energy for which people yearn is precisely that which
only God can give. We must not underestimate the urgent calling of Jesus of
Nazareth, because there is no other source of life for the Church of the
twenty-first century.

Are we therefore to be passive? Does this mean that we are to do nothing? No! It only seems passive, as any trust in God often does. It would be a
cheap grace if we were to stand on the sideline doing nothing. But there is
nothing as active as an active obedience to God. If this active obedience is a
risk, it stands firm in the teachings of Jesus, and the Church must be willing
to take that risk because the Church is now in exile in many parts of the
world. The hope of the Church is never generated by the Church or among
the believers. The hope of the Church is always a gift of grace.

Nothing illustrates this grace better than two of the parables of Jesus of
Nazareth. In the first parable recorded by Matthew, Jesus told a story about
the kingdom of God. He said that the kingdom was like a farmer who employed day laborers. Some were hired early in the morning, some during the
mid-morning, some around noontime, still others in the middle of the afternoon, and the last were hired about an hour before the closing time. Then it
was time to pay the laborers. There was no doubt that the first crew expected
to be paid first and more than all the rest. The farmer paid first the last crew

that joined. Then he paid all the workers the same amount. When the crew that started early in the morning received their pay, they were taken aback as they found out that it was the same amount that all the others had received. They complained loudly and bitterly, as they should, and grumbled that it was unfair, as they must. The action of the farmer was a violation of the religious and moral sense.[53]

Luke recorded the second parable, which is also about the kingdom. According to him, Jesus told the parable of the kingdom, saying that it is like a king who invited guests to a banquet. The purpose of the banquet was to celebrate his son's wedding. Those who were invited, as special guests for the feast, did not come. But the king was creative and generous. He sent his servants to go and remind the invited guests that everything was ready. But the guests made a light of it, and started making excuses. According to Matthew's account of the parable, some guests were even cruel to the servants whom the king had sent, mistreating many and killing others.[54] The king himself was enraged and sent his troops to destroy the destroyers. Finally, the king asked his servants to go to the main street (where they were sure to find loiters who congregated to gossip). Since the invited guests proved to be unworthy of the king's invitation, the king then invited "everyone" who could be found. "Those slaves went out into the streets and gathered all whom they found, both good and bad; so the wedding hall was filled with guests." [55]

There are three main points in these two parables:

(a) In the first place, elements of surprise are to be expected in the gathering for the kingdom of God. We do not know exactly what God will do, and we know not who will be "in" and "out" of God's kingdom. Perhaps it is a surprise that almost four hundred million of the African population today claim to be Christians. In the first parable, one would expect that a particular system would be in place for hiring the workers. In the second parable, we would expect the banquet to be called off and rescheduled. In both cases, the behavior of the farmer and the king caught us off guard. In other words, God could act in an unpredictable manner in gathering people for the kingdom. E. P. Sanders put it this way: "Jesus described a topsy-turvy world."[56]

(b) In the second place, God has other people, who we do not know directly, who are equally worthy of his kingdom. Therefore, the universality of God's love extends to the end of the earth and to everyone. The parable of the Great Banquet shows that all our logic cannot fathom the extent of God's love. We do not know whom God will count "in" and whom he would count "out." Perhaps the concept of "in" and "out" does not exist for God. Therefore, we should not think that God values us alone or more than others. To repeat E. P. Sanders: God's kingdom is coming whether we are ready or not, and God will include whomever God will. God will include people who we think are unworthy and may exclude people who we believe are entitled to the kingdom. God's compassion makes everyone worthy of God's kingdom, for God created us and also redeemed us.[57]

(c) Finally, we do not receive God's forgiveness or approval because we have repented. We are not entitled to God's kingdom because we have reordered our lives, turned around, and abandoned our old ways. We are acceptable to God because we know the love of God. It is this love that woos us to God's kingdom. Therefore, we repent our sins not to show God that we merited God's kingdom, but because we know that God loves us.

A Summary

While John the Baptist used religion as an instrument for faith (and for salvation), Jesus minimally saw religion this way. In the view of Jesus, religion has very little to do with doctrinal certainty but a stimulus to promote justice and godliness. Religion is more than a cultic or religious activity, but rather a way of life or a way of being. Thus, religion can be a path that leads to a principled faith.

To summarize, we would see that in the context of the modern Church in South Africa, religion needs faith in order to keep it from producing impetuous and chaotic movements. This is why the message of John (a call for God's creation to be religious) needs the balance of the message of Jesus (a call for God's creation to a principled faith). In other words, religion needs faith in order to keep it from reducing human life to impersonal, detached calculations. The purpose of religion is not to cure bad people or make bad people better by obliterating their evil deeds and make them whole again. Religion often makes people go from bad to worse since they can hide their evil intentions under the banner of their religions. This is what Christian Afrikaners in South Africa did for generations under apartheid. Faith, on the other hand, which does not capitalize on the holiness of the few, has the ability to make all human beings whole, restoring a broken creation and a fractured world. This cannot occur easily, however, without the vehicle of religions. Thus, faith needs religious context in order to express itself, and the context of repentance proclaimed by John the Baptizer can complement the principled faith embedded in the recognition of the love of God. In order for faith to be relevant to humanity and serve the totality of the human condition, a sense of repentance as proclaimed by John the Baptizer is important.

Notes

[1] Leander E. Keck, *The Church Confident: Christianity Can Repent, but It Must Not Whimper,* (Nashville, Tennessee: Abingdon Press, 1993), 58.

[2] David Frawley, "The Missionary Position," BJP: News Reports, http://www.bjp.org/news/feb1799.htm.

[3] David Frawley, "The Missionary Position," BJP: News Reports, http://www.bjp.org/news/feb1799.htm.

[4] Ibid.

[5] See Gauri Viswanathan, *Outside the Fold: Conversion, Modernity, and Belief* (Princeton, New Jersey: Princeton University Press, 1998).

[6] Henry Venn was the secretary of the Church Missionary Society (CMC) in the late 1800s. He proposed that the purpose of the missionary was not to create an Anglican Church on the mission field but an indigenous Church that is rooted in the customs of the people. Indigenous Churches, thus created, will follow three-self formulae: it will be (1) self-supporting, (2) self-governing, and (3) self-propagating. Rufus Anderson, working separately in America, made a similar proposal for missionaries from the United States.

[7] V. Y. Mudimbe, *The Invention of Africa: Gnosis, Philosophy, and the Order of Knowledge* (Bloomington & Indianapolis: Indiana University Press, 1988), 47 ff.

[8] Mudimbe, *The Invention of Africa,* 48.

[9] Jean and John Comaroff, *Of Revelation and Revolution: Christianity, Colonialism, and Consciousness in South Africa* (Chicago & London: University of Chicago Press, 1991), p. 54. See also the second volume in the trilogy, *Of Revelation and Revolution: the dialectics of modernity on a South African frontier* (Chicago & London: University of Chicago Press, 1997).

[10] At the annual Yale-Edinburgh Conference in 2002, Brian Stanley of Cambridge University presented a brilliant paper about conversion at the University of Edinburgh, Scotland. The title of the paper was: "Conversion to Christianity: The Colonisation of the Mind." In the paper, he argued that the term "conversion" is not always appropriate to qualify the experience that takes place when an individual becomes a Christian. He argued that the word "transformation" is a preferred option because neither the receptor nor the missionary has a full control of what takes place in the process of conversion.

[11] The Yoruba people in West Nigeria use the word "*ironupiwada.*" "*Ironupiwada*" means turning completely from one way of life to another. Literarily, the word means a change of one's inner being that will be reflected in one's character. This word aptly describes the concept of "conversion" in the New Testament.

[12] Acts 14: 27.

[13] See Andrew F. Walls, *The Missionary Movement in Christian History: Studies in the Transmission of Faith* (Maryknoll, N.Y. and Edinburgh: Orbis Books and T. & T. Clark, 1996), 28 ff.

[14] Walls, *The Missionary Movement in Christian History,* 51-2; See also *The Cross-Cultural Process in Christian History: Studies in the Transmission and appropriation of Faith* (Maryknoll, NY and Edinburgh: Orbis Books and T. & T. Clark, 2002), 67–8.

[15] *Ubuntu* is a Zulu word that can be roughly translated to sharing and caring or "fellowship." But the Zulu people believe that it means more than that. In their awareness, *ubuntu* translates into an impetus to give rather than to receive for the common good of the community. This is unique to South African cultural experience, but it has been rejuvenated with new Christian identity. The word "*ubuntu*" has entered the vocabularies of the diverse population of South Africans, analogous to the word "Christian fellowship."

[16] Karl Marx's father, a Jew, was the first to convert to Christianity in his extended family ring. We can assume that Karl Marx's father wanted his son to have a successful intellectual career, and that becoming a Christian will facilitate this dream for his son. Karl Marx himself recognized that he was a Jew and respected his grandfather as a Jewish rabbi. See John L. Esposito, Darrell J. Fasching and Todd Lewis, *World Religions Today,* (New York: Oxford University Press, 2002), 162

[17] Paul Johnson, *A History of the Jews* (New York: Haper & Row, Publishers, 1988), p. 312. Also quoted in H. H. Ben Sasson (ed.), *A History of the Jewish People* (trans., Harvard 1976), 826.

[18] Gustavo Gutiérrez, *A Theology of Liberation* (Maryknoll, New York: Orbis Books, 1973), 8.

[19] Jaroslav Pelikan, *The Vindication of Tradition,* p. 65. See also Leander E. Keck, *The Church Confident,* (Nashville, Tennessee: Abingdon Press, 1993), 45.

[20] Second National Meeting of United Church of Christ Women in 1986. *Names of God Litany* (St. Louis, MO: Chalice Press, 1995): No. 11.

[21] Janet Martin Soskice, *Metaphor and Religious Language,* (Oxford: Clarendon Press, 1985), 148.

[22] Ibid.

[23] Ibid.

[24] E. P. Sanders, *The Historical Figure of Jesus,* (Middlesex, England: Allen Lane—Penguin Press, 1993), 233.

[25] Ibid. 203.

[26] Ibid.

[27] Harold Coward, *Pluralism: Challenge to World Religions* (Maryknoll, New York: Orbis Books, 1985), 17.

[28] See Krister Stendahl, "Notes for Three Bible Studies," in *Christ's Lordship and Religious Pluralism,* ed. G. H. Anderson and T. F. Stransky (Maryknoll, New York: Orbis Books, 1981), 10 ff.

[29] Sanhedrin 4, 5. See also Paul Johnson, *A History of the Jews* (New York: Haper & Row, Publishers, 1987), 155.

[30] Franz Mussner, *Tractate on the Jews: The Significance of Judaism for Christian Faith* (trans., Philadelphia 1984), 180ff.

[31] See Proverbs 8:22ff.; Ecclesiastes 1:1–5, 26; 15:1; 24:1ff.; 34:8.

[32] Paul Johnson, *A History of the Jews,* 179.

[33] Ibid.

[34] E. P. Sanders, *The Historical Figure of Jesus,* 63ff.

[35] Paul Johnson, *A History of the Jews,* 144ff.

[36] Belkin, op. cit., 134ff.

[37] Paul Johnson, *A History of the Jews,* 159.

[38] Ibid. 131.

[39] John 4:1–38.

[40] Matthew 5:25–34.

[41] Matthew 5:25–34.

[42] Luke 10:38–42.

[43] Luke 8:2

[44] Mark 7:25–30.

[45] Luke 8:1–3

[46] See Charles Villa-Vicencio, "Mission Christianity" in Martin Prozesky and John de Gruchy, eds. *Living Faiths in South Africa,* (Cape Town and Johannesburg: David Philip, 1995), 64–5.

[47] Ibid.

[48] Paul Johnson, *A History of the Jews,* (New York: Harper and Row, Publishers, 1987), 21. See also Thomas Cahill, *The Gifts of the Jews: How a Tribe of Desert Nomads Changed the Way Everyone Thinks and Feels.* (New York; Nan A. Talese Publishing Group, Inc. 1998).

[49] W. F. Albright, "The Song of Deborah in the light of Archaeology," *Bulletin of the American School of Oriental Research,* 62 (1936); H. M. Orlinsky, "The Tribal System of Israel and Related Groups in the Period of Judges," *Oriens Antiquus,* I (1962). Paul Johnson, *A History of the Jews,* (New York: Harper and Row, Publishers, 1987), 21.

[50] This term "amphictyony" is used to denote the gathering of neighbors in ancient times to defend a common religious center. It was commonly associated with an association of like-minded neighbors or states in ancient time to defend a common religious beliefs.

[51] Bert Hoedemaker, *Secularization and Mission: A Theological Essay,* (Harrisburg, PA: Trinity Press International, 1998), 14.

[52] Walter Brueggemann, *The Prophetic Imagination,* (Philadelphia: Fortress Press, 1978), 79.

[53] Matthew 20: 1–16.

[54] Matthew 22:5–7

[55] Matthew 20:10 (NRSV).

[56] E. P. Sanders, *The Historical Figure of Jesus,* 197.

[57] Ibid.

❀ Chapter Two
THE FAILURE OF
MISSIONARY'S SUCCESS

In the last chapter, we examined the roots of the Church in the New Testament and analyzed some of the problems the Church is facing today because of the privileges associated with the Church. South Africa is a rich land that attracted both British and Dutch Colonialists. The Dutch also brought to South Africa controversial Calvinist interpretations of Christianity and many exploited the wealth of the land and subjugated its peoples. Even today, after 300 years of insidious oppression of the majority, Western Christian investors continue to "harvest" gold, diamond, uranium, copper, coal, and other natural resources from South Africa for fabulous profits, but the majority of South Africans continue to languish in poverty. This has created an ethical dilemma for a large number of people, especially Christians, who want to disassociate their faith from apartheid and neo-imperialism. This is our focus in the next two chapters. This chapter focuses specifically on the failure of the missionary's successful activities in South Africa. We will look at the beginnings of missionary works in South Africa. We will also look at the beginnings of the missionary's work around the Cape and the alignment of the missionary-initiated Churches with the message of John the Baptizer.

The Failure of Missionary's Successful Activities

Nothing is as concrete as the failure of missionary's success in South Africa. The missionaries in Africa were not unfamiliar with the failure of their remarkable success. What does this mean? The missionary's success in Africa in general, and in South Africa in particular, is obvious. At the end of the 20th century, Africans were cemented in their literary and cultural traditions with the West; Africans were wearing Western clothes; and Africans started to think as if they were Americans or Europeans.

There are at least two kinds of the failure of missionary's success that we must look at: First, there was the failure of the loss of the goal attained. That is, there was the appearance of an unforeseen problem associated with the success. We can call this "a paradox of failure within success." A physical example in modern warfare is the construction and reconstruction of nuclear plants by developed nations. The successful construction is dovetailed by the worry of sending the heated water of the plants to the ocean, and this subsequently destroys the marine life in the ocean. The success is inadvertently damaging to the ecological measure in place. Human consumption of the fish from the ocean that has been polluted by the heated water from nuclear plants can invariably cause dreadful diseases, such as cancer. Consequently we are diminished by the successful construction of the nuclear plants. In just the same way, we can split atoms, but the success creates the problems of disposal of the waste. The Indians eliminated the danger of poisonous snakebites by killing them, but the countryside is overrun by rats that snakes would have consumed. In Sri Lanka where citizens do not often kill snakes for religious or cultural reasons, there are few rats (success) but poisonous snakes have claimed the lives of many (failure).

An improved medical care in the West reduces infant mortality. It also fosters longevity of life. This brilliant success, however, has resulted in overpopulation, hunger and lower standard of living for the majority. Similarly, good roads and highways facilitate driving, but they also cause pain when there are fatalities on the roads, air pollution, and disfiguring of the countryside. Likewise, the marvelous invention of the telephone, computers, e-mails, and the like, enables us to communicate faster and more effectively, but they have almost destroyed the art of writing letters.

The missionary's efforts in South Africa created the new possibilities for all South Africans in their spiritual landscape. There are Church buildings and Western-style hospitals. This success, however, has caused the gradual death of ancestral mores and the decay of authentic African traditions. Early missionaries wanted Africans to adopt the European way of life, and the adoption of Western lifestyles has created a new literary tradition for Africans. This is a success that has also created a psychic damage for the indigenous population and a crisis of African identity. This has also made it difficult to re-Africanize the indigenous population. What missionaries jointly intended for the indigenous population in South Africa was to accept the Christian faith. This worthy goal also emancipated them from their ancestral mores. Thereby, they were deracinated from their traditional environment. Missionaries also provided European way of life for Africans. There is little doubt that the intension was for Africans to adopt Christianity in European draping. In the process of accepting the Christian faith, however, there was a gradual collapse of traditional African values. The new ways undercut civic duty and the African traditional loyalty to the community. They place high value on otherworldliness and prize Christian asceticism. In an essay entitled: "Blessed are the Powerful: Christian Righteousness and the Redistribution of Power" Cornel du Toit stated it best:

> Christianity is imperialistically orientated. There is only one truth to which all must bow and this truth must be spread all over the world, no matter what the consequences may be for non-Western, indigenous cultures. This is naturally not exclusive to Christianity and is innate to many other religions.[1]

This would not have happened if Africans themselves were the responsible agents for crafting the essential categories of Christianity in their particular context without the intermediary of European Christians. In *Out of Every Tribe and Nation: Christian Theology at the Ethnic Roundtable,* Justo L. González articulated it best when he stated, "The fact that there are four 'gospels,' and that from them we may derive different conclusions and perspectives, is of fundamental importance for Christian missionary enterprise."[2] It is consistent with the New Testament covenantal relationship with God to suggest that believers from different historical and existential backgrounds will see their faith differently and that their worldviews do have definitive effects on the shape their understanding of the Christian faith would take. Therefore, human existential condition has important contributions to make in shaping their understanding of God and their Christian identity. More than any other religion, it is clear from the beginning that the nature of the Christian faith was sufficiently plastic that subtle differences in the conditions of its growth and life could affect it profoundly. Expansion of the faith does not so much depend on the nature of the Christian doctrine as much as on the adherents of the faith who maintained that it was not for believers to first be intellectually convinced and then convert to Christianity, but through the love of the Christian community were the believers transformed.

The second failure of the successful missionary activities in South Africa is the "Constantine" ambiguity. It is more acute and needs an urgent attention. This is where the goal achieved is destroyed by the success. This is what makes certain aspects of missionary activities on the continent counterproductive. The goal of missionary movements in Africa was, no doubt, to gain converts and multiply their numbers. This is a worthy goal, and no one would quarrel with missionaries in their attempt to increase the number of converts into God's kingdom. But what often happens in Africa, and particularly Southern Africa, is that the Church becomes overrun with members who depended heavily on the missionaries both emotionally and theologically.

One of the major challenges for Christian missions in Africa today is the identification of Christianity with wealth and prosperity, against the enduring spiritual values of the African simple life. Also, missionaries are constantly under the danger of making theological and cultural mistakes and there is no place for them to hide. Their vulnerability becomes multiplied when they have to do everything on the field or return home because of the overwhelming condition of the situation they were ill prepared to deal with themselves. This pseudo-conversion to mainline missionary Churches in South Africa undermined God's Kingdom and raises question about what it means to be converted. A conversion (transformation) to Christianity has to be genuine and sincere. Otherwise the converted would likely relapse into the old customs and habits of life. A cross-fertilization of Christianity with the traditional religions, on the other hand, has the potential to sustain Christianity when the new and the old become interwoven in the lives of the devotees.

Sebastian Castellio, a Church historian in the sixteenth century, put this failure of missionary's success quite bluntly: "one who forces people into the Church is like a man, who, to augment the wine, fills the barrel with water. He [obviously] has more—but what's it like?"[3] There is little doubt that the expansion of the Church in Africa required certain accommodation of the modes and mores of the indigenous population for it to be successful. When Africans entered the missionary-initiated Churches, they came in with their past, their Africanness, and their religious worldview that was marked with the eloquence of ancestral wisdom. Thus, an amalgamation occurs that may be enrichment, though more often, the missionaries view it as a perversion of the Church. Thus, while numbers wreck the goal, this has been an unavoidable religious phenomenon from the time of Constantine. M. Thomas Thangaraj was insightful in the following statement:

> The Edict of Milan (313 C.E.) by Emperor Constantine changed the situation of persecutions to a setting in which Christianity was bestowed with royal favor. Every attempt was made by Constantine to stabilize his empire through the building up of the Christian Church. It was Constantine who called the first ecumenical council for the purpose of settling divisions among Christians over issues of doctrine and practice. He encouraged the construction of big Church buildings, known as basilicas, with great pomp and glory. Constantine's mother, Helena, was involved in the recovering of relics connected with the life, ministry, death, and resurrection of Jesus. Constantine declared Sunday as the weekly holiday in 321 C.E. He humanized criminal law on the basis of Christian principles. Clergy and bishops

were elevated to powerful positions. Thus Christianity came to be the most favored religion of the empire.[4]

As in the time of Constantine, these large congregations in Africa often require skillful managements that missionaries are ill equipped to provide. The load of ministry becomes totally unmanageable, creating a serious burden of "Church" growth. This is not to say that the Church should not increase in numbers. What is obvious is that missionaries had more on the plate than they could chew. There are ways of handing the problems, but missionaries are not often willing to listen to the indigenous people and incorporate the management skills the local people could provide.

In a post-colonial world, modernity became the unenviable result in many parts of Africa. One can even say that if colonialism brought modernity to Africa, the rejection of Western colonialism by leaders trained by the Church became the mark of a new beginning of post-colonial Christianity. A political backlash was inevitable, including a bid by Church leaders in Africa for political independence and a rejection of some Western values, such as capitalism and political individualism. Thus, the arrival of missionaries propelled a new beginning, both religious and political, for the majority in Africa. Questions that the majority of the missionary-producing Churches in the West were anticipating included how Africans could pick up the pieces of the past and begin to adopt the Western way of life, rejecting their ancestral language and culture. But ironically, it was the presence of missionaries that drove the majority of Africans back to the ancestral language and culture. In this sense, missionaries in Africa indirectly helped Africans bring to light the significance of their ancestral language and culture. This has been the consistent argument of the Yale scholar and historian of Christian missions, Lamin Sanneh.[5]

Thus, we can say that missionaries also favored a recovery of sight for the indigenous life and place values on the recovery of political and economic independence and a restoration of indigenous values and community life. This, however, was only an indirect result of the missionary activities in Africa. The paradox of Western military and missionary presence in Africa is that Western values, such as a sense of dignity and equality, lent support to the African indigenous efforts to undermine colonial and religious domination. This is similar to the way Mohandas Gandhi (1869–1948) campaigned for the freedom of his people in India after learning the language of the oppressors well enough to use it to challenge the authority to practice in India what was preached in Britain.

In a book on World Religions, John L. Esposito argued that when the number of converts to Christianity grew, Africans developed their own indigenous forms of Christianity in "revolt against the tight control missionaries sought to maintain over African Christianity."[6] But it is not so much that

Africans converted to Christianity in the way most Christians in the West traditionally assumed. Their liturgical liveliness, the use of the Bible, and the nature of their evangelicalism make one conclude that Africans have not so much converted to Christianity as much as converting the God of the missionaries to their own spiritual awareness and existential religious needs. Hence, Philip Jenkins asserted that in Africa, "Christian missionaries were not so much breaking new grounds as reopening ancient and quite familiar mines."[7] Elsewhere on the continent, missionaries were met with enthusiasm that would have been difficult to explain if not because we realize that the indigenous people in Congo, for example, are rediscovering what had been the national religion only a century or so earlier.[8] This will be very clear as we examine the African Church in the modern African-American Spirituality.

The African Church in African-American Spirituality

During the second half of the 20th Century, two schools of thought emerged in the study of the people of African origin and their beliefs: (1) The first school is the Afro-centric school championed by cultural anthropologists.[9] This school sees Africa as the ancestral home of black people in the Diaspora.[10] One of the most celebrated leaders of this Afro-centric school, also known as Africanism,[11] was Melville J. Herkovits. The contention of this school is that the experiences, religions, worldviews, and values of Afro-Americans may best be seen in light of clearly defined traditions and life-styles that have defined them over time and migrated with them to every part of the world, beginning in the era of enslavement.   (2) The second school of thought is simply termed "Atlanticism."[12] The chief proponents of this school are predominantly sociologists of religion. These scholars agree with the Afro-centric school that Africa is the ancestral home of Black people in the world. They believe, however, that the currents of a dynamic world have altered the religious beliefs and cultures of Afro-Americans. In his book, *The Negro Church in America* published in 1963, E. Franklin Frazier articulated the view that during slavery Afro-Americans lost one identity—their African heritage or the quality of their "Africanness"—and acquired another, being Americans. He postulated in this hypothesis of deculturization, therefore, that Afro-American worldviews evolved independently of an African influence. According to him, Afro-American culture began without any African antecedents because slavery was so devastating in America that it destroyed all African elements among Afro-Americans. Slavery in the United States destroyed the African family institution and the indigenous African social and religious structure. It also put blacks in close contact with whites, from whom Afro-Americans learned new patterns of thought and behavior that they subsequently adapted to their own cultural and religious idioms.[13]

In the past decade or so, a new school of thought called the "Atlanticist school" has taken Frazier's view to a new level of scholarship. It is too simplistic, the Atlanticists claimed, to say that the dynamic culture and religious currents of the Western civilization have not influenced people of African descent as they have influenced all other people in the Western hemisphere. They contend that there has been a cross-fertilization of religious and cultural ideas. As Isidore Okpewho stated:

> It seems only reasonable to expect that, after so many centuries of expatriation from Africa, the New World Black sensibility would find it increasingly difficult to keep faith with its ancestral sources (which, we must add, have scarcely remained the same), given the urgency of contingent forces. After a while it becomes hard to draw lines, with any degree of calibrative accuracy, between what is *truly* African and what is not, despite our most cherished ideological convictions.[14]

Like all others in the Western hemisphere, modernity and the pluralistic age of Western societies have influenced Afro-Americans in a way that has implications for the essence of Afro-American religious life and identity. Thus, in the several centuries that black peoples have been living in the Western societies, their belief systems have not remained intact and pure. There is a further complication that would be of interest to both Atlanticists and Afro-centric advocates alike. It is of theoretical relevance to religious historians that African cultural and religious history is not solely dependent on indigenous roots. Societies in Africa have long been shaped by major external forces and have been subjected to non-indigenous factors stemming from the neighboring continents of Asia and Europe even before the enslavement years.[15] Thus, African civilization itself has been shaped by great migrations of people across waters and from distant lands, from other continents and cultures.

The argument here is that Afro-Americans, in their co-existence with a broad spectrum of different peoples and religions, have themselves been able to fashion a new religious culture in response to what they have encountered. Their response does not merely depend on the religious categories of Africa, their ancestral home—or on the hybrid religious climate that has inevitably become their "home" away from home—but on a cross-fertilization and creative mingling of both.

Afro-Americans have responded to religious pluralism by looking into their religious roots in Africa and culling a new religious identity that owes its creation to the multiplicity associated with the age of religious pluralism itself. It seems that the issue of extracting an African religious identity, however, is beclouded by at least two forces of Euro-American intellectual property:

(1) The first is the very habit of Afro-Americans to search for their identity within the Atlanticist tradition in a nebulous air of postmodern doubt. When African Americans do this, they restrict their religious identity to a category that only theorizes blackness and excludes Afro-Americans from all but the periphery of a true embrace of their African religious roots. This does not mean that Afro-Americans are no longer "Africans" because they read the works of Jacques Derrida, shop at Prada, drink Coca Cola, and watch David Letterman's late night show.[16] The accident of Western historical conditions that have shaped the Afro-American religious experience have not obliterated or negated the energy of the past in Afro-American religious expression. The Afro-Americans, Afro-Europeans, Afro-Asians, and all Africans abroad everywhere, do not stop being "Africans" because they are various and live in different locations.

(2) The second intellectual force forming the response of Afro-Americans is the tradition that celebrates the dissolution of the walls between various religious identities in a pluralistic age. All religions are not the same. Religions have permanent "essentials" in their particularity and identifiable idioms or languages. There is something fixed and eternal in the particulars within the mixture of multi-religiosity and multi-culturalism.

Afro-Americans belong as perfectly to this new age as to the religious world of the African peoples. They call themselves Christians, Muslims, Jews, Hindus, and Buddhists. Yet they accept gladly their link with the people they believe are their kin in a distant land of Africa.

As religious thinkers look closely at the response of Afro-Americans to the age of religious diversity, and as they draw insights into the sources of periodic conflicts between Christianity and Islam in Black religious consciousness, for example, we must ask the following questions: (a) What does it mean to say that one has an African ancestry in a religiously pluralistic culture? (b) Is one's ancestry enough to account for certain psychic factors associated with one's encounter with the divine in a different religious tradition? In other words, does one have to be of African birth to be religious in a certain way? (c) How did Africans manage to create a viable religious life for themselves after they were enslaved in the Americas? (d) How were they able to negotiate the social, political, cultural, and spiritual encounter in the world of multi-religiosity? (e) What criteria are we to use to measure their success, as since 1619 they have been forced to co-exist with other peoples as a result of the unkind forces of history and social circumstances? (f) How successful have they actually been?

In connection to modern Muslim-Christian relations, Colin Chapman provided a tentative answer to some of these questions. He recollected an experience of a Western Christian who lived among Muslims in Turkey, and stated: "It has become harder and harder for me to imagine or even want them to convert...we should be talking about coexistence rather than conversion."[17] Thus, Christians should be talking not only about "conversion" in relation to non-Christians. They should also be talking about mutual enrichment and transformation, as well as a constructive co-existence that will include mutual teaching and learning. Perhaps, it is how we are in our religious identity that matters most to God. The tension in the modern Muslim-Christian relation is not borne out of a simple great divergence between Christianity and Islam, but out of certain theological similarities amidst essential differences. Chapman stated it best: "Could we not believe that Muslim ideas about God...might...come a little closer to those revealed in the Gospels?"[18]

These questions and our responses to them could not possibly be exhaustive, even though scholarship indicates that enormous attention has been paid to this subject in academic circles, symposia, and international academic conferences.

All in all, it is rather clear that Afro-Americans and their progeny confronted a host of religious environments and built a dynamic religious life for themselves. Thus, many factors contributed to the spirituality of Afro-Americans today, and these factors are from many sources. A more practical question beneath the surface of intellectual awareness is a bigger and more fundamental issue: how did Afro-Americans build a religious life on ideologies of selfhood that have guided their efforts to adjust to the world in which they find themselves? How did they respond to religious pluralism in a spiritual way? Isidore Okpewho gave one answer when he stated:

> ...the slaves held on stubbornly to their ancestral mores not only as a political statement but [also] as a psychological necessity, and found ways of masking their African customs with [a] superficial veneer of European icons when their owners sought to erase their African memories. Long after emancipation, and during reconstruction, the old sense of roots continued to express itself even when time had steadily taken a toll on memories of Africa.[19]

African-descended Americans found religion a useful outlet for reassuring themselves of the enduring indigenous values they found lacking in the culture of whites, who controlled their lives in bondage and in freedom. Therefore, the cliché that "it was easier to get the Israelites out of Egypt than for Moses to get Egypt out of the Israelites" is not only applicable to the non-religious life of Afro-Americans but also to their religious life. The religious energy of the past was not destroyed by geographical boundaries. But we could say, as some scholars have done, that Afro-Americans are practicing "anti-racist-racism"[20] in their religious and political beliefs. It is also clear that Afro-Americans have responded to the age of religious pluralism in at least three ways: (1) in their confession and profession of the essential categories of the Christian faith, the Islamic faith, and Judaism (2) in rearticulating the religious traditions traceable to their ancestral home in Africa and cross-fertilizing it with the new traditions in the Western world, and (3) in ideological, political, and social perspectives.

The profession of an African-centered interpretation of the Christian faith in the Western world by Afro-Americans is more of an act of confession and re-affirmation of the Christian faith in an age of multiplicity of religions, than an assimilation of European cultures and Protestant Christianity. If we would move beyond the actual historical circumstances that have called "the black interpretation" of Christianity into play, we would find ourselves in the zone of basic human responses to which Africa as a place of ancestry of Afro-Americans holds no special claims. Thus far, a good deal of energy has been employed in arguing for African origins of Afro-American religious expression, dress, music, dance, speech, literature, food, culture, sports and the performing arts. There is justification to continue to invoke a sense of African origin at crucial points of creativity in Afro-American life, and scholars are quite justified in turning "essentialist" lights on those aspects and categories of Afro-Americans that mirror continental African traditions. It is now more important, however, to channel scholarship and energy into highlighting and celebrating the sheer creativity with which the blacks of the New World (without African antecedent) have triumphed over efforts to erase their racial memories and have created a viable religious existence for themselves. John S. Mbiti's argument on the inseparability of the religious from the secular in continental African daily life and outlook has its basic character and roots in Afro-American social and historical realities that are peculiarly African in origin. But we must explore new factors created by the climate of religious pluralism surrounding the paths blacks have had to cut for themselves beyond the encumbering mists of ancestral antecedents. We need to shake religious pluralism from an obsession with intercontinental burden brought by the new world order and the process of globalization, and devote attention to some of the humble dimensions of black religious experiences. Some of the steps include the way blacks have made Christianity, Islam, and Judaism viable by creating new and idiosyncratic cultural contexts for them. Another step is to examine the social context in which religion is embedded in the Diaspora.[21] Religious continuities between Africans and Afro-Americans will be fully grasped neither by sociologists of religion, who do not see that African spirituality belongs to the human spiritual quest and collective spiritual consciousness, nor by cultural anthropologists, who do not ask questions about the social and economic environment leading Africans in the Diaspora to examine and question the theology behind human conditions of hopelessness. Afro-American spirituality has taken confident-building measures. Collectively, this religious phenomenon is a way the universe is trying to re-discover itself.

The Afro-American congregations are strong. At the end of the 20th century, eighty percent of the Black congregations in the United States, for example, claimed to be Protestant.[22] There is a conscious effort, we would assume, of Afro-Americans to want to find spiritual and ethical meanings in their history and to want to do so within the context of Christianity, Islam, or Judaism. As C. Eric Lincoln stated, "The Black Church evolved not as a formal, black 'denomination,' with a structured doctrine, but as an attitude, or a movement."[23] Reaffirming the Christian faith, Afro-American Churches are a part of the Black sacred cosmos in a religiously pluralistic society. In a sense, their Christian understanding and confession are a moral alternative to European Christianity and North American mainline denominations. Their Christian response is not, however, to exhibit an aberrational attempt to mimic mainstream white culture, but to see it as a point of departure in their authentic African Christian response to the age. There are, for example, exceptional elements that distinguish Afro-American Christian identity from European Christianity and culture. But there is an historical divergence as well.

In his pioneering work, *Major Black Religious Leaders: 1755–1940*, Henry J. Young gave a detailed account of how Richard Allen (1760–1831) began the African Methodist Episcopal Church (AME). Richard Allen and a small group of blacks usually attended St. George Methodist Episcopal Church in Philadelphia without any serious resentment from the white members of that Church. When the number of blacks attending St. George grew significantly, Allen recollected: "they moved us from the seats we usually sat on, and placed us around the wall."[24] The area reserved for blacks during worship was referred to as "the Negro pew."[25] Absalom Jones, William White, and Dorus Ginnings, who were also members of St. George Methodist Episcopal Church, supported Richard Allen in proposing a new Church for blacks. These men did not want to detach themselves from St. George Methodist Episcopal Church. They knew, however, that an independent black congregation would offer them a sense of dignity they did not receive at St. George. Although the white members of the congregation threatened that they would disown Allen and his friends if they formed a separate church, Allen and his friends left St. George. It was this action that gave rise to the beginning of the African Methodist Episcopal Church in the United States in 1794, and Allen subsequently purchased an old frame building and officially opened it for worship in the same year.[26] In 1799, Bishop Asbury ordained Allen as a deacon. Absalom Jones, who originally started the Church with Allen, organized a separate congregation called African Protestant Episcopal Church (APEC) following a disagreement on ecclesiastical matters. In 1816 all the AME Churches gathered in Philadelphia to elect their first bishop. Daniel Coker was elected but resigned the next day to support Richard Allen, who was consecrated by ordained ministers at the same meeting.[27]

Almost all African initiated Churches in the United States tend to be evangelical, and as Christians in South Africa did to the European missionary's faith, it is important to see that Afro-Americans did not so much convert to Christianity as they converted the God of Christianity to their own spiritual awareness and existential condition.[28] Preaching is based, for example, on biblical stories from the Hebrew Scriptures and the Christian Gospel. This, however, is not without practical applications. Holiness and Sanctification are emphasized in their charismatic preaching, and sermons are directed to converting the unchurched people to Christianity. A prominent part of their sermons is the social teaching that often emphasizes an egalitarian way of life—what they did not receive in white Churches. One of the most profound responses of Afro-American Protestant Movement to Christianity, however, is a broad Civil Right Movement of Christian activism for which the 1960s was only a small segment. This response also created an internal influence on Afro-American culture itself. Henry J. Young observed: "The black Church became the vanguard of social activism."[29]

It is important here to mention that although religions in the parent continent of Africa are as varied and diverse as African cultures, there have been unified themes as well. Africa itself is a large collection of societies shaped by an unusually large variety of influences, and Christians from different regions of Africa are often shaped by the particularities of their cultures. One of the unifying themes in the Afro-American faith community was the social activism championed by Afro-American Christians during the Civil Right years. In the 1940s and 1950s, Christians in Africa and Afro-American Christians fought for political freedom simultaneously in ways that we can say were mutually influential. It is important to note, for example, that the day Kwame Unkrumah[30] was sworn in as the president of the newly independent Ghana in 1957, seven African American students were admitted to a public school in Arkansas for the first time in U.S. history without a protest. Hence, most of the early Christian leaders who fought for political independence in African nation states were Christians who had received missionary education, but later converted Churches to political platforms similar to Afro-American use of Churches in the 1940s and 1950s in the United States.[31]

It is in their style of worship and social activism, however, that Afro-Americans carried over a measurable imprint of their Africanness to the United States most forcefully, and not in the substance or essence of their faith. This does not mean, however, that Afro-Americans did not respond in substance to the traditions of the parent continent of Africa.

In the religious world of Afro-Americans, much of the Africanness mirrored in the African pantheon of divinities has been appropriated second hand from other places across the Atlantic. Thus, Afro-Americans have to redesign, almost on a clean slate, a new spiritual identity without a direct connection with Africa. More than that, Afro-Americans have to redesign new roles for those old divinities and their manifestation because the African religious antecedent has been partly broken and needed to be refashioned and then welded.

In *Flash of the Spirit,* Robert Farris Thompson sees "ancient African organizing principles of soap and dance as a key element in the evolution of cultural forms in the New World Societies."[32] Yet, this idea is not shared universally. Paul Gilroy has voiced his resistance to African origins we can trace to E. Franklin Frazier, whose debates in the 1940s with Melville Herskovits provided fuel and much energy for the studies of Africans in the Diaspora. The religious fervor of the black people arrives from many corners to the New World, and there are many factors responsible for its continuity other than just the trans-Atlantic slave trade. For instance, language has an important role to play in the creation of rhetoric on the black American pulpits. Therefore, effective communication has played a decisive role in the emergency of Afro-American spirituality far more than a pure African ancestry.

If we must consider Afro-American religious expression as an offshoot of African spirituality, but judge the source of inspiration of Afro-American religious expression primitive, while considering the product to be modern, elegant, and robust, certain inconsistencies would be found in the internal logic and further weaken the argument that a pure and direct antecedent existed between Afro-American spirituality and Africa. A flight from "home" is always a curious paradox, because nothing could be more particular than the recognition that a cultural and religious location, however unsuitable or unstable, always has inherent psychological authority over one's spiritual destiny, even when it does not enjoy the authority of participation in the journey that leads to an anticipated spiritual destiny fashioned by religiosity. One does not deny the home location, yet one must not hold on to it if one wanted to participate in the journey fully. When searching for a place to relocate Afro-American religious identity, one will both find it and lose it at the same time by solely looking for it in Africa.

The relationship of Black cultures to multi-religious society must deal with both positional and spiritual identity. There is no doubt that the Black world has grown to the point that it hardly makes sense to take a unidirectional view that will give privilege to any geographical region above all others. The geographical and ideological boundaries between Afro-Americans and Africans must be dissolved. The ideological boundaries that distance has erected between Africa and the New World are artificial borders. More than thirteen percent of the U.S. population has African ancestry. The new waves of African immigrants to both Europe and America suggest that over a million people of African birth now classify Europe and North America as their first homes.[33]

But in the final analysis, this constructed geographical position, in a fundamental sense, is also a statement of identity. Religious dialogue is now more open than ever before. This is not unrelated to the open dialogue about race and race relations and the impending recognition of the classification "mixed race" for some categories of Americans that do not fit into any of the official racial categories.

One of the ways to understanding the religious life of Africans in the Diaspora is not to see it as an ontological phenomenon, or as a theory or a doctrine, not even as a permanent icon that is accumulating. It has to be considered as an attitude, an ethos, a philosophical life brought by necessity. African religious or spiritual awareness is also subject to historical and theological limits that are imposed on it, and devoted followers possess the possibility of going beyond inherited religious awareness.

Africans in the Diaspora are bringing their own building blocks to the construction of a universal religious civilization. In a comprehensive study, *The Black Church in the African American Experience* (1990), C. Eric Lincoln and Lawrence Mamiya identified important aspects of Afro-American religious experience. There is little doubt that a strong correlation exists between traditional African religions and Afro-American religious experience. The stimulus for Afro-American religious practice is, however, beyond traditional categories of Christianity. The religious practice of Afro-American is tied to the specific cultural ascendancy of African American Protestantism rather than to Roman Catholicism. It was American Protestantism that accorded legitimacy to the institution of slavery in the United States. Therefore, it was to Protestantism, not to Roman Catholicism, that the early slaves were exposed. But the Afro-American interpretation of Christianity within the broad domain of Protestant tradition is not without the mirror of traditional African religions.

The concept of God in black religious experience continues to be tied to the Yoruba concept of *Olodumare*[34] in West Africa—the ancestral home of most slaves in the United States, particularly those who settled in New Orleans and South Carolina. The black Churches in America are also related to West African traditional religions in a conceptual and moral way. Sociologists of Religion call this "a black sacred cosmos."[35] That is to say that a parallel universe of spirituality similar to European Christianity is now emerging among Afro-Americans. One interpretation is that Afro-American Churches are not an aberrational attempt that copied mainstream white Christian culture, but rather a response to the age of religious pluralism with a focus that exhibits exceptional elements that distinguish Afro-American religious expressions from European Christianity and culture.

Afro-American Churches are new religious and moral alternatives to North American mainline denominations, and they are an important contribution to the age of religious pluralism. We can identify at least three stages that have led to the birth and rebirth of Afro-American contributions: (1) The uncritical acceptance of Protestantism in North America by Afro-Americans,

(2) The intellectual stage or the stage of intense examination of Protestant Christianity by Afro-Americans, and (3) The stage of participation and of rebirth of the African Christian heritage.

During the first stage, which corresponded to the enslavement years, African Americans had to assume European Protestantism uncritically; they accepted the Protestant Christianity because it was the only denomination to which they were exposed. Protestantism also exploited Afro-Americans by asking them to accept their position of servitude with meekness and humility.[36] In a Catechism, slaves were coached to utter the following answers to the questions the minister posed:

> Question: Who gave you a Master and a Mistress?
> Answer: God gave them to me.
> Question: Who says that you must obey them?
> Answer: God says that I must.[37]

This does not mean, however, that the slaves were not practicing traditional African religions in secrecy without the knowledge of the slave owners.

The second stage coincided with the era of emancipation and produced many articulate Afro-Americans. These Afro-Americans were emboldened to interpret Protestantism in a way that fostered cross-fertilization between African traditional religions and Protestant Christianity in the United States.

It is here that one sees a clear similarity between the enslavement years and the years of political oppression by the apartheid government in South Africa. Church leaders in South Africa were emboldened to re-interpret the acquired Protestant Christianity, using the same vocabularies of faith that whites used to put them in bondage, to also win their freedom from whites. Both anti-slavery African-Americans and South Africans anti-apartheid Church leaders, employed similar methods (and vocabularies of Christianity) to secure civil liberty, although they were generations apart.

The third stage only began during the last half of the 20th century, when Afro-Americans started to reclaim their African heritage as a legitimate medium of God's revelation. In this sense, one can say that Afro-Americans are making the same claim that the South African majority black population was also making, that no language or culture or religion can be a final destination or a sole gatekeeper of God's revelatory act. Perhaps what is radically unique about the third stage is that it has become a birth process in which traditional African religions are no longer regarded as paganism but have come to be practiced in public and endorsed indirectly (and uneasily) within the domain of Protestant Christianity. This is a stage of Afro-Americans participating in interreligious dialogue. There is an element of indirectness in this participation because traditional African religions have also survived in

North America by blending with Protestantism. Even then, it is in the style of worship, not in doctrinal substance or speculative Christian teachings, that Afro-American religious experience mirrors African traditional religions more completely. The survival of traditional African religions in South America, however, is quite different.

Afro-American Christianity in South America

While Afro-American religious experiences have transformed Protestantism in North America, Afro-Brazilian, Haitian, Cuban, and Caribbean religious experiences have transformed Roman Catholicism in South America. Perhaps we can draw from a language example to see the way Afro-Americans have responded to the modern age of multi religiosity. Maureen Warner-Lewis noted:

> The significance of the recovery of African language texts in this century emphasizes the dialectics of change and evolution, in that African languages have coalesced with European languages to create new languages indigenous to the Caribbean—the Dutch, French, English, and Spanish Creoles, yet African languages, in out-surviving that fusion have themselves been reshaped in phonology and syntax by European language forms.[38]

The acquisition of indigenous African languages involved a dynamic process of performance. Subsequent generations of Afro-Americans preserved the phrases in songs, legend, and prayers. An analysis of Yoruba songs recorded in Trinidad indicated an effective and informational range of themes that restored personality to their original singers and that also reflected their traumas and religious beliefs.[39] The coexistence of African-derived liturgical liveliness and European religious resourcefulness on American soil gave birth to the layering and creative contribution of African American to the age of religious pluralism.

It is now a commonplace to say that myths construct the world of African Americans, especially in their association with elements of African religious traditions. Elements of Traditional African Religions were first exported from West Africa to Brazil in the 16th century, but they did not flourish until the 19th century. Afro-Brazilian religions mirror African Traditional Religions substantially and contextually by strongly emphasizing performances. Speeches, drumming, dances, and sacrifices are common in Afro-Brazilian religious expression. Ceremonies that embody traditional African religious substance are often colorful and dramatic and, even, ecstatic. They evoke the age-old power of divinities and saints.

There is no doubt that in Brazil, the old divinities of West Africa have been transformed into the Roman Catholic Saints so that devotees can become legitimate worshippers in local and national assemblies. In Brazil, divination remains vitally connected with comparable functions in West Africa. Divination invokes the help of the spiritual world for those who are suffering misfortune in the world of the living. Afro-Brazilian religions, like the traditional religions in West Africa, strongly emphasize function. *Orishas* of the Yoruba people in West Africa and Roman Catholic Saints have been given pluralistic-age legitimacy, and there is a cross-fertilization between the two among the Roman Catholics in Brazil. Although Afro-Brazilian religious experience and its connection to West Africa have not been supported or encouraged openly, and the religious practices that can be traced to West African are often forbidden and sometimes persecuted, the association of *Orishas* with the Christian Saints has given Afro-Brazilians certain legitimacy among the predominantly Roman Catholic populace of Brazil.

Even Vodoo in Haiti is not unconnected to the traditional religions of the people in West Africa. Among the Caribbean religions, none has gained the attention of religious historians in the contemporary world as much as the Haitian Vodoos. Many Afro-American worship practices take roots in West Africa, but the substance of Afro-American religious activities in North America cannot be traced to West Africa alone. Afro-American religious life has undergone certain refinement, and the age of religious pluralism has facilitated the cross-fertilization of traditional African religions with Christianity.

The paradoxical effect of African American religious history is this—while Europeans assailed Africa in the 19th-century to teach Africans how to worship like Europeans, African Americans are in both Europe and in the Americas, teaching the people of European descent how to worship like Africans. For example, there are people of European descent in many immigrant Churches in the Americas and in European countries today, clapping hands, reporting their visions and dreams, and worshipping God as if they were Africans.

African Americans will face many challenges in the future as they continue to express Christianity through African idioms. These challenges include, but not limited to, the following: (1) A decay of the extended role of families, (2) mobility of labor and social fragmentation, (3) poverty and demographic shifts from the rural to the urban areas, (4) distraction from traditional agrarian concerns and demands in an age of information and technology, and (5) the abuse of the environment and how this would affect human dignity.

These challenges will alter the cross-fertilization process between Christianity and traditional African religions by Afro-Americans. This is also an indication that their contribution to the age of religious pluralism has not been completely cemented with the religious beliefs associated with the ancestral home of Africa.

To be sure, traditional African religions are greatly misunderstood. Nevertheless, the religious beliefs of West Africans continue to be seen as reminiscent of ancient African traditional religions as they linger and take new forms within Christianity as practiced by Afro-Americans.

One can draw three conclusions from the response of Afro-Americans to the age of religious pluralism. First, the age has assisted Afro-Americans to make profound contributions to religious civilization. Second, and like South Africans, Afro-Americans have used religion as a catalyst for self-rediscovery and a stimulus for resisting injustice. Third, religious awareness is complex, and, for both Afro-Americans and South Africans, it is a particular human effort by which they have re-discovered their existence and shaped civilization in the world.

One phenomenon of the American life that has affected the adjustment of Afro-American to the society remains the singular nature of the American diversity. It is not uncommon for Afro-Americans to claim that although they have been in the Western world for several generations, they still do not feel at home. They are constantly reminded of the color of their skin in the American society that is yet to accept them as "legitimate." One of the daunting questions is, "how long would Afro-Americans have to live in the American society to be fully integrated, and what roles does the Church have to play to accelerate that process? This is not an easy question and it would take more efforts by the Church to lead the society in the process of a full adjustment and integration of Afro-Americans. This is a daunting task because eleven o'clock hour on Sunday morning remains the most segregated hour in the American society. This is a particular failure (racial disharmony) of the missionary's success (Afro-American congregations) in North America.

The Church in a New Key

The Church in other non-Western countries provided abundant evidence of the failure of missionary's success. In Korea, for example, there are some Presbyterian Churches in Seoul with more than 12,000 members in the sanctuary that was built to seat only 4,000. On any given Sunday, it is over-crowded three times over. Consequently, the Church is in danger of becoming a theater and the ministers slipping into the roles of actors.

In South Africa, the problem of this failure is compounded by an acute shortage of trained ministers to be the shepherds of the large population of South African Christian congregations. But the failure of missionary's success is even more acute, stretching back by more than four centuries.

The success of the mainline Churches is not only against a background of relentless European settlement and conquest of new territories and the African resistance, but also against powerful, but less visible, international economic and political forces aimed at enriching Europeans and their white surrogates.[40] As a fully established religion of European powers, Christianity migrated with them when they entered South Africa. Not only this, Christianity also came as a result of missionary activities that followed immediately, and the non-Christian indigenous population has been practicing Christianity for at least four hundred years.

But here lies the failure of a successful missionary activity. The Dutch Reformed Church wielded power and became an organ of the government. The role of the Dutch Reformed Church in formulating and maintaining the oppressive system of apartheid should not be underestimated. But the other Churches also played a role in making Christianity a religion of compromise in the face of oppression. In *Facing the Truth: South African faith communities and the Truth and Reconciliation Commission* (1999), a well-crafted work edited by James Cochrane, John de Gruchy, and Stephen Martin, the contributors stressed again and again that the Churches of all denominations served as (a) agents of oppression, (b) victims of oppression, and (c) opponents of oppression simultaneously in South African apartheid years.[41] In a way, apartheid was the Church against the Church. The wounds are not only offensive, but have also affected the Church's credibility as agents of healing in a fractured society of the post-apartheid years. Thus, the wounds of the past are not only *within* the Churches, but they are also *between* the Churches and faith communities.[42] But there is no other faith community in South Africa that put its credibility on line the way the Church did. The apartheid era was partly the Church's doctrine of election against the Church's doctrine of grace. It was God's sovereignty versus God's *soteriology* (the doctrine of salvation), and Calvinism versus Augustinianism. The Dutch Reformed Church could be the worst offender, but other Churches and religious communities were not entirely blameless.

It should be noted that the Church did not deliberately seek power; however, the government needed the Church to justify its system of oppression. Thus, the state conferred power to the ecclesiastical body, and the Church could no longer rescue or ransom the prisoners and those who are marginalized or persecuted by the state. In this sense we can say that the Dutch Reformed Church ceased to be the solution and became the problem, collaborating with the apartheid government to push back the frontier of poverty for the majority of South Africans.

The Broken Cisterns of the Dutch Reformed Church

We are largely confined here to a reflection of the Dutch Reformed Church and the limited expectations of her broken cisterns. Her language and her way of knowing and reasoning in the 1940s and 50s were confined to the ideology coined by apartheid, and she drew her confessional stance from the intellectual climate that sustained the unjust system of apartheid. Therefore, there are very limited public places in which serious and sustainable hope for the majority can be associated with the Dutch Reformed Church. But what is lacking in the body of believers of this old tradition of the Reformed is what is most needed—a way out of exile so that the Church could redefine herself as an organ of renewal. The Dutch Reformed Church is herself a victim of apartheid, not just its surrogate. Therefore, South Africans of today would be judicious to pay a closer attention to the religious causalities of oppression during those dark days, so that they can make ways for members of the society to receive new gifts and opportunities to serve and worship God in a new South Africa. This means that the Reformed Church could "repent," but there is no reason for whining and whimpering. This public and personal spiritual and collective recapitulation is necessary for a new beginning.

For one thing, a collective recapitulation would create a public arena for the articulation and redefinition of gifts that fall outside the conventional rationality of the apartheid years. Without this, the Dutch Reformed Church could falter and enter entropy or ultimately become a footnote in the history of Christianity in South Africa. But it should not have to be that way, and for it not to be, the DRC must provide a new engine, not just a refueling, to articulate her new life in Christ. From what I experienced in South Africa, I know full well that there are many laymen and women who can put the pieces of the puzzle together and make genuine a new life in the Church that is slowly emerging. Part of this recreation, no doubt, would be difficult, just like any birth or rebirth. The process would also involve a dissatisfied coping, a grudging trust in God, and a managing that dares not to ask too much of the government of the new dispensation or of other Christians. This is because what has been regarded as the "strange other" has now become a real partner in conversation. The fear of the Dutch Reformed Church is comparable to that of the black constituency during the apartheid years. This fear, however, is unfounded because institutional Christianity itself is not the gospel. It mirrors imperfectly the God who forgives and accepts. My perception is that a repentant Dutch Reformed Church, personally and corporately, would enter a new arena of conversation with other Christian Churches so that hands can be joined to rebuild South Africa in hope and mutual forgiveness. For such a state of forgiveness and cooperation is the state of affairs not only when a Church is in exile, but is also characteristic of most situation of a ministry of reconciliation. In this sense, the Dutch Reformed Church could become enlivened in South Africa and be the embodiment of a renewal in the new South Africa.

When one confronts personal sins, privately or in public, one can face the enemies within with confidence, if not with enthusiasm. The question facing the Dutch Reformed Church today is partly whether there is anything to be said, done, or acted upon in the face of the ideology of hopelessness that now surrounds her. Is there a ray of light in the wilderness, and how can one now experience a renaissance within one's unfruitful ideology of the past?

For a genuine renewal to take place, one must cut through the despair and penetrate the dissatisfied coping that seems to have no end or resolution. There is not much a theologian or an anthropologist can do in such a situation of hopelessness and a crisis of identity. Therefore, we suggest three basic and modest tasks: (1) offering new Christian symbols that will show the universality of Christ and his message without discrimination, (2) bringing to a public expression hope that was once denied through land redistribution, and (3) speaking a new metaphorical language about the real newness that comes to us in Christ and redefining our situation in South Africa.

The Task of the Church in a New Dispensation

The task of the Dutch Reformed Church under a new dispensation is to imagine prophetically. This means bringing to public expression those very hopes and yearnings for the majority that have been denied or suppressed so deeply for so long that we no longer know they were there. This may require that the Church express to the state her vulnerability, and it may also require that the Church ask difficult questions. While the Dutch Reformed Church under apartheid was one of the assimilationist collaborators with the state, she must recognize that she also harbored deep theological and intellectual ambiguities that held at bay the heterogeneous standard and universal components of the Christian faith.

Two of these ambiguities are characteristic of the nature of the biblical text and of the Christian tradition themselves: (1) first, there is the unitary canonical text that can be shown to have, at its heart, possibilities for multiple interpretations and meanings, and, is therefore, susceptible to distortion, manipulation, exploitation and fracture; (2) second, not completely unrelated to the first, there is the insistence of the devoted followers of Christ that the text can be subjected to endless reworking inside and outside the Church tradition or prophetic school. Therefore, the text, and the faiths based upon it, can be used for political and ideological gains.

Thus, the Dutch Reformed Church must now make concerted efforts to move theological discussions in the post-apartheid era beyond these ambiguities of past religious and ideological categories. It is also the responsibility of other ecclesiastical bodies in South Africa to re-localize theological discussions and to look at the possibilities of securing Christianity within the domain of theocentricism. A God-centered faith has the possibility of healing the wounds of division that has been created in the body of Christ in South Africa.

In doing this, the Church must also raise key questions such as: what room is there in South African religious context to affirm the plurality of biblical interpretation in the post-apartheid era? In what ways can theology bridge the gap between biblical inclusivism and theological exclusivism within the locale of religious plurality? What is the salvific significance of the formation of the Church? If the Church is the watchdog of the society, then who is the watchdog of the Church? Can salvation pertain to the redistribution of earthly goods and power without diminishing its traditional meaning of the restructuring of the soul? How can the Church or the society proclaim freedom to all without empowering all?

This task was more eloquently expressed in James Cochrane's article: "Religion in Civil Society: Readings from the South African Case" when he stated that "there are no *a priori* reasons why the Churches in South Africa, or other religious groupings for that matter, cannot transform the role they played in the past in resisting apartheid, into one that builds [democratic values]."[43] Restating the point of Archbishop Hurley, a leading anti-apartheid cleric of the Roman Catholic Church, Cochrane further elucidated the point that any sense of an "established" Church could no longer be sustained.[44] Therefore, "Christianity will no longer seek to influence society directly through its political institutions, nor even perhaps through cultural and educational institutions. It will address its message to the conscience of people."[45] Thus, the sustainability of the Christian faith in South Africa as a credible light for the society would not depend on its identity as an established religious institution. Rather, the Church would be a community of individuals that share their faith, hope and courage on the streets and in the market place.

A further task of the Dutch Reformed Church deals with bringing hope to the people through mirroring for them the hope of Christ.

One of the most remarkable things that Jesus ever asked his disciples, his followers, as well as his more distant sympathizers to do was to live truthfully and transparently, as he himself lived, in the presence of God. He never urged them to build an alternative society that would be the Church. The Church was the vision of the early followers who were determined to proclaim the good news of the resurrected Lord. Jesus himself did not urge the creation of an alternate social entity, and no Bible passage says: "create a small group of reformers." Jesus taught people to be committed to his way of justice, compassion, and holiness, and they were not to be merely passive. It is by living right because they know God's love for them that people could participate meaningfully and enter the kingdom of God. There was nothing that we could ever do to merit the kingdom, and nothing can be done within our natural constitution to bring about that kingdom. Jesus was not even willing to assign places for his disciples in it. That the kingdom draws near does not mean that we can make it come. Individuals cannot get together with others of like mind to create the kingdom by reforming social, religious, political or ecclesiastical institutions. Thus, the lives of Christians on the streets matter more than their lives when they congregate. The analogy of three Christian football players comes to mind. The first was approached what he would do if the second coming of Christ were to meet him on the soccer field. He responded by stating that he would go to a nearby Church to pray so that the Lord's second coming would meet him while praying to God. The second player echoes the sentiment of the first, but said that he may not have time to reach a nearby Church to pray. Therefore, he would kneel down on the soccer field to pray. The third player stated that he would continue playing football because he did not have to show his faithfulness to the Lord in any dramatic fashion. Practicing our faith on the street corners and wherever we are would go a long way to healing the wounds of the past in South Africa. Christianity is not just a matter of confession and believing, it is also an attitude and a way of life.

The second task deals with a new symbol for the Church. But a new symbol will require moving back into the deepest memory levels of the confessional stance of the Dutch Reformed Church and activating those very symbols that have been the basis for contradicting hope. In other words, if we cannot teach old dog new tricks, we can make a new dog out of the Church. Therefore, from this symbol it would be imperative for the Church to have the courage of its convictions. But more importantly, it would be important for the Church to have the courage to challenge those convictions. Certainly, a new symbol means agreeing with God about an alternative future for all South Africans. In creating a new symbol, three tasks are necessary: (a) the first task is for the Church to mine the memory of her faith, using the tools of hope, not fear. (b) the second task is to recognize how the past controversial Calvinistic theological stance defined the reality of oppression for the majority in South Africa. (c) finally, the task of the Dutch Reformed Church would include the use of the tools of hope (with both eyes open) to share with her membership that the Church has been misleading and that this is, in part, because of unavoidable universal human nature and the ambiguities of historical events. Out of our own anguish and amazement, we must know that the nature of Christianity is also self-correcting.

The failure of missionary's success in South Africa led, in part, to the unholy alliance between the Dutch Reformed Church and the apartheid government. An expression of hope and idioms of true Christianity had to be recovered through a protest of other Christian denominations in South Africa that, ironically, will also include members of the Dutch Reformed Church, who would be disgruntled by the unholy alliance between the Church and the apartheid government, and who will not create a dichotomy between righteousness and justice. They believed that the hope and idioms of true Christian ethos were forfeited when the Dutch Reformed Church aligned herself with the state. Therefore, Christianity became a source of spiritual embarrassment in South Africa. This is not for the Dutch Reformed Church only, but also for other Christians. One of the ways out of this embarrassment is for the Churches of all denominations to join hands and face the fact that the Church herself is evolving.

The failure of the missionary's success in South Africa was, thus, partially responsible for the alliance of the Church with the state. As the Church disclaimed the black majority, labeling traditional black congregations as the "mission" as opposed to "the Church," so did the state by undercutting the black population. The way out would not be and cannot be on the basis of theological or ideological grounds. Rather, it would be almost both apologetic and lyrical in the sense that it must touch the minds and souls of hopeless persons at many different important points of faith. More than that, however, is the anthropological issue that a quest for renewal must raise. That is to say that the human interpretation of the divine nature is always temporary and inconclusive, and is characteristically fraught with human frailty. Human knowledge about God can only bring partial truth about the divine, and far beyond our interpretation resides another depth that reason and imagination cannot fathom. The covenant between God and all faith communities in South Africa would be rekindled when this anthropological quest is further elucidated. This must also be communicated in an attitude of listening. It would be about God and not completely about South African society; it would be about faithfulness to the path God has created and about God's faithfulness. To regain respect in the Christendom, the Dutch Reformed Church in South Africa will have to embrace anew the humble practice of giving and receiving.

A Summary

As we come to the end of this chapter, it is important for us to note that the earliest Dutch colonial authorities in South Africa regarded the indigenous population as inferior and they believed that it was both lawful and expedient to keep the native South Africans in subjection. This is not dissimilar to the way the early American forefathers perceived the Native American population. To this day, Native Americans (and African-Americans to a lesser extent) have not been fully assimilated *de facto* as citizens of the

United States. The assimilation of immigrants from non-European countries to the United States of America is still an incomplete process.

It is the painful struggle against apartheid by the indigenous population in South Africa that prevented this from occurring in modern South Africa. But the Church still has important roles to play in the process of achieving a full integration of all the racial groups in South Africa.

The urging is to rekindle hope that is fractured, and to bring the Church to the understanding that a parochial interpretation of the biblical text to accommodate unsustainable political ideology will not stand the test of time. The biblical text cannot be domesticated for political and ideological gains. Just as slavery in the 17th and 18th centuries was the hidden curse of Christianity in the Western world, apartheid was a hidden curse of its propagation in South Africa in the 19th. But just as the evil of slavery could not prevail in the 20th-century, although it has resurfaced in form of racism, the courage of Church leaders of the 20th century in South Africa did not allow apartheid to prevail beyond the 20th century.

It is hoped that the gesture of the Church would heal part of the wounds and smoothen the rough edges created by apartheid, and would rekindle hope to the public expression of the Christian faith within the tradition of the Dutch Reformed Church in the 21st-century.

Although the failure of missionary's success meant for South Africans an internal bondage, creating internal religious damage for the majority of Christians, the Church has the responsibility to forge a new direction so that this failure could generate some success.

Notes

[1] Cornel du Toit, "Blessed are the Powerful: Christian Righteousness and the redistribution of Power" in *Religion and the Reconstruction of Civil Society,* John W. de Gruchy and S. Martin, eds. (Pretoria: University of South Africa, 1995), 238.

[2] Justo L. Gonzáles, *Out of Every Tribe and Nation: Christian Theology at the Ethnic Round-table* (Nashville, Tennessee: Abingdon Press, 1992), 27.

[3] Sebastian Castellio, Conseil à la France Désolée (1562, reprinted in 1967), 46.

[4] M. Thomas Thangaraj, *The Common Task: A Theology of Christian Mission* (Nashville, Tennessee: Abingdon Press, 1999), 107.

[5] See Lamin Sanneh, *Translating the Message: The Missionary Impact on Culture* (Maryknoll, New York: Orbis Books, 1989).

[6] John L.Esposito, Darrell J. Fasching and Todd Lewis, eds. *World Religions Today,* (New York: Oxford University Press, 2002), 94.

[7] Philip Jenkins, *The Next Christendom* (New York: Oxford University Press, 2002), 34.

[8] Philip Jenkins, *The Next Christendom,* 34.

[9] See *The African Diaspora: African Origins and New World Identities* (1999) edited by Isidore Okpewho, Carole Boyce Davies, and Ali A. Mazrui, (Indianapolis, Indiana: Indiana Uni-

versity Press, 1999). Many entries in this work suggested that the first school of thought is "Afro-centric."

[10] In this book, I am using this term "Diaspora" to denote black people in the United States, in Cuba, and in Brazil. This is because people of African descent in these parts of the world exhibit unique religious identities that are different from the black people of the parent continent of Africa as well as the black people in Europe or Asia.

[11] Africanism is the study of those elements of culture found in the New World that are traceable to an African origin. This area of Cultural Anthropology has been a neglected but not uncontroversial area of academic inquiry in the United States. It was resurrected in 1941 when Melville J. Herskovits published a pioneering work, *The Myth of the Negro Past* (Boston: Beacon Press, 1958; originally published in 1941).

[12] Ibid.

[13] E. Franklin Frazier, *The Negro Church in America* (Boston: 1963).

[14] Isidore Okpewho, "Introduction" in Isidore Okpewho, Carole Boyce Davies, and Ali A. Mazrui, eds. *The African Diaspora: African Origins and new World Identities*, (Bloomington, Indiana: Indiana University Press, 1999), xviii.

[15] See J. D. Fage (with William Tordoff) *A History of Africa* 4th edition (London: Routledge, 2002). Chapter one is especially very helpful because the authors discussed the origins of African society.

[16] Michael J. C. Echeruo "An African Diaspora: The Ontological Project" in Isidore Okpewho, Carole Boyce Davies, and Ali Mazrui, eds. *African Diaspora: African Origins and New World Identities* (Bloomington: Indiana University Press, 1999), 3–18.

[17] Colin Chapman, "Time to Give Up the Idea of Christian Mission to Muslims? Some Reflections from the Middle East." *International Bulletin of Missionary Research,* Vol. 28, no. 3 (July, 2004): 112.

[18] Ibid. 116.

[19] Isidore Okpewho, "Introduction" in Isidore Okpewho, Carole Boyce Davies, and Ali A. Mazrui, eds. *The African Diaspora: African Origins and new World Identities*, (Bloomington, Indiana: Indiana University Press, 1999), xv.

[20] Jean-Paul Sartre considered the legitimate aspirations of early Afro-Americans of his days as practicing "anti-racist-racism." Almost all the major philosophers in the West shared his view—David Hume 1711–1776, Immanuel Kant 1724–1804, Jean Jacques Rousseau 1712–1778, and Francois Marie Arouet known to us as Voltaire 1694–1778. But all did not hide their racism, suggesting that Africans were naturally inferior to Europeans in mental ability. David Hume even argues that there never was a civilized nation of any other complexion than white, nor even any individual eminent either in action or speculation. No ingenious manufacturers amongst them, no arts, no science. He further claimed that a uniform and constant difference could not happen, in so many countries and ages, if nature had not made an original distinction between breeds of men. For details, see Philip D. Curtin, *The Image of Africa: British Ideas and Actions, 1780–1850.* Madison: University of Wisconsin Press, 1964).

[21] An example of this (from linguistic point of view) is the success of the French and English languages on the African continent. Today, it is estimated that over 360 million Africans speak the English language as their second language and more Africans speak the French language than the Frenchman. Therefore, the preservation of the French culture partly depends on the viability of that language by Africans if we assume that language and cultures cannot be separated effectively.

[22] In *Black Man's Religion: Can Christianity be Afrocentric?* Glenn Usry and Craig S. Keener made the claim that the Christian faith should not be said to be a "white man's" religion and that "The Black church remains the most prominent social institution in the Afro-American community today." (Downers Grove, Illinois: InterVarsity Press, 1996), 11. C. Eric

Lincoln and Lawrence H. Mamiya gave this statistics that 80 percent of all black Christians are in the seven major Black denominations. See their book, *The Black Church in the African American Experience* (Durham and London: Duke University Press, 1990), 1.

[23] See C. Eric Lincoln, ed. *The Black Experience in Religion: A Book of Readings.* (Garden City, New York: Anchor Books, 1974), 3.

[24] Henry J. Young, *Major Black Religious Leaders 1755–1940.* (Nashville, Tennessee: Abingdon Press), 28.

[25] Ibid..

[26] Ibid., p. 29. See also Richard Allen, *Life Experience and Gospel Labors,* p. 12.

[27] Ibid. 30.

[28] Paul Rading insightfully wrote that the Christian God provided the African-American slaves with a "fixed point," and rather than being converted to God, they converted God to themselves. For the details, see Paul Radin, "Status, Phantasy, and the Christian Dogma," in God Struck Me Dead: Religious Conversion Experience and Autobiographies of Negro Ex-Slaves (Nashville, Tenn.: Social Science Institute, Fisk University, 1945), i–ix. See also, Margaret Washington Creel, "Gullah Attitudes toward Life and Death" in Africanisms in American Culture (Bloomington, Indiana: Indiana University Press, 1990), 74.

[29] Ibid. 39.

[30] Kwame Nkrumah, the Father of African Nationalism, was the first President of Ghana when the country gained political independence from Great Britain in 1957.

[31] For a good study of how Danish missionaries trained Christian leaders to fight for political independence through social activism, see Niels Kastfelt's work, *Religion and Politics in Nigeria: A Study in Middle Belt Christianity,* (London: British Academic Press, 1994). Here, the author established the fact that one of the most significant political functions of the missionaries was their contribution to the making of new political elite by training them in mission schools.

[32] Quoted in Isidore Okpewho, Carole Boyce Davies, and Ali A. Mazrui, eds. *The African Diaspora: African Origins and New World Identities,* (Bloomington, Indiana: Indiana University Press, 1999), xxii.

[33] See Michael J. C. Echeruo, "An African Diaspora: The Ontological Project," and Maureen Warner-Lewis, "Cultural Reconfiguration in the African Caribbean" in Isidore Okpewho, Carole Boyce Davies, and Ali A. Mazrui, eds. *African Diaspora: African Origins and New World Identities,* (Bloomington, Indiana: Indiana University Press, 1999).

[34] For a comprehensive study of *Olodumare*, see E. Bolaji Idowu, *Olodumare*: *God in Yoruba Beliefs* (London: Oxford University Press, 1969). *Olodumare* is the traditional deity of the Yoruba people, and the name means "the supreme being of mysterious qualities to whom every being returns."

[35] C. Eric Lincoln, and Lawrence H. Mamiya, *The Black Church in the African American Experience,* (Durham: Duke University Press, 1990).

[36] See, Henry J. Young, *Major Black Religious Leaders: 1755–1940*, (Nashville, Tenn.: Abingdon Press, 1977).

[37] See Benjamin Quarles, *The Negro in the Making of America* (New York: Collier Books, 1969), 71.

[38] Maureen Warner-Lewis, "Cultural Reconfigurations in the African Caribbean" in Isidore Okpewho, Carole Boyce Davies, and Ali Mazrui, eds. *The African Diaspora: African Origins and New World Identities* (Bloomington: Indiana University Press, 1999), 20.

[39] Ibid. 21.

[40] See John W. DeGruchy, *The Church Struggle in South Africa* (Grand Rapids, Michigan: Eerdmans Publishing and Cape Town: David Philip), 1986.

[41] James Cochrane, John de Gruchy & Stephen Martin, eds. *Facing the Truth: South African faith communities and the Truth & Reconciliation Commission,* (Cape Town: David Philip Publishers, 1999), 170.

[42] Ibid., 171.

[43] James R. Cochrane, "Religion in Civil Society: Readings from the South African case" in James R. Cochrane and Bastienne Klein, eds. *Sameness and Difference: Problems and Potentials in South African Civil Society.* South African Philosophical Studies, I: The Cultural Heritage and Contemporary Change Series II, Africa, Vol. 6 (Washington, D.C.: The Council for Research in Values and Philosophy, 2000), 26.

[44] Ibid. 27.

[45] Ibid.

Chapter Three

THE SUCCESS OF MISSIONARY'S FAILURE

Let us now swing to the other side of the pendulum of the missionary activities in South Africa, and examine the success of the missionary's failure. The success of the missionary's failure in South Africa is perhaps more important than the failure of the missionary's success we examined in the previous chapter. This is especially from the point of view of the historical developments of Christianity in Africa as a whole. The focus of this chapter is to examine recent developments of Christianity in South Africa in light of the success associated with the perceived failure of early European missionaries. The inland advance of other living faiths in Africa has not prevented Africans from turning their hopes toward Jesus Christ. Most South Africans have been susceptible to the elevating influence of the gospel, if dissatisfied with what their fellow South African Christians did to discredit the message under apartheid.

It is important to note that the success of missionary's failure has origin in the life and ministry of Jesus himself as God's viceroy and potentate.[1]

In the minds of many, the crucifixion of Jesus was a failure because the Son of God died. One of the first reactions is that it cannot be possible for God's son to die. Perhaps for a moment, it seemed so to Jesus himself. Hence, he cried: *"Eloi, Eloi, lema sabachthani?"* translated "My God, my God, why hast Thou forsaken me?"[2]

The cross on which Jesus Christ died, however, has become a powerful symbol, and what appeared to be a failure has sustained million of Christians across many generations. The resurrection itself is not only a vindication of the life of Jesus and his ministry, but also a representation of the most important success of the failure of the cross and its necessity. It is in this light that one can say that the message of the missionaries in South Africa is also a success of failure. Although it was imperfect in its method, exploitative in its social strategy, and a form of cultural violence in its manipulation of the existing indigenous religions and cultures, Christian missionary activities in Africa show a brilliant success.

For example, black Christians led the way in South African resistance against apartheid. Chief Albert Luthuli, who won the most coveted Nobel Prize for peace in 1960, and Robert Sobukwe, the founder of PAC, were devoted Christians. Whatever the failures of the Christian missions in South Africa may be, black leaders attended mission schools where liberal education was promoted. This, in no small measure, assisted to nurture black leaders as they articulated their outcry against apartheid on behalf of all South Africans. Mission is not only about converting South Africans, but also about missionaries and their descendants being converted.

Two examples would further illustrate the point of the success of missionary's failure in Africa. Most European empires of the medieval periods have now become history. The Roman Empire fell, but Roman civilization endured in many forms all over the world. The system of law of the Roman government in its adumbrated form has been translated into many democracies in the modern world. The French wanted to make North African colonies an extension of France but failed. The success of this failure, however, is that most North African acquired the French taste and way of life. There are now more Africans who have abandoned their native tongues (failure) in favor of the French language in North and Central Africa (success). Perhaps, more Africans speak the French language today than the number of the native speakers in France. The French imperialism failed, but the French civilization survived, and the essence of its culture was transmitted successfully.

The same can be said about the British Empire. It arose as quickly as it disintegrated. But the British Empire was only marginally a failure, so far as the empire was concerned. One cannot say that the English's best days were in the past any longer. In a way, the best days of the English people just started in the Commonwealth, in the universal employment of the English language as a medium of commerce, and in the extension of the British culture in the non-Western world. The language has become the language of civilization and, one may add, it has become the medium of communication between diverse groups all over the world. The British Empire is gone; it failed on many fronts and for many reasons, but the legacy has been transmitted to many cultures of the world with a brilliant success.

Many European Churches initialed brilliant missionary programs on the African continent in the eighteenth and nineteenth centuries. At best, many people in these missionary-producing countries of Europe are today nominally Christians. The missionary programs in Africa survived, but at home in the West, Christianity is no longer a major religious phenomenon. In his work, *The Next Christendom,* Philip Jenkins took a full measure of the changing face of the Christian religion. Jenkins has shown that Churches have not only grown most rapidly in the Southern hemisphere, but have also, and most fundamentally, taken account of the enduring values of the Christian faith.[3]

Post-apartheid Landscape of Religions

According to 2002 statistics, the total South African population was estimated as 40,583,639, and religions as a percent of the population are as follows:[4]

Denomination	Population	Percentage
Mainline Churches	14,567,569	35.9
African Independent Churches	10,668,515	26.3
Pentecostal/Charismatic Churches:	2,683,314	6.6
Other Churches	2,139,344	5.3
Total Christians in South Africa	30,058,742	74.1

Other Religions	Population	Percentage
Muslims	553,583	1.4
Hindu	537,428	1.3
Jewish Faith/Hebrew	68,060	0.2
Eastern Faiths	10,069	0.0
Other Faiths	1,937,337	4.8
African Traditional Religions	7,418,420	18.3
Total South African population (2002)	40,583,639	100.0

Religious practices of the peoples of South Africa can be characterized as comprehensive and broad. Virtually 80 percent of the total population professes some kind of faith. Like many other countries in Africa, religion continues to be a significant social force. But unlike most countries, religious practices cannot be completely understood in South Africa apart from its geographical, ideological, political, cultural, and historical context. Information of their historical developments provides the character of South African dominant religions.

Almost three-quarters of South Africans report a Christian affiliation. Devoted followers are found in both the oldest form of Christianity such as the Ethiopian tradition, and the newest form such as the Zulu Zionists.[5] While Pentecostal and Charismatic Churches continue to grow, mainline Churches are still by far the largest Christian denomination in South Africa, claiming 35.9 percent of the total population. The major mainline Churches include the Anglican,[6] the Methodist,[7] the Lutheran,[8] the Presbyterian,[9] the United Congregational,[10] the Roman Catholic,[11] the Dutch Reformed Church,[12] the Baptist,[13] and the Greek Orthodox.[14] Their historical developments vary from one denomination to another, but their missionary activities and evangelistic work in South Africa stretch back by more than two centuries. The history of mainline Churches in South Africa is not only against a background of relentless European settlement and conquest of new territories and the African resistance, but also against a powerful, though less visible, international economic and political forces aimed primarily at enriching Europe and its white surrogates by exploiting helpless indigenous population.[15] As an established religion of European powers, Christianity migrated with them as they entered South Africa. It also came as a result of the missionary activities to the non-Christian indigenous South African population. But while the white settlers tried to Christianize South Africans, the indigenous population wanted to Africanize Christianity[16] in local idioms. This is the decisive context in which one should look at the historical development of Christian denominations in South Africa beginning in 1488 when the first known Christian contact took place. This contact predates 1652 when the Dutch coastal trading practices, with no interest in settling in South Africa, led to a much more potent form of European interests in the region.

It should be noted that not all Churches in South Africa have historical origins in European countries. There are some Churches in South Africa that trace their historical origins to other African countries. There is at least one Church in South Africa with historical origin in India. The Reverend John Rangiah, for example, was a son of an Orthodox Hindu priest in India before he was converted. He became a member of the Lone Star Baptist Church in the Natal region. The flow of indentured servants from Indian to Natal took him to South Africa, and this later had a Christian effect. There was a need for Christians to have a Telegu minister in Kearsney at the turn of the century. In 1903, Reverend John Rangiah was ordained and started the First Indian Baptist Church in South Africa in December of that year. John Rangiah's grandson, Pastor M. Rangiah, followed his grandfather's footstep and was a minister to the Indian Christian population in Kwa Zulu Natal before he died in 2001.[17]

The historical origins of Christianity in South Africa have many turns, but the earliest Christian control of the Cape passed from the Dutch to the

British hands around 1806, and the way opened for a steady influx of English-speaking Christians with their own division into denominations—the Anglican, the Methodists, the Lutheran, the Presbyterians, the Congregational, Catholic, Baptist, and the like—thereby increasing the divided state of Christianity. In due course, this exacerbated the fragmentation of the black South Africans who lined up according to the Christian denominations they inherited from Europeans.[18] Although this appeared to be good for the souls of black South Africans from a Christian point of view, it was a political disaster because a divided Church meant a divided people. Opportunistic politicians in South Africa then took measures that eventually led to insidious subjugation and racial segregation. It took the Church more than half a century to come together and combat the evil of oppression, exploitation, and racism, and to come face to face with apartheid. Mainline Churches in South Africa today carefully balance the unholy alliance of the Church, especially the Dutch Reformed Church with the apartheid government, against the important positive liberating resources black Christians have found in Christianity.

In South Africa, religion is not neutral and does not transcend human conflicts.[19] During the apartheid era, Christianity was trapped in apartheid,[20] making the faith rather problematic and its ethical teachings controversial. Thus, the Christian faith entered a crisis of identity in post-apartheid years. Apartheid left South Africans clannish with sectional groups and religious loyalties.[21] Christian Theology in South Africa was embroiled in major ideological struggles and, as a result, created more divisions within the Church.[22] But during the immediate years after the dismantling of the apartheid system, Christians started moving away from the terrible legacy of apartheid to rediscover Christianity and cultivate fresh perspectives on what a Christian ethos can be in a new society, especially in fostering democratic values. Hence, Christians started coming together, regardless of their racial or ethnic affiliation, for a shared common value or a common loyalty that encompasses nationalism. By claiming democratic values, Christianity has a fruitful effect in the lives of the peoples, restoring the credibility of the faith in South Africa. Salvation is not only about the soul, but also, and in light of its original Hebrew meaning, about the restoration of health and redistribution of earthly good and power. Thus, the characteristics of a saved society are consistent with democratic values of freedom, the right to self-determination, equality of dignity, honoring legitimate interests, and promoting responsibilities of the citizens.

The South Africa during apartheid was different from the South Africa immediately following its demise. Whereas South African society was at a brink of collapse under apartheid, communities with private self-interests have been relatively united afterwards.

The Children of Adam and Eve in South Africa

(a) Hinduism 1.3%

Hinduism in South Africa as in other places in the world is a broad religious tradition, incorporating a great variety of cultural, philosophical and religious elements that are at least 4,000 years old. In South Africa, however, the word "Hinduism" is not often used to describe the religion. Devoted followers prefer the term *sanathana dharma* (the eternal way) to sum up their religious tradition. South African Hindu communities are the third largest in the world following India and Sri Lanka. This should not be a surprise because outside of India, the largest Indian population in the world is in South Africa, and 80 percent of South Africa's Indian population lives in Kwa Zulu Natal. Consequently, Natal has been the bastion of Hinduism in South Africa.

Hindu constitutes 35 percent of the population of Durban, a major seaport, and 18 percent of Pietermaritzburg, both in Kwa Zulu Natal. In 1857 when there was an acute shortage of labor in the sugar industry in Natal, it became necessary for the government of South Africa to import indentured laborers from India. As these Indians disembarked in Durban so was their religion, and approximately 90 percent of these workers were Hindus from the Tamil- and Telugu-speaking communities from the Southern Indian State of Madras (now Tamil Nadu).

What is unique about Hinduism in South Africa is that in spite of their miserable working conditions on the sugar estates of the Natal north and south coasts, Hindus demonstrated their religious commitments by building small shrines and temples. The oldest of these is the *Equefa Perumalsami* temple near Umzinto, built in 1864. Today, South Africa has four main streams of Hinduism: (1) *sanathanism*, (2) *Arya samaj,* (3) neo-Vedanta, and (4) Hare Krishna.[23] The last three of these are often collectively referred to as neo-Hinduism or Reformed Hinduism. *Sanathanism* emphasizes the practical and ritual dimensions of Hinduism, whereas the others emphasize the precepts. Minor differences regarding details of worship, ritual and social customs continue to exist between these branches of Hinduism, but nearly all South African Hindus believe in an interminable process of reincarnation governed by *karma*, the universal and impersonal law of cause and effect. This means that the essential 'self' (soul in Christianity) of each human being, that is immortal and indestructible, is repeatedly reborn in a variety of different life forms. Also, most Hindu's places of worship in South Africa are adorned with the symbol of Divine Reality. This ultimate Reality is conceptualized in three forms as the so-called *Trimurti*, consisting of Brahma (the creator), Vishnu (the Preserver), and Shiva (the Destroyer).

Brahma is seldom worshipped (even in India), and no Brahma temples are in South Africa. Perhaps the most important feature of Hinduism in South Africa is the importance of *dharma* (duty and moral obligation). This includes such principles as telling the truth, living a pure life, exercising forgiveness, practicing self-control, goodwill, generosity, and protecting all living beings.

Vegetarianism is one way to avoid the pollution associated with contact with dead animals. All South African Hindus observe a number of religious festivals. The caste system that is associated with Hinduism in India is eroded because of the influence of Christian education and the openness of the South African culture.

The most celebrated Gujarati Hindu in South Africa is Mohandas K. Gandhi (1869–1948) who spent approximately 20 years of his productive life in Natal, arriving in May 1893.[24] A month after his arrival, Gandhi found himself embroiled in South Africa's political problems when he was evicted from a first-class train compartment at the Pietermaritzburg train station even though he had a first-class ticket. In 1894, the Natal Indian Congress was founded, and Gandhi served as its first secretary. It was from South Africa that Gandhi's non-violent philosophy was fully developed, and this method of passive resistance would vibrate in the United States during the Civil Right Movements.

(b) Judaism 0.2%

One other unique element in the South African religious fabric is Judaism. Its relationship with Christianity is unlike anywhere else in the world. Africa has some of the poorest as well as some of the wealthiest Jews. While the Black Jews of Ethiopia are culturally Africans, they have often claimed to belong to "the lost house of Israel." The modern Jews of South Africa on the other hand are culturally Europeans, but they have often claimed that they belonged to South Africa no less than the Zulus. The Jews belonging properly to South Africa are the Lembas.

Only the United States surpasses South Africa as the destination of Jewish immigrants from Europe (particularly from Lithuania) at the end of World War II.

Most of the Jews in South Africa, therefore, are descendants of the Lithuanian immigrants who fled the political domination and anti-Semitic persecutions under Russia-controlled Lithuania. As a result, most Jews in South Africa have *Anglo-Litvak* origin. Exactly here stands the reason why South African Jewish community is one of the most organized Jewish communities in the world. The Jewish population in South Africa is relatively thin, approximately 0.2 percent of the total population. But South African Jews are by no means insignificant or a homogeneous population. For example, Zionism is an integral part of Jewish life in South Africa. This international movement that mobilized supports for a Jewish homeland in Palestine has strong supports as well as oppositions among Jews in South Africa.

The political Zionists have argued that the problems of Jews worldwide would only be solved effectively by creating a Jewish State.[25] A strong support comes through the gradual disclosure of the horrors of the Nazi death camps. While World War I made the Zionist state possible, it was World War II that made it essential, whatever the cost. There are vocal oppositions to this, however, from Jews who argue for a messianic Zionism not brought into existence by political establishment of a Jewish state. Also, Jews in Johannesburg, the commercial capital of South Africa, are different from Jews in Cape Town, the political capital. Johannesburg is represented as the center of Jewish religious life, but Cape Town remains an important focus because early Jews in South Africa first settled there.

It can be argued that although Cecil Rhodes (1853–1902), an imperialist Englishman, was responsible for opening South Africa to mineral wealth, the Jews of South Africa were the ones that created the financial institutions to sustain the wealth. The Jews have always been involved in precious stones (particularly diamonds) and they played vital roles in South African deep-level mines and in the financial systems that raised capitals to sustain them. Such Jewish personalities as Alfred Beit, Barney Barnato, Louis Cohen, Lionel Phillips, Julius Wehrner, Solly Joel, Adolf Goertz, George Albu and Abe Bailey would be remembered for transforming South Africa from a rural agrarian economy to one of the world's most vibrant and largest mining economies.

There are also Jews in South Africa whose presence is important to the general religious fabric of the country. The majority of South African Jews are labeled "unobservant orthodox" partly because there is no guilt feeling for not observing the precepts of Orthodox Judaism in dietary matters. This flexibility to kosher laws is the reason why relatively more Orthodox Jews in South Africa often see Reformed Judaism and teachings as heretical, while Reformed Jews often see those who are more orthodox as fanatical.

(c) Islam 1.4%

Muslims are approximately 1.4 percent in South Africa. Islamic religion in South Africa, however, implies more than what it symbolizes elsewhere in Africa. It implies a new language, a new concept of law and government and a new standard of dress and architecture. This is partly because under apartheid, the majority of South Africans saw Islam as an alternative to an oppressive system of apartheid under the Christian banner.

In 1991, Ebrahim Moosa expressed typical South African Muslim suspicions of Western human rights assumptions. According to him, Islam has always rejected racism and, has from the beginning, had heroes of resistance to apartheid. Muslims have not always felt comfortable working alongside other liberation movements, fearing that their own struggle, undertaken in obedience to God's revealed will, might be contaminated by those whose motives may be different or impure. Muslims recognize that liberation struggle is consistent with Jihad, an idea that provides a basis for recognizing human dignity. Understood within the frame of human dignity, Jihad is best understood not as a defensive war against outsiders, but as a struggle within. Thus, Jihad is a struggle against selfishness, injustice, and racism on the part of the individuals or groups. It is within this frame of human dignity that Muslims joined hands with Church leaders in South Africa to fight oppression under apartheid, understanding that the greatest Jihad is the one directed at selfishness and purification from greed and self-centeredness.

Early Muslims arrived in South Africa at the Cape approximately six years after Jan van Riebeeck of the Dutch East Indian Company arrived in April 1652. Muslims arrived, however, not to join hands with the colonizers, but to protect them against indigenous insurrection. Hence, they were called *mardyckers,* protecting the colonizers against the incursion of the indigenous South African population.

In South Africa, a mosque has a dual role: (1) it is a place of worship, and (2) it provides space for intellectual, social and political gatherings. This has been the roles of a mosque since the first one was build in 1804 on Dorp Street in the Cape.

The egalitarian spirit of Islam is an important factor for its growth in South Africa, especially because it can serve as an alternative for the underclass and the dispossessed indigenous black population. Unlike Christianity under apartheid, Islam does not justify discrimination on the basis of race, and white devotees participated regularly along with Indians, Coloured, and Blacks at Islamic functions and during pilgrimage to Mecca.

In South Africa, respected Muslim scholars never defended apartheid according to Islamic law. Controversial Calvinistic theologies, on the other hand, sustained aspects of apartheid in South Africa among both educated and uneducated devotees. Thus, the low success rate in converting Muslims to Christianity in South Africa has frustrated Christians who are more sympathetic to apartheid ideologies. Christians in this category often viewed Muslim upward social mobility with scorn and deep bitterness.[26]

Popular Islamic practices in South Africa include the use of talismans, and amulets to word off evil spirit (*azimat*), the communal celebration of Prophet Muhammad's birthday (*milad or mawlud*), and occasional collective prayers to bless the dead. The traditional distinction between Sufism (Islamic mysticism), or between the Sunnis and the Shiites is not as strong in South Africa as it is in North African countries. Some of the most beautiful mosques in South Africa are in Kwa Zulu Natal, built by Indian Muslims whose descendants migrated to South Africa from India as indentured laborers to work on the sugar-cane fields of Natal.

In South Africa, Islam is more nomocentric in its public character than Christianity, thereby elevating its status of the law as in rabbinic Judaism. There are seven fundamental teachings that underpin Islamic ideology in South Africa: (1) an understanding of the article of faith, (2) prayer five times a day, (3) learning and remembering God's appellation by the use of beads, (4) service and honor of fellow Muslims, (5) sincerity of intention, (6) avoiding idleness, and (7) doing evangelical work. Most of the *ulama* and Islamic scholars in South Africa were trained in the Middle East. But a synthesis of Southeast Asian Islam and elements of indigenous cultures have most definitely had effects on South African Muslims. It has also given South African Islam its visible cultural flexibility and adaptability to the extent that Islam and Christianity coexist more amicably in South Africa than in most places in the modern world.[27] Also, Muslims and Christians in South Africa had a common enemy—apartheid.

(d) Christianity 74.1%

During the apartheid era, the government tacitly tolerated the practice of non-Christian religions. Christianity, especially the *Nederduitse Gereformeerde Kerk* (Dutch Reformed Church—DRC), enjoyed an unparalleled support from the apartheid government. All other religions were regarded as the "other"—a reflection, perhaps, of a pervasive European mentality that saw non-Christian faiths as anti-thesis to Christendom. The DRC was the Church of the government and its political roles in South Africa during the apartheid years were great, giving unquestioned legitimacy to apartheid system. There were also Christians, however, on the forefront of the struggle that dismantled it.

In May 1996, however, one of the first actions of the parliament after the dismantling of apartheid was the approval of the final version of a new constitution that provided for the establishment of a commission for the promotion and protection of the rights of all religious and linguistic communities. Thus, South Africa returned to a secular state and does not have an "official" religion. This, however, need a refined translation in South African context.

Unlike in the United States where the majority assumes that the phrase "one nation under God" in its Pledge of Allegiance means that the citizens believe in God, in South African context, the majority would translate such a pledge as meaning that the citizens believe that believing in God is consistent with the values of a secular state. Genuine freedom is rooted in religion because one of the major pillars of a true human happiness is religion. As freedom is rooted in religion, so is the ability to express one's religious values rooted in genuine freedom. Thus, South African new constitution identifies and guarantees freedom of worship and prohibits discrimination on the basis of religion. All South African citizens now have legal protections without discrimination on the grounds of religious beliefs, even when it is realized that certain elements of Christianity and its traditions oppressed the majority for more that two generations.

Therefore, the success of Christianity and its adoption as the state religion during the apartheid years was not completely a blessing. Christianity became an acid that corroded the government and stiffened African spirituality. Hence, missionary Christianity as the indigenous people understood it became an anathema, and the majority had to convert the God of Christianity to their own ancestral spirituality. Thus, the creativity of the indigenous population became the salvation of the faith that was once proclaimed in a foreign draping.

Modern Origins of Christianity in South Africa

The initial proclamation of the Christian faith in South Africa took place around 1488 C.E. This corresponds to the time when earliest Portuguese landed in the Cape area. It is estimated that approximately thirty-three million South Africans are professing Christians and the number continues to grow.

The chief controversial issue of Christianity, and the one that dominates South African society at large includes the great racial, linguistic and cultural heterogeneity of its people. This classification by race continues to exert a strong influence on the social life of the people and their faiths. Despite the new constitutional prohibition on discrimination based on race, the psychic damage that apartheid left behind in the black communities is strong. The view that blacks are intellectually inferior to other racial groups has been rendered regnant in South Africa, but it is not yet totally extinct.

The Church and Cultural Confrontations

South African mainline Churches are similar to European Churches and are on similar steps in regards to architecture and liturgy. In this way, one can say that the missionary Churches were transplanted from Europe to South Africa. They were also established initially along the coasts in the 19th century, but took roots elsewhere after the discovery of gold and diamond in the mainland, particularly in Kimberly. Johannesburg, the commercial capital of South Africa, was established as a result of this "gold rush" and continues to carry the mark of material success of the 19th century.

It would appear from the success of Christianity that traditional African religious paradigms have succumbed to the Christian faith in its European draping. Yet, this would be an exaggeration and it would be reckless to make such a sweeping general assumption. Although they have been rendered renegade, indigenous religious beliefs have not been supplanted or extinct, and they are not totally crushed out of existence by Christianity. One of the major difficulties is that what we know about the indigenous religions in South Africa before the arrival of Christian missionaries was largely derived from the accounts of early observers and interlocutors whose religious bias often produced misunderstandings. Recent studies have defended the suspicion that Christianity has not displaced the traditional indigenous beliefs, nor reduced them to a subsidiary position. On the contrary, both systems of belief co-exist in a loose relationship of cross-fertilization. Thus, rather than showing themselves as discrete and contradictory faiths, Christianity and indigenous traditional beliefs appear to share a single continuum and, often, they are interwoven as an organic religious system. Hence, John Mbiti asserts that as Africans pass from their indigenous religious and traditional values into Christianity, they do not need to walk very far before walking on familiar terrain of religious consciousness.[28] This is because African religious insights—and all its active features of ancestors, diviners, herbalists, sorcerers, and witches—have real and compelling affinity with that of the biblical religions, and South African religious past is not totally discontinuous with the new awareness illuminated by the arrival of modern Christian missionaries. While traditional African belief has survived in its own right among over 18 percent of the population, it has also blended into Christianity. Thus, South African traditional religions continue to endure as a "skein" threaded into the weft of the Christian faith. Certain elements such as the veneration of ancestral spirits as well as ritualistic dancing have been deeply incorporated into Christianity, while others blend imperfectly and uneasily with Christian teachings. Thus, the unveiling of a tombstone after burial can be both an African as well as a Christian rite. As a result of the adumbrated or skeletal form of African traditional religious beliefs within Christianity, black South Africans have a more formidable range of religious resources to draw upon as they order their lives, and in the resolution of personal problems, than their counterpart white Christians or among those who have only retained a purely African or a purely European religious framework.

In the mainline Churches, the Church also served another function during apartheid—it became a place where funerals were conducted for the victims of police brutality and state-sponsored killings. Thus, the Truth and Reconciliation Commission (TRC) was created to address the past so that all South Africans could move forward. In 1995, Nelson Mandela appointed Archbishop Desmond Tutu to head the commission. On December 16, 1995 Archbishop Desmond Tutu announced that the TRC had been charged with the awesome task of facilitating a process of national healing in South Africa.[29] The purpose of the Commission was to grant amnesty to those who committed politically motivated crimes under apartheid if they came forward to testify truthfully and face the victims or their families. The TRC revealed the "altar of Satan" on which hundreds lost their lives in senseless killings, and Eugene de Kock would go down in South African history as the most notorious criminal and the incarnation of evil under apartheid. Perhaps, it would require another Book of Job to state the psychological damage and the collective problems that apartheid created for all South Africans. What is remarkable about the TRC, however, is its Christian character, an indication of the success of missionary's failure in South Africa. The TRC was not a witch-hunt commission and was not set up as the Medieval Christian inquisition for producing a certain kind of truth so that heretics could be exposed and censored according to the design of the Church. From the beginning Tutu made it clear that the commission intended to stay on responsible Christian platform of sacramental confession and renewal. He stated: "We will be engaging in what should be a corporate nationwide process of healing through contrition, confession and forgiveness."[30] All of South Africans were consulted in the process and many people responded, regardless of their religions or denominational affiliation. It was as if South Africa was ready for the ritual of confession, contrition, national mourning, healing, and renewal. Thus, this Anglican Church leader led his nation in a national ritual of repentance and he invoked Christian vocabulary to do so. Perhaps, South Africans saw Christianity at its worst and at its best during the TRC hearings. In many ways, the hearings represented the most important public confession and forgiveness in the last half of the twentieth century. Through the TRC, Tutu challenged South African Christians and all other faith communities to come together so that the present victory over apartheid, and the future hope of a new beginning, could be celebrated. According to him: "Our churches, mosques, synagogues and temples will be able to provide liturgies for corporate confession and absolution."[31] Informed by his own profound

Christian journey, Tutu established the narrative framework of the commission as an essentially a Christian narrative of confession, contrition, forgiveness and reconciliation.

The religious character of the commission was transparent, and horrific stories of abuse and gross violation of human rights were told in ways that enhanced the religious character of the commission. Bodies of religious representatives like the DRC and the Zion Christian Church, at the TRC felt that it was their chance for contrition, confession and forgiveness. Tutu crafted the TRC so well that in reality, it promoted the image of God who loves and forgives. The philosophy behind the commission was that one must face the past, however horrific it might have been, and bounce back by God's grace. Nothing demonstrated this more forcefully as the book he wrote about his experience as the chair of the TRC.[32]

Christianity has also left an indelible mark on South African culture, particularly on Music and literary tradition. This is probably one of the most permanent imprints of the success of the failure of early missionaries. In traditional Zulu dance and performing arts, for example, one sees the impact that Christianity has made. But it is not certain whether it is Christianity that has surrendered to the cultural idioms of South Africans, or if it is the South African cultural norms that have been conquered by Christianity in the cross-fertilization process between the two. What is clear, however, is the mark of the success of Christianity in South Africa through the establishment of Indigenous Churches.

The African Indigenous Churches (AICs)

Members of the African Initiated Church (AIC) are 26.3 per cent of the South African population. The leadership of the mainline Churches is generally slow or unwilling to ordain Africans as pastors, and reluctant to give them full responsibility in financial matters, or admit them as equals. Missionaries generally refuse to relax ultimate white control of the missionary-initiated Churches. Tired of being treated as inferiors, the AIC leaders made attempts to break the shackles of white domination while retaining some form of ecclesiastical structures of the white Churches. While the missionary-related Churches proselytize, the AIC draws membership from either family members or indiscriminately from other Christian denominations.

In the AICs, members wear white clothes to Church and do not wear shoes or jewels during worship services or religious activities. Perhaps, this is in reference to the command Moses received from God to take off his shoes because he was on holy grounds. One can also infer from this that the AICs take the Bible literarily as a book of remembrance.

Closely associated with the mode of dress is the significance of dancing. Dancing, members of the AIC believe, links the physical world with the supernatural world. This is an important cross-fertilization between the Christian faith and the traditional religious worldview. The AICs have also embraced Leviticus-style sensitivity to diet. They forbid the intake of harmful substances because a healthy body is the only body suitable as the Temple of the Holy Spirit. The intake of traditional Zulu medicine is also strictly forbidden.

In the AICs, all that European missionaries taught Africans to discard as evil were brought back as legitimate medium of Christian worship. If the arrival of European missionaries in the 18th and 19th centuries represented the 'first conversion' of South Africans to Christianity, what AICs represents is the 'second conversion.' They are not radically different from the mainline denominations, but many of their Church activities are not familiar to mainline Christian worshipers. Their liturgical liveliness can be characterized as Christian, as African, and as different. Europeans have returned to the mainline Churches in the missionary-sending communities overwhelmed by the vigor and the rapid expansion of African Christianity. In South Africa, if there were to be one word to characterize them, it would be "Zion." There are over 4,500 different groups of Zionists in South Africa and the number continues to grow. The distinctive elements of worship include dreams, visions, healing, and the experience of the Holy Spirit.

What is remarkably different, however, and this is their contribution to the development of Christianity worldwide, is not the political reconstruction of an unjust South African society, but the "mending of the lives" that have been twisted by the oppressive system of apartheid. Cooperatively, they salvage the individual members by supporting them economically, socially, and spiritually. Converts are largely from adults that are troubled by misfortune fueled by injustice. A large congregation of AICs is an indication of a victory over sorcery. Members eschew all worldly pursuits and cultivate a semi-ascetic approach to life that stresses diligence, sobriety, frugality and saving against spending. The unity and cohesion of the AICs is based on the principles of shared responsibility and mutual support. This impetus to give for the common good is called *ubuntu*. *Ubuntu* means to be open and available to others and be willing to reveal one's vulnerabilities and affirm the vulnerabilities of others. In the spirit of *Ubuntu* one does not feel threatened because others are more capable and self-confident. What matters in *Ubuntu* is to know that we belong to each other and to the greater whole. When one of us is humiliated, oppressed or marginalized, we are all diminished. Archbishop Desmond Tutu put it this way: "*Ubuntu* gives people resilience, enabling them to survive and emerge still human despite all efforts to dehumanize [and vilify] them."

The closest one gets to a "black Messiah" in South Africa is Isaiah Shembe (1870–1935). He was the founder of the Zulu Zionist movements, and in 1911 started the Nazareth Baptist Church in Kwa Mashu (near Durban), thereby transforming Christianity from a white, European-dominated settler religion, to a vibrant black-majority religion rooted in the Zulu idioms and cultures.

Pentecostalism in South Africa

While AIC represents distinct African initiatives, the Pentecostal/Charismatic movement in South Africa is a part of a global Christian phenomenon. In the West, one should not underestimate the revival meetings of John Wesley, Dwight L. Moody, Ruben A. Torrey, and Charles G. Finney because they represented an important precursor that ignited twentieth-century Pentecostalism worldwide.[33] In South Africa, however, Pentecostalism existed along the path of indigenous Christianity, and moved along the same channels created by the African Initiated Churches, particularly the Zionist movements. There is a little surprise, therefore, that they share many spiritual characteristics. One can trace the historical origins of Pentecostalism, however loosely, to the Los Angeles meetings conducted by an African-American, William Joseph Seymour, in April 1906 at Azusa Street, and to the Apostolic Faith Mission of 1908.[34]

One of the unique features of Pentecostalism in South Africa, however, is its trans-denominational character. Its members have interactions with members of other religious bodies—Christians and non-Christians. Having no need for Church buildings or trained clergy, it regularly established itself indiscriminately and sporadically at the backyards of important neighborhoods in black townships and major cities. Baptism with the Holy Spirit is the most important qualification for leadership, and members are pushed away from alcoholism, petty crimes, gambling, corruption and promiscuity in preparation for the coming of the Holy Spirit.

In a society that was notoriously segregated by race under apartheid, Pentecostalism represented an empowerment for blacks and gave them an alternative way to re-order their social lives. This further represents a brilliant "success of the failure" of the missionaries in South Africa. Social life is organized around Church meetings and the nuclear family, where they learn self-discipline and a puritan work ethic.

There are certain factors that make Pentecostalism appealing to white and black alike in South Africa. Pentecostalism, for example, is a conglomeration of a number of Christian traditional beliefs that include: (1) justification by faith in Jesus Christ, (2) sanctification by means of spiritual baptism, and (3) a positive stance on divine healing. Factors that characterize Pentecostal Churches in South Africa include: *glossolalia* (ability to speak in tongues), shaking and prostrations under the power of the spirit, and instances of divine healing. These factors make it appealing to all racial groups in South Africa.

Perhaps, what has often escaped scholarly attention about the religious life of South Africans is that what Islamic religion represents to black Americans, who continue to carry the scar of racism, is what Pentecostalism represents for black South Africans.

The weakness of the people in position of power is in their failure to realize that a disproportionate use of force against the weak eventually corrupts the society as they attribute more value to their own lives while the values of the weak languish in valueless-ness. The power of the weak, on the other hand, lies in their ability to accept their sufferings but constantly hope for a better future. On the long run, it is not the weak that needs the strong, but the strong that needs the weak. Thus, both the strong and the weak in South Africa will continue to depend on each other.

Pentecostalism is growing rapidly in South Africa partly because it is free from missionary supervision and has also adopted, unapologetically, an Africanized version. Thus, religious features that are regarded as typically "African," such as the warmth and dignity of the people, as well as a corporate existence, are unique to South African Pentecostal experience.

One of the reasons the mainline Churches are losing members to the Pentecostal Churches is not only because of the success of indigenous definition that the Pentecostal Churches have given to Christianity, but also because they have adapted well to the demographic shift from the rural to the urban centers. The mainline Churches find it difficult to adapt to the new trend of urbanization, but the poor in big cities prefer Churches that are small group oriented, where basic human needs are met. This can only mean that any Church that identifies with her members at grassroots level, addresses their existential needs, and helps them face and deal with the personal realities confronting them, will thrive.

A Summary

Thus, South Africans are intensely religious, and their faiths today can be characterized as comprehensive. Virtually 80 per cent of the total population professes some kind of faith in a recognized world religion. Like many other African countries, religion continues to be a significant social force, and its practice cannot be completely understood apart from its geographical, ideological, political, cultural and historical context. Christians of various denominations are by far the largest religious group.[35] This is a mark of the success of Christianity, although Christian missionaries failed in many cultural aspects in South Africa.

Before the arrival of European missionaries around 1488 C.E., South Africans were followers of African Traditional Religions (ATR), and more than 18.3 percent of South African population still practices them today. Other religions in South Africa include Islam, starting in 1658 C.E.; Hinduism beginning in 1857 C.E.; and Judaism beginning before 1669 with a record of a small number of Jews that converted to Christianity.

The success of missionary's failure has translated to these various religious communities in South Africa. And with little or no visible hierarchy to hinder the work of the laymen and women in South Africa, missionary and non-missionary Churches are becoming agents of healing to hurting communities in post-apartheid era. Though missionaries exhibited paternalism and failed to endorse indigenous creativity in South Africa, the success of their work is unparalleled in modern history, transforming Africa as a whole into a paradise for sociologists and psychologists of religion. Withdrawing creatively from the political and religious scenes, missionaries have given way to African leadership. It means that Africans themselves have to emancipate the faith they have inherited and give it indigenous definitions.

It was at the funerals of the victims of state brutality that a new interfaith ecumenism of Hindus, Jews, Christians and Muslims surfaced, establishing unprecedented common moral foundations and platform from which to oppose the apartheid system. Thus, apartheid was a common enemy, and there was a decline of religious particularity but greater emphasis on religious humanism and universalism in South Africa. It was from the wreckage of apartheid that a new South Africa with new initiatives for inter-religious dialogue has now emerged.

Traditionally, Christianity has been a cementing factor in South African society. It was the killings and state brutality under apartheid that further strengthened the unity of the different religious groups and divided communities for the promotion of social justice. The main features of Civil Right activities in South Africa in the 1980s and early 1990s, for example, were protest marches, political rallies, and funeral services for victims of state brutality. Out of the ashes of the 1980s emerged South Africa with a multiple religious heritage—Christianity, Islam, Hinduism, Judaism, and African Traditional Religion—all vying for social justice. This is also the first time in her modern history that South Africa faces the real prospect of true multiculturalism and religious plurality.

In South Africa, religions have been greatly affected by political and economic factors. It is also true, however, that they too have been influenced by religions. One does not need to revisit the hen-egg debate here: did the

Church invent apartheid or did the politicians? By association, the Church seemed guilty and it is worrisome that Christian mission has been discredited in South Africa today. As politicians entered the Church to worship, Christians also entered the house of parliament to debate racial issues. Yet, the Church is challenged as a reconciling body to transcend the accidentals and embrace the essentials. An unjust social structure cannot be the platform upon which the future of South Africa will be constructed.

Although the Church should not carry the lion share of the blame for apartheid, it is also the case that the Church did not stand strongly against it at the beginning. Some Black congregations depended on their White "mother Churches" financially. Therefore, they possess little leverage to denounce apartheid publicly. But more and more missiologists came out strongly against the traditional policy of apartheid in the 1980s. By the mid 1990s, the traditional justification of apartheid on theological grounds was all but dead even in the Dutch Reformed Church. Therefore, it is possible, and we can assume this interpretation with a reasonable degree of probability, that the spiritual life of all South Africans at the beginning was nurtured without one racial group dominating another (white Churches dominating black Churches). The Churches where most Afrikaners belonged later propelled the insidious agenda of political oppression. One interpretation for this change is that Afrikaners had to survive because they too suffered discrimination under British rule. The prevailing white supremacy Afrikaners inherited from the British was transferred to the indigenous South Africans. Politicians assisting them, the Churches, out of necessity and pragmatism, provided the theological framework and the blueprint for racial division. It is the theological blueprint for racial segregation that politicians received with both hands.

There is also a remarkable spiritual transformation of black South African's, not only political and economic transformation. Perhaps, after South African religious experience, it would be quite difficult to see Christianity in the same way. While there clearly has been a major Christianizing of black South African, so too has there been a major Africanizing of Christianity by black people, to the extent that it probably does not make much demographical sense today to talk about the European-derived mainline denominations as the "mainstream" denominations in South Africa. The African Initiated Churches, the Pentecostal, as well as the Evangelical Churches, are now at the central stage of Christianity in South Africa. And it makes more sense to see them as the "mainstream" Christian denomination in modern South Africa.

It was the killings and state brutality under apartheid that united all these different religious groups and divided communities. Thus, one does not see himself as a Hindu or a Jewish or Christian or Muslim to join protest marches against apartheid. All the children of Adam and Eve joined hands to fight a common enemy—injustice of apartheid. Perhaps, this is the most important success of missionary's failure on the continent of Africa as a whole.

The multiple religious heritage—Christianity, Islam, Hinduism, Judaism, and African Traditional Religion—all vying for Africa's spiritual allegiance, have become interwoven into the fabric of religious life of South Africans, to the extent that it has become difficult to define a particular religion. It is worthy to note that as the vocabulary to justify apartheid was crafted by Christians, so was the vocabulary that secured civil liberty for the majority of South Africans. This was reflected most boldly in the truth and reconciliation commission (TRC) headed by the most reverend Desmond Tutu.[36]

But what is more intriguing in modern Africa about the adoption of Christianity by the majority, is how Christianity stands against African Traditional Religions and confirms African way of life at the same time. African religious traditions render Christianity valid by providing a soft environment for Christian expansion. At the same time, Christianity provides an alternative to African way of life and religious awareness. What Europeans missionaries have condemned as witchcraft, heathenism, or, less felicitously, a delusion, early African Christian leaders took seriously. They interpreted them in contrast to Christian way of life and as a departure from the traditional spiritual force. As ancient traditional religious shrines burst into flames, Christianity is confirmed as the real alternative to the ancient religious awareness. Africans know the power of darkness too well and they often provided interpretations to the Old Testament with keen perceptions, to the amazement or embarrassment of European missionaries.

Major challenges remain in South Africa, however, and they include the creation of conditions for eliminating widespread unemployment, poverty, and HIV/AIDS that persist in the country. Christians and other religious communities can be mobilized to address these problems and tackle them effectively. Determined attempts are being made by post-apartheid government and Christian communities to improve the lives of all South Africans.

The most celebrated statesman in South Africa's modern history is Nelson Mandela, the African National Congress (ANC) leader and the first non-white President. In a spirit of forgiveness, Mandela crafted the country's transition to full democracy through painstaking negotiations with the last white President, F. W. de Klerk. The stature of Mandela has dramatically enhanced South Africa's prestige internationally.

Perhaps, the end of apartheid in South Africa demonstrates in modern history that there is no permanent hiding place for a systematic injustice perpetrated by one group of human beings against another. Religious communities, Christians and non-Christians alike, put the broken pieces of apartheid and magnified oppression together. The roots of these religious communities can be traced largely to non-African soil and missionaries would be promi-nent in their background.

Notes

[1] Kenyan Scholar, Douglass W. Waruta titled his contribution to *The Faces of Jesus in Africa* "Who is Jesus Christ for Africa Today? Prophet, Priest, Potentate." See Robert J. Schreiter, ed. *Faces of Jesus in Africa* (New York: Orbis Books, 1991), 52–69.

[2] Mark 15:34.

[3] Philip Jenkins, *The Next Christendom: The Coming of Global Christianity* (New York, New York: Oxford University Press, 2002).

[4] See Jurgens Hendriks and Johannes Erasmus, *Journal of Theology for Southern Africa* Vol. 109 (March 2001): 41–65.

[5] See Ali A. Mazrui, *The Africans: A Triple Heritage* (Boston, Massachusetts: Little, Brown and Company, 1986), 157.

[6] The Anglican Communion is very strong in South Africa. Most Anglicans are adherents of the Church of the Province of Southern Africa, comprising 23 dioceses (including Lesotho, Namibia, St. Helena, Swaziland and two dioceses in Mozambique). The Anglican Commun-ion has more than one and a half million members.

[7] The Methodist Church in Southern Africa has more than two and a half million members.

[8] Lutheran Communion in Southern Africa (LUCSA) includes: Angola, Botswana, Malawi, Mozambique, Namibia, South Africa, Swaziland, Zambia, and Zimbabwe. Lutheran Com-munion has approximately one and a half million members.

[9] The Presbyterian Church of Africa has more than one million members.

[10] The United Congregational Church of Southern Africa has approximately 350, 000 mem-bers.

[11] South Africa has four Roman Catholic archdioceses (Bloemfontein, Cape Town, Durban, and Pretoria), twenty-one dioceses, and one Apostolic Prefecture. In 2000, it was estimated that the Roman Catholic has three and a half million members in South Africa or approxi-mately 8.3 percent of the total population. The most powerful Catholic body in South Africa is the Southern Africa Catholic Bishop's Conference (SACBC).

[12] The Dutch Reformed Church *(Nederduitse Gereformeerde Kerk)* consisted of the Dutch Reformed Church with more than a million members; the Uniting Reformed Church also has more than a million (mainly Coloured and Black) members. The Reformed Church in Africa, predominantly Indians, has approximately two thousand members.

[13] The Baptist Union of Southern Africa has approximately 290,000 members. In late 1980s, the Baptist Convention of South Africa was formed (predominantly Coloured and Blacks).

[14] There are approximately 20,000 Greek Orthodox members in South Africa.

[15] Read John W. De Gruchy, *Christianity and Democracy: A Theology for a Just World Order* (Cape Town: David Philip, 1995), 165–192.

[16] Robert J. Schreiter, ed. "Jesus Christ in Africa Today" in *The Faces of Jesus in Africa* (Maryknoll, New York: Orbis Book, 1991), viii.

[17] N. M. Israel and his wife, Mrs. Ragi Israel, have written about the history of the Indian Baptist work in South Africa and they have articulated their views about how the Baptist work among the Indian population started in Natal. Their knowledge of history is admirable and the information here is based on the author's interviews with them while in South Africa.

[18] While Christianity is a cementing tool in many parts of Africa, uniting different ethnic groups, it is a weapon of division in certain regions. Uganda is a good example where one can only be an Anglican or a Roman Catholic with open, often contentious, animosity toward the

members of the other denomination. See Paul Gifford, *African Christianity: Its Public Role* (Bloomington, Indiana: Indiana University Press, 1998).

[19] Bonganjalo Goba, "The Role of Religion in Promoting Democratic Values in a Post-apartheid Era" in *Religion and the Reconstruction of Civil Society,* John W. deGruchy and S. Martin, ed. (Pretoria: University of South Africa, 1995), 189.

[20] See Charles Villa-Vicencio, *Trapped in Apartheid: A Socio-theological History of the English-speaking Churches* (Maryknoll, New York: Orbis Books, 1988).

[21] The theological base for this clannish ideology has its roots in the theory of Ham which is based on a peculiarly strange exegesis of Genesis 9:18–27. It was a theology of exclusion and it has foundational presupposition that argued that black people are naturally inferior to whites and other races. This theory played a pivotal role in Afrikaner nationalism. It provided, for example, legitimacy for political self-interest of the Afrikaner, and it was the engine that drove their theological and national exclusiveness. See Bonganjalo Goba, "The Role of Religion in Promoting Democratic Values in a Post-apartheid Era," 191.

[22] Ibid. 195.

[23] See Paul Maylam, *A History of the African People of South Africa: From the Early Iron Age to the 1970s* (Cape Town: David Philip, 1986).

[24] In May 2003, South Africans commemorated the 110th anniversary of Gandhi's eviction in Pietermaritzburg, South Africa.

[25] The Dreyfus Trial of 1894 in France played a pivotal role in convincing the Jews world-wide that a permanent homeland was of necessity. Alfred Dreyfus, a Jew, was a captain in the French army and was falsely accused of selling secret documents to Germany. In 1894, he was convicted and sentenced to life imprisonment on the basis of forged documents. The real traitor was Esterhazy but was acquitted despite overwhelming evidence against him. Public protests of this travesty of justice were insufficient to override the tide of popular anti-Semitic feelings that underlay the scandal. A respectable novelist, Emile Zola, wrote an editorial protesting the injustice, and he was sent to prison for doing so, an unfortunate casualty of the notorious case. Later, a French army officer came forward and admitted that he forged the documents used to convict Alfred Dreyfus, and then committed suicide. When the case was re-opened, surprisingly Dreyfus was again found guilty but was given a presidential pardon and declared innocent in 1906. This trial had a profound influence on Theodor Herzl (1860–1904) who followed this case with great passion as a journalist. It was Herzl who ignited the campaign for a Jewish homeland that is now called the Zionist Movement, rejecting the concept of Jewish assimilation worldwide. Read John L. Esposito, Darrell J. Fasching and Todd Lewis, *World Religions Today* (New York: Oxford University Press, 2002), 164–65.

[26] Read Andrew Wheatcroft, *Infidels: The Conflict between Christendom and Islam 638–2002* (London: Viking Penguin Books, 2002).

[27] Even in certain African nation state, Muslims and Christians do not often co-exist amicably. Nigeria is notorious for atavistic hatred between Muslims and Christians and hundreds of people have lost their lives in senseless killings. Read Niels Kastfelt, *Religion and Politics in Nigeria: A Study in Middle Belt Christianity* (London: British Academic Press, 1994).

[28] John S. Mbiti, "Christianity and East African Culture and Religion," *Dini na Mila* 3, no 1 (May 1968): 4.

[29] David Chidester, "Stories, Fragments and Monuments" in James Cochrane, John de Gruchy and Stephen Martin, eds. *Facing the Truth: South African Faith Communities and the Truth and Reconciliation Commission* (Cape Town: David Philip Publishers, 1999), 134.

[30] Ibid.

[31] Ibid.

[32] Desmond Tutu, *No Future Without Forgiveness* (New York: Doubleday, 1999).

[33] Harvard University Professor, Harvey Cox, did a comprehensive study of Pentecostalism worldwide. In 1965, he wrote *The Secular City* and argued that the dominant theme of modern society was secularism. He described how secularism was causing the Church to die in the city. But thirty years later, this learned Professor retreated, stating that religion should be taken seriously in the modern world, especially in the cities. He argued in *Fire From Heaven* (1995) that Christianity is strong in the cities of the world, from the East to the West, from North to South. Read Harvey Cox, *Fire From Heaven: The Rise of Pentecostal Spirituality and the Reshaping of Religion in the Twenty-First Century,* (New York: Addison-Wesley Publishing Company, 1995).

[34] Most of the earliest leaders of Pentecostal Movement in the United States were African-Americans. It was Charles Harrison Mason, for example, that started the Church of God in Christ in 1897 and led it into the Pentecostal movement in 1907, now the largest predominantly African-American Pentecostal denomination in America. It is symbolical that Martin Luther King, Jr. gave his last sermon (I have been to the mountain top....) at a Church named after Mason in Memphis (Mason Temple) before his assassination in April 1968. Read Harvey Cox, *Fire From Heaven,* 67–80.

[35] Christians in South Africa are approximately three quarters of the total population. This means that Christians have a higher percentage in South Africa than in any other African nation state.

[36] The Most Reverend Archbishop Tutu has written about his experience as the Chair of the Truth and Reconciliation Commission. Read Desmond Tutu, *No Future Without Forgiveness,* (New York: Doubleday, 1999).

❋Chapter Four
POST-WESTERN CHRISTIANITY IN SOUTH AFRICA

Perhaps one of the most important developments of Christianity in the twentieth century was its transition in South Africa from a white, European-dominated religion to a vibrant black-majority religion rooted in African idioms and cultures. At the same time Christians in South Africa became engaged in the struggle against social, political, and ecclesiastical domination, using the vocabularies of their faith to secure civil liberty.

This chapter argues that the unintended consequences of the early European missionaries in South Africa are the new forms that Christianity has now taken. These unintended outcomes transcended the original intentions of both the integrationist[1] and segregationist[2] Churches under the control of the missionaries.

In this chapter our emphasis is on early European missionaries. They envisioned the values of indigenous Church leadership under the three self-formulae of self-supporting, self-governing, and self-propagating in the 19th century. But the African-initiated Churches rooted in African cultures and spiritual values in the 20th century were least anticipated. This ultimately led to the demise of non-indigenous control and effectively supplanted non-native authority in South Africa.

The chapter further argues that a major unintended consequence of missionary's efforts in South Africa was that the Churches "planted" by early missionaries continue to fall by the wayside. The indigenous Churchmen and women are leaving them behind, determined to take control of the life of the

Church and use the Church institutions to end political and ecclesiastical domination.

Certain questions are raised in the chapter: What room is there in South African religious context for biblical interpretation within the indigenous cosmological systems in post-apartheid era? In what ways can new theological developments bridge the gap between biblical inclusivism and theological exclusivism within the context of religious plurality? In the new South African context, can salvation also pertain existentially to the redistribution of the earthly goods and power without its traditional meaning of the restructuring of the soul? How can the Church proclaim freedom for all without empowering all?

The Church and the Abuse of Structured Power

There is a familiar story in the fifteenth chapter of the book of Acts. The earliest disciples of Jesus were predominantly Jews. When the Church was gaining institutional strength, Jewish Christians were troubled that Gentiles were also becoming Christians and referring themselves as "the people of the way."[3] The apostles wanted to resolve this problem, and perhaps they were jealous that God was blessing the Gentiles as God was blessing the Jews. Therefore, they sent a group of delegates to Jerusalem to find out from the ecclesiastical authority what Gentiles must do before they could become Christians. This would not have occurred in such a dramatic way if not because early Christians considered themselves a sect within Judaism.

In a spirit of compromise characteristic of early Christians, the apostles in Jerusalem concluded with certain discomfort that the Gentiles could be Christians without first becoming Jews or performing the religious rituals associated with Judaism. They envisioned that their decision would not present any danger to the Jewish religious rituals or jeopardize its hollowed traditions. In this familiar story, we are left with an unavoidable question. Did the apostles realize the long-term impact of their decision? Did they have any thoughts that Gentiles would soon outnumber them in Church membership? Had they realized this, would the apostles in Jerusalem have been happy with their decisions? When Gentile followers later abandoned animal sacrifice, ceremonial washing, worship on the Sabbath, and the wearing of veils, how did this affect the decision the apostles made in Jerusalem?

This old question seems to have resurfaced in the development of South African Christianity. The question, however, is not whether South Africans should or should not adopt the religious rituals and traditions of early Europeans in order to be classified as Christians. The question now is whether European missionaries thought carefully before embarking on missionary journeys to South Africa more than two hundred and fifty years ago. Did they know that by the beginning of the 21st-century, Christianity would be growing more rapidly in Africa than in Europe? Would they have embarked upon their missionary journeys to Africa if they knew that South African Christians would be capable of using the vocabularies of faith to secure political freedom from the leaders with ties to European missionaries? Did early missionaries envision the creative roles of religions in politics that African Christians have crafted?

In 1786, there was an important conference of the Baptist ministers in Northampton, England. At that meeting, the young William Carey, later to become one of the most successful missionaries to India, raised the question of mission to the unknown places such as Africa. Carey was told: "sit down young man. When it pleases the Lord to convert the heathen, he will do it without your help or mine."[4] There is little doubt that most early Europeans regarded Africa and the Orient as esoteric, if not barbaric, hidden, or heathen. The push to converting the heathens was also a push to civilization, according to the dual mandate. Beneath this thin veneer of religion was also a desire to glorify Europe for sending missionaries as explorers. These missionaries entered South Africa with a different definition of the Church from the definition of the Church in Europe.

The term "Church" in the consciousness of early European missionaries was different from the Church in South Africa. The "Church" was always in Europe, but the Church in Africa was regarded as a "mission work" not to be confused with the "Church" in Europe. This dichotomy between the "Church" and "mission work" was a theme in the relationship between the missionaries and the indigenous people of South Africa. The Church became associated with Christians in the Western world. Mission, on the other hand, was associated with all the people that have been converted or would be converted to Christianity.

South Africans continued to be in need of an authentic Christian identity, whether they have accepted Jesus Christ or not. The split between what the Church is and what the mission is, has always been a characteristic of Protestant Christianity in South Africa. Therefore, Christ was divided from the beginning of missionary activities in South Africa.

The object of the Church Missionary Society (CMS) was the development of Native Churches with a view that missionaries will ultimately settle in South Africa, monitoring the progress of their missionary work as the master supervises the apprentice perpetually. The strategy developed to reinforce this rests on the three-self formulae proposed by Henry Venn.[5] That is, the missionaries should plan for an indigenous Church that is a self-supporting, self-governing, and self-propagating (extending) congregation.[6] Venn, however, used the term *euthanasia of mission* to describe this process.

Although this term means that the missionaries would stop being in South Africa at some point, the very fact that they needed to set up this three-self formulae plan, acknowledges that there would be a tendency for the missionaries not to leave the mission field. This means that the three-self formulae could become a way of prolonging the life of missionaries on the field. This way, the life of the indigenous Church would perpetually depend on the supervision and control of the missionaries—monitoring the indigenous Church in South Africa indefinitely.

The true spirit of the three-self formulae was in the founding of the "Ethiopian" Churches, and L. N. Mzimba justified the establishment of Africanized Christianity when he stated that the purpose was "to plant a self-supporting, self-governing and self-propagating African Church [that] would produce a truly African type of Christianity suited to the genius and needs of the race, and not a black copy of any European Church."[7] Even here, the real intention was to formalize missionary presence in South Africa.

The 19th century missionary program on the continent in general and in South Africa in particular, came to a critical point when World War I broke out in Europe—the Christian heartland. Although the war was not the end of the missionary euphoria, as some scholars have suggested,[8] it was the beginning of the end of the enthusiasm that had gathered at the Missionary Conference at Edinburgh in 1910. To be sure, World War I (1914–1918) disrupted the smooth running of the missionary operations in European countries and undermined the claim of optimism and of the Western Christian superiority. But the fatal blow to the spirit of utopia expressed in the ambitious agenda of the missionaries—to teach Africans how to establish God's Kingdom on a native soil—was World War II (1939–1945). The indigenous religions of the peoples of Africa were regarded as devoid of any eternal value before the war. This propelled European missionaries to convert Africans from what was termed "heathenism." The fatal blow came when World War II broke out in Europe.

Most African Christian leaders were sensitive to the psychological cause of the war (a cause that many Europeans would disclaim), but not to its immediate military cause—the violation of the territorial integrity of Czechoslovakia and Poland in 1939. But the two causes are closely linked. The cause of the war *de facto* was the Berlin Conference of 1884–1885 when European powers divided the continent of Africa. Many African Church leaders knew that a violation of African sovereignty at the Berlin Conference would embolden European countries at home and whet their appetite for annexation in Europe. In 1935, for example, Italy under Mussolini violated Ethiopia's sovereignty by an invasion. His partial success emboldened the Nazi and Fascist dictators at home. If European powers could collectively subjugate a distant land without serious resistance from the indigenous people, the Nazis concluded, the weak countries at home were also up for grasps. Thus, Nazi Germany's invasion of Poland in 1939 could be traced psychologically back to Italy's own aggression in Ethiopia in 1935, and both could be further traced back to the collective aggression of Europeans at the Berlin Conference in 1884–85. Therefore, the real cause of World War II was not only military but also psychological.[9] Does this mean that World War II (1939–1945) was Africa's revenge against Europe for what Europeans did to Africans at the Berlin Conference in 1884–85? Could this be a "Divine Vengeance" upon Europe similar to the classical Greek concept of Nemesis? Did African ancestors wake up in 1939 to punish Europe for the partitioning of their children? Is Europe divided today for the arrogance of 1884–85? Did Africa come back in the 20th century to exact revenge for what happened in the 19th century?

What is even more relevant for our purpose here is that when World War II broke out, it did in the heartland of Christendom, and effectively called into question the justification for missionary activities in Africa, which was relatively at peace. Hence, the dichotomy between the "Church at home" in Europe and the "Mission Work" in Africa was undermined. African soldiers were conscripted to fight a war they knew little about and defended the same Europeans that had colonized them.

But the net result of World War II was beneficial to Africans. They sensed for the first time the vulnerability of Europe and the weaknesses of the crown. In like manner, non-Christian religions were no longer conceived as the primary "enemy" of Christendom and of the missionary movement. On the contrary, devotees of non-Christian religions in Africa became accepted allies in the longer war against misery, oppression, poverty, and secularism. Furthermore, Western cultural superiority started to disappear with the same speed as the Christian superiority that was encoded in Western cultures. This is what actually paved the way for the fading of the Church-Mission dichotomy of the post-war era in South Africa.

At the end of World War II missionary attitudes and emphases on propagating the Gospel were no longer geographical and racial. Devotees of non-Christian religions had fought side by side in Europe with Christian soldiers. This deeply affected the attitude of South Africans about the dichotomy between Christians and non-Christians. At the end of the war, non-Westerners started to see their religions as appropriate for them in their particular cultural and ideological contexts. The ugliness of wars in Europe opened the eyes of Africans to be more appreciative of their motherlands. The word "Evangelization" was introduced as the responsibility of all to save all. This is one of the reasons why at the International Mission Conference in Willingen, (The Netherlands), in 1952 the theme was: "The Upbringing of the Younger Churches as a part of the Historic Christian

Community."[10] This title would not have been used in the pre-wars era. Stating that African Churches were "younger Churches" also meant that European Christians were beginning to come to terms with their African brothers and sisters. The focus of Christian mission remains, however, on the Western world and its mission-sending status.

The Church and the Stigma of Racism

Europeans learned during World War II that there is only a kaleidoscope of religions and cultures without a measure of racial or cultural superiority. Yet, no Protestant Churches in South Africa accommodated blacks and whites in a single structure. Protestant Churches, especially the Methodists, reproduced the Church-Mission dichotomy by separating their "Church" work for whites from the "Mission" work for black South Africans. David Thomas asserted, "Despite their enormous and growing numerical superiority, the mission wings were considered far less important than the Church wings."[11] One of the ironies of a divided Christianity in South Africa was that blacks were not called "missionaries" although their willingness to proclaim the Gospel to fellow South Africans and the willingness of the converts to adopt Christian practice and liturgy to local cultures were undoubtedly the major reasons why black South Africans were probably the most successful missionaries of all.[12]

The Lutheran Missions had a lot more in common with the proponents of the segregationist/apartheid ideology than with those of multiracial congregations. It is no accident that one of the leading architects of apartheid in the 1950s was W. W. M. Eiselen, whose father was a German missionary to South Africa.[13]

Politicians exploited the Church to entrench racial segregation. Nowhere was this more obvious than the Nederduitse Gereformeerde Kerk—the Dutch Reformed Church (DRC). Although the DRC had established Federal Council in the 1940s, she had no single multiracial body to express the unity of the Church she proclaimed.

Although the motives for establishing "sister Churches" or "younger Churches" were initially based on racial considerations, they were later justified by the three-self formula.[14] The support of the General Missionary Council in South Africa for the concept of the separate "native Church" was apparently a step ahead at the time, but this was not good news for the indigenous South African Christians. This is because the missionaries still expected such a Church to be under their control and anticipated the indigenous Churches to be within their ethos and theological orientation. Even missionaries that were originally in favor of the indigenous congregations under the three-self formulae, showed hostility towards any indigenous Church that was not under the guidelines and theological bent of the missionaries.[15] Most missionaries disapproved strongly, for example, the establishment of the African-initiated Churches, calling it a syncretistic religion.[16]

It was not only the Conservative wing of missionaries in South Africa that disapproved African ecclesiastical autonomy. The "liberal wing" of Missionary Organization also disapproved African initiatives. Initially, missionaries within the General Mission Council (GMC) endorsed the territorial segregation as being in the best interest of the African people. At first it may seem as though the missionaries within the GMC were characteristically magnanimous towards the indigenous people by allowing them freedom within the three-self formulae. But they exploited the three-self formulae to formalize Church segregation. Thus, even the liberal wing of the GMC was not blameless. This became clearer when the missionaries in the GMC endorsed the Land Act of 1913 that gave 87 percent of the land to the white minority, and left the large black majority with only 13 percent. The "Christian Express," a forerunner of the missionary publication "South African Outlook," voiced support for the GMC. When bitter criticisms started flowing to the GMC office from every corner of the country, the authority of the GMC fired back that its support for the Land Act was based on the fact that it was piloted through the Parliament and those who framed the Bill had good intentions towards the African people.[17] In a recent article, J.J. (Dons) Kritzinger stated: "By the 1950s there was a general consensus in the Afrikaans Reformed Churches that differences in language and culture 'or race' provided enough reason for separate Church formation."[18]

Furthermore, there was a continuous criticism within the GMC itself, indicating that there was by no means a uniformity of opinion among the liberal missionaries on the question of racial policy. Thus, territorial segregation continued and was promoted in missionary circles well into the 20th century. Edgar Brooks based his pioneering work, *The History of Native Policy,* on his doctoral thesis of 1923. It is a well-documented scholarly work showing that the hands of missionaries were not clean on the issue of racial segregation in South Africa.

In 1926, leaders of the Anglican, Presbyterian, and Methodist Churches met with the leaders of the DRC and agreed, "It is not necessarily contrary to Christian principle to seek to develop and uplift Native life separate from European life."[19]

The Christian Council of South Africa (CCSA) was founded in 1936 to replace the GMC. Over the next three decades, the CCSA lost touch with the black political and Church leaders. When it was formed, black Church leaders assumed that the CCSA was replacing the GMC in order to create a platform for missionary's true liberalism that would be sympathetic to the aspirations of the black people. In the very year that it was formed, however, militant black opinions began to turn against white liberals because of their failure to stop the 1936 legislation that removed African voters from the common roll in the Cape Province.[20] There was no official reaction from either the remnant of the GMC or the new CCSA to the legislation. It can be said that all the attention and energy were directed at that time to the creation and restructuring of the CCSA. When this was accomplished, however, the presence of the DRC members in the CCSA proved to be too strong, and it prevented CCSA liberal members from saying anything against the legislation.

In Faith and Fear: Migration to the Urban Centers

Unjust legislation did not go unnoticed in the 1930s and '40s. The first wave of reaction against unjust distribution of land came from the Church of the Province of Southern Africa (CPSA). Members emphatically rejected the abolition of the black vote in the Cape. When the legislation became law in 1936, the South African Outlook attacked the legislation and criticized it bitterly. But this was because of the fear of what the Province of South Africa, which had initially launched a wave of criticism, might say. Already, missionaries had started to see that the expansion of Christianity and its rapid growth in Southern Africa could not have been solely because of the success of their efforts.

In the 1930s and early 1940s, a demographic shift began in South Africa. The indigenous people began to leave the rural areas, where factors that promoted traditional religions and values were found,[21] and started migrating to the urban centers, where there were factors that promoted Christianity. Therefore, the acceptance of Christianity by the black population can be attributed, in part, to the demographic shift from the rural to the urban centers. This is also one of the main reasons CCSA lost the close contact it had enjoyed with African political leaders in the rural areas in the early years of the century. The South Africans who migrated to the urban centers were not motivated by religion but by a strong desire for political freedom. Hence, these South Africans left the missionaries behind in the rural areas, resulting in both isolation and ineffectiveness for the missionaries. Missionaries that were left behind in the rural areas were psychologically paralyzed. Scholars have reframed this positively, however, stating that "the heartland" of missionary's success in South Africa was in the rural areas. It is accurate to state that missionaries were successful in providing education (often against the wishes of the apartheid government) for the remnants of black South African village dwellers."[22] The majority of black people, however, were more interested in migrating to the urban centers. They were least interested in the religious education provided by the missionaries in the rural areas. Missionaries should be credited for understanding more than most that the power base of white South Africans would be undermined if blacks were educated. Thus, missionaries worked against the apartheid government to educate black South Africans, although black South Africans were more interested in migrating to the urban centers than staying for missionary's instructions in the villages. One of the most popular slogans among blacks in the 1950s was: "revolution first, then education." It is no accident that the policy of the government tightened in the 1950s to control the urban centers where black South Africans were heading. This subsequently led to the notorious pass laws of the 1950s, which sought to control the flow of the blacks to the urban centers. The migration to the urban centers paid off politically, even if it was a failure religiously. Africans began to see Christianity as a tool they could use to secure political freedom. Therefore, the mass "conversion" to Christianity in the urban centers was not motivated by spiritual desire as much as it was a political strategy.

Most newer militant generation of black nationalists, like Anton Lembede, who in the 1940s was one of the leading thinkers of the Africanist wing of the ANC (which merged into the Pan Africanist Congress [PAC] in 1958), and Robert Mangaliso Sobukwe, the President of that organization, did not have close ties with white missionaries or Churchly organizations—although they were devout Christians. Unlike the older generations of ANC leaders, who had strong ties with missionary Churches, the younger generations of South Africans that migrated to the urban centers cared very little about membership in the missionary-initiated congregations.

Beginning in the 1920s, the GMC and CCSA reacted vigorously to the actions of Afrikaner nationalism in government. But among the liberal missionaries there was no evidence of a positive or negative feeling about Native African nationalism. What was absent from the CCSA documents and statements at this period was any mention of black political organizations, particularly the ANC. The missionaries and Churchmen involved in the CCSA were largely opposed to the African nationalist development in the 1940s and 1950s. In the Defiance Campaign of 1952, for example, the CCSA only yielded to the pressure from the Churches outside South Africa by issuing a statement in January of that year to answer the question asked by overseas Churches relating to matters of wide campaign for human rights in South Africa. But why didn't the CCSA speak specifically on human right issues in South Africa? The CCSA defended its lack of involvement by calling for a national convention. It appealed to the authorities to refrain from legislation or administrative action that could aggravate racial tension and to abstain from exacerbating the problems of organized resistance.[23] In 1952,

Blaxall reported on his return from the International Missionary Conference held in Willingen, the Netherland, that:

> While the meetings were in progress the passive resistance campaign started in South Africa, paragraphs appearing in the columns of the English, Dutch, German and French newspapers. Interests aroused were astonishing, but once again it meant difficult questions. At Willingen, and subsequently in Holland and England, I was constantly asked why [is it] that Churches [in South Africa] do not come out solidly in moral support of the resisters? In my replies I stressed the practical difficulties of our country in getting agreed expressions of views, but I said that probably most of the Churches would make statements at their annual conferences.[24]

After studying the views expressed by the individual Churches themselves, the Executive Board of the CCSA stated that, while it had profound sympathies for the non-Europeans Christians and understanding of the motives that had given rise to the Defiance Campaign, it nevertheless felt "bound to point out that obedience to the law is a Christian duty, and that disobedience is only justified when such obedience involves disobedience to the dictates of [one's] conscience."[25] We can assume that Blaxall's statement was an accurate representation of the reflection of the Church in general.

Two Churches, however, came out to support the Defiance Campaign in 1952: (1) the Bantu Presbyterian Church, and (2) Port Elizabeth African Ministers' Council (an organ of the Cape Midlands Non-Denominational African Ministers' Association). Through their ministers and elders, the Bantu Presbyterian Church issued a statement declaring: "Since our people are not in the possession of the political instruments which make for peaceful change...we are compelled to see a certain necessity in their choice of passive resistance as the only way open to them."[26] The secretary of the Port Elizabeth African Ministers' Council and the Cape Midlands Non-Denominational African Ministers Association jointly issued a statement that African Churches in the Eastern Cape would take their stand in support of the Defiance Campaign.[27]

These unequivocal declarations of support for a direct political action were typical of the stance of the younger Churches in the two-third worlds. They contrast sharply with the ambivalence and contradictory statements of the missionary-controlled congregations. Even the statements of missionary-producing liberal congregations are always hesitant and carefully measured.

In 1958 the Treason Trial was widely reported and gave the ANC a high profile. Yet the CCSA failed to take a stance or respond to the rising tide of Black Nationalism. When members of the CCSA made statements in public, they were usually diplomatic and well calculated, refraining from what could be deemed controversial. There is no evidence to suggest that the attitude of CCSA was less ambivalent even after the Defiance Campaign of 1952. Under apartheid, few Christian denominational leaders stood in support of African nationalism, and most did not have the courage of their conviction. The few leaders that supported African nationalism, however, changed the course of South African history in significant ways.

We can only conclude that, when European missionaries entered South Africa to Christianize the indigenous population, they did not foresee that their success would be subject to what David Thomas called "the law of unintended consequences."[28] Some of the unintended consequences include the ways the indigenous converts seized the ideology and institutions of European Christianity and Africanized them. Thus Africanized, the Churches were turned to political institutions to undermine white racial dominance in both Church and state. This is one of the reasons why the descendants of European missionaries in South Africa had to reconstitute Christianity and develop new theories of conversion and race relations. Little did Christians, both white and black, know that the segregationist ideology and its political by-product, called apartheid, would bring to light the deep division among the people in South African multi-pigmentation society.

Segregationist Ideology and Economic Dependency

The segregationist ideology of Afrikaans-speaking Churches in South Africa was much closer to the thinking of the missionaries at the international missionary and ecumenical movements of the world in the 1930s and 40s. The liberal and more integrationist ideology in South Africa was quite contrary to the missionary vision in the world. What the International missionary communities meant about segregation was in keeping with Henry Venn's positive three-self formulae. That is, the Church in South Africa should be self-supporting, self-governing and self-propagating. Thus, it was quite appropriate to have separate black congregations under these formulae. At home in South Africa, the segregationists interpreted this formula to reinforce the oppressive form of segregation—apartheid. What Henry Venn envisioned positively was interpreted in South Africa negatively to reinforce segregation. The integrationist ideology was also misinterpreted in South Africa, and had very little support abroad. Furthermore, the integrationist ideology could not be sustained in South Africa because it undermined black identity in Church life.

At a people's congress in 1950, the concept of separate development emerged. The Federal Mission Council of the Dutch Reformed Church called the congress to discuss the "native question." Particularly active in the drive behind this congress was G. B. A. Gerdener, Professor of Missions at Stellenbosch University, one of the most advanced educational institutions in

South Africa (located just outside of Cape Town). J. Kinghorn summarized the outcome of the conference:

> South Africa was described as [a] cosmos of nations [that is, not races], each with a unique character and culture but at different stages of development. The only Christian way to safeguard every culture and to avoid friction and abuse was to separate the nations, thus providing room for the organic development of each according to its special needs [capacities].[29]

The concept of a South African community of autonomous states was born at this congress, and Hendrik F. Verwoerd, when he became Prime Minister in 1958 began to implement those resolutions of the congress that appeared to him to be consistent with practical politics. Kinghorn further noted that, until the late 1980s, all the Churches had carried forward the ideal of separate development, which to them was the embodiment of a true biblical justice under South African conditions. The attempts of liberal Christians to dignify the policy with the new terminology of "separate development" failed hopelessly, and it continued to be known and vilified simply as apartheid.

One of the first cases of formalized segregation in South Africa could be linked to the Christian Council of South Africa (CCSA). In 1963, the government officials of the Bantu Administration Department (BAD), escorted by police, visited the Wilgespruit Fellowship Center near Roodepoort, and insisted that in the future, government permits must be obtained for all non-whites using the center.[30] The Wilgespruit Center was originally established in the 1950s by a group of laymen and women with the expressed purpose of creating a multiracial conference venue. The goal was to foster a multi-racial dialogue at an informal setting and for white and non-white brethren to enjoy the facilities. In this sense, the Church, through the Center, represented the first community with a new vision for a non-racial future in South Africa. The Center was situated adjacent to the Enzenzeleni School for the Deaf and Dumb, of which Blaxall was the Principal. Since the Center did not have a legal Custodian of its own, members asked the CCSA to become the legal trustee and caretaker of the property when the members bought it in 1956.[31] Technically, it meant that the CCSA was actually the owner of the Wilgespruit Center, and it was to the CCSA Executive that Blaxall himself, as well as the warden of the Center, reported the permit demand of 1963.

In view of the difficulties this posed for the holding of inter-racial conferences at the Center, the CCSA Executive agreed to send delegation to the Minister of Bantu Administration to ask for the granting of a blanket permit to cover all functions. The minister refused the delegation's request. In 1966, the local municipality reinstated this rigidity and further divided blacks and whites by refusing to grant permits to allow any indigenous African to stay at the center overnight.[32] It was not until 1968 that the CCSA, now reconstituted as SACC, referred to separate development as "a false faith," which was being presented as "the way for the people of South Africa to save themselves in the name of Christianity." In 1968 statement further declared:

> The Christian Gospel requires us to assert the truth proclaimed [to] the first Christians, who discovered that God was creating a new community in which differences of race, language, nation, culture, and tradition no longer had power to separate man from man. The most important features of a man are not the details of his racial groups, but the nature which he has in common with all men and also the gifts and abilities which are given to him as a unique individual by the grace of God; to insist that racial characteristics are more important than these is to reject what is most significant about our own humanity as well as the humanity of others.[33]

An important lesson from this was that the government couldn't legislate segregation by race at all levels of social intercourse.

Both schools, segregationist and integrationist, were swept away by the indigenous Christians in South Africa. Christians then moved to the forefront to establish a new multi-pigmentation Christian ideology that gave birth to a new South Africa. If the proponents of the apartheid had used the three-self formulae to their own "advantage," the establishment of autonomous indigenous Churches was beginning to produce unintended consequences. It became clear from the early 1970s that the Black *Nederduitse Gereformeerde Kerk* (NGKA) was going her own way.[34] A demonstration of new thinking in the NGKA came in November 1973 when a meeting of a hundred NGKA ministers issued a statement denouncing apartheid as "unChristian." Thus, there were strong calls for an end to structural divisions based on race within the Church. Black NGKA leaders and those of the Lutheran Churches found enough in common to begin a service of consultations together, which in time led to the formation of a new black organization, the Association of Black Reformed Evangelical Churches in South Africa. As a further indication of the trends of thinking in this Church, it should be mentioned that Allan Boesak, a leading exponent of black theology, increasingly recognized as a leader of Black Nationalist resistance to apartheid in South Africa, was a product of the NGKA.[35] The Black Nationalist movement, with Boesak as a leader, engulfed apartheid and the theology of ethnic Church planting on which it was based. Also, Black Christian Nationalist movements engulfed liberalism and neo-liberalism. This, however, does not translate to economic prosperity for the majority of blacks whose ideology ushered in liberation to South Africa. If we assumed that the Church has always been for the poor and the marginalized, we must also maintain that it is when the Church loses herself in the service of others that she would begin to rediscover herself. In South Africa, this means that it is when the Church can show herself as genuinely African and no longer an import in her modes of theological thought and appreciation, in her life, worship, and activity, can the Church in South African experience hope to make an effective impact on neo-African society.

When this is realized, then mission would then be the responsibility of the whole Church, and applicable to whites as well as blacks. The mission/Church dichotomy will be permanently abolished.

In the Methodist Church we saw the beginning of the process of a rediscovery in 1944 when the Methodists changed the Missionary Society to Missionary Department and resolved the Mission/Church dichotomy once and for all. The Church of the Province of Southern Africa (CPSA) abolished the Mission/Church dichotomy in 1961 following the Methodist resolution in the same year that stated that the fundamental Methodist Missionary policy was to "go to every place where men are without Christ...to spread scriptural holiness throughout the land by the proclamation of the evangelical faith." To be noted here is the deliberate omission of "converting the heathen" and a stress, instead, on the universality of human need for the message of salvation in Jesus Christ. A year earlier, in 1960, the Presbyterian Church of Southern Africa (PCSA) had changed her African Mission committee to the Church Extension Committee.

The new South Africa of black majority in ecclesiastical and political life is an unexpected outcome of an historical process that had begun more than 500 years earlier, when the first European missionaries left the shores of Europe to "convert the heathens of Africa." Had they realized that a vigorous Africanized Christianity would replace the faith they were taking to Africa half a millennium later, would they have been more cautious about their decision to assail to Africa? It is a twist of irony that today Africans, and devotees of non-Christian religions from Asian countries, are in Europe. If their presence is not intended to convert Europeans, they have at least turned Europe into a multi-religion society that is more reflective of the Christian faith in the African world.

Another component to the South African mission and conversion story was religious tolerance. Steve Biko articulated this when he stated:

> African religion in its essence was not radically different from Christianity. We also believed in one God, we had our own community of Saints through whom we related to God, and we did not find it compatible with our own way of life to worship God in isolation from the various aspects of our lives.[36]

In 1976, Allan Boesak made a profound and powerful statement about Black Theology when he stated:

> Black theology is a theology of liberation. Black theology believes that liberation is not mere "part of" the Gospel, or "consistent with" the Gospel, but is the content

and framework of the Gospel of Jesus Christ. Black theology takes seriously the black situation, black experience, and it grapples with the suffering of black people under oppression.[37]

We can say that ultimately, South African Nationalist movement "saved" Christianity from been exclusively a "white man's religion" just as early Gentiles saved Christianity by accepting it from the hands of the Jews who had initially followed Jesus. Perhaps, Christianity's Africanization was its most important development in the 20th century, and after the development of Christianity in Africa in general, and South Africa in particular, it would be hard to see Christianity in quite the same way. Christianity in South Africa will be at its best, however, when it offers the best opportunity to Africans, so that there would be new thought patterns freeing all Africans from inferiority complex to realize their God-given potential.

Resistance through Silence

There were many dramatic moments at the hearings of the Truth and Reconciliation Commission (TRC). Perhaps the most important moment that signaled a transfer of dignity to the indigenous South African leaders occurred during the faith hearings of the TRC. Bishop Edward Lekganyane of the Zion Christian Church (ZCC) in Moria was asked to address the commission. A careful reading of the transcript of the proceedings conveys much of what can be said to be least expected. One can feel the drama of unexpected challenges to the white establishment through the power of silence.

Archbishop Desmond Tutu called the highly esteemed Bishop Edward Lekganyane to the stand. Archbishop Tutu introduced him as "one of the outstanding leaders, religious leaders, in our country." Everyone acknowledged that Bishop Lekganyane had significant influence on a very large section of the population,[38] and Tutu stated that this was demonstrated by the fact that a former state President as well as other political leaders have been in Moria to see Lekganyane. His introduction was extempore, and it was extremely significant that Archbishop Tutu referred directly to the highly controversial visit by President P. W. Botha to the Zion Christian Church's nationally popular Easter celebrations at Moria in the midst of the 1985 uprising and resistance. It was also significant that he referred to the more politically acceptable visits of Nelson Mandela and F. W. deKlerk in 1993 and 1994 as those "other political leaders."

It was clear that the chair of the commission was interested to hear directly from Edward Lekganyane. One can even say that Tutu was interested in hearing some explanation for the political act, symbolic, perhaps, of so many South African critiques of the Zion Christian Church. His next few remarks indicated that he was aware that he was treading on extremely thin ice, wanting to affirm the Bishop, but at the same time wanting to hear how he will explain this and other politically sensitive issues. In an unexpected form of resistance, Lekganyane demonstrated that one way to gain back dignity was by silence:

> Archbishop Tutu: We are looking forward to hearing from you that submission that you are going to be making to the TRC as we look to what happened in the past [P. W. Botha's visit?] and in what manner you may have suffered [the justification for Lekganyane to talk of the abuse the members of his congregation have suffered], and what contributions you believe you may be wanting to make, or able to make to the healing and reconciliation of this beautiful country we all love so much. Thank you, Ndade.

One can picture the Archbishop, whose moral authority in the proceeding to this date has been universally acknowledged, leaning forward in anticipation to hear the Bishop speak, perhaps for the first time. And then, the drama began. Two others took to the stand, and the Bishop remains seated, smiling benignly and not saying one word. Archbishop Tutu was taken aback and stated: "Is it Bishop Lekganyane who is going to testify, or are you going to do so? I'm not quite certain. [Turning to Lekganyane] Bishop, are you going to say anything?" Tutu, a cultivated and learned figure himself, was probably thrown off guard. He sounded almost pleading. The ZCC representative, Immanuel Lothola, took the microphone and stated that the Church Council had already decided that he, Lothola, and not the Bishop, was to make the official submission. Tutu, however, attempted to make a come back and stated: "Yes, your Council is free to determine how you want to do this…but if at the end of this we are asking questions, is the Bishop going to reply?" Even to this question, the only verbal response came from Lothola, who stated: "Chairperson, speaker Thomas Mahope will reply to the questions." To this unexpected response, Tutu retorted: "Only he?" But again, Bishop Lekganyane was only smiling. Lothola then stated: I will reply to the questions as part of this panel. The exchange between Tutu and Lothola then commenced as follows:

> Tutu:　　We want to know who, you see, if it is the two of you only that are going to be spokespersons.
> Lothola: That is correct, yes.
> Tutu:　　Now I don't know, some of your congregation members are here. I don't know whether they will be happy to go away without hearing a word from their leader.
> Lothola: Chairperson, thanks for your concern, but that has already been addressed, the congregation is aware of the situation and I can assure this commission that they are more than happy.

Tutu: Yes, all right. I wish I had such a congregation. Thank you very much and
          will the two of you then please stand.

At the hearing of a commission that is loquacious and constituted by words through submissions and testimonies, it was silence that spoke most loudly and voluminously, and ultimately the event that arrested the attention of everyone because of the drama of silence in the room. There has been a "poverty of dignity" for the blacks during apartheid years, but it is this kind of drama that gave back the dignity that all South Africans desired.

Thus, a gesture of refusal flamed the testimony of the ZCC in a profound way. It was a statement that maintained that South African indigenous congregations would not be reduced to a foreign category or even to the language of the oppressors. The indigenous Christians did not have to justify themselves in terms that were analogous to oppression and injustice. This dramatic act of resistance was a unique way of expressing independence.

Speech and silence also framed the other two AIC submissions. Mr. Mpanza of the amaNazaretha stated, for example, "Even though my speech is prepared in English I will speak in Zulu, because most of the members of my congregation consists of people who cannot read or write English."[39] There is a double gesture in this: (1) we are able to do things on the terms of the missionaries who taught us how to speak the English language, but (2) we have chosen not to do so in order to preserve our identity and have our dignity back as a people.

Ntongana of the Council of African Instituted Churches (CAIC) represented another voice of refusal: "my ancestors, my clan, refused that I write down a submission."[40] The invocation of the ancestor points beyond the earthly authority that is equally resistant to the present condition of the people.

Silence is a form of resistance that can also be seen in another form—that of the mystical destabilization of power through prayer. Mpanza argued that Isaiah Shembe (1870–1935), for example, taught his followers to respect the authorities, "but promised that through our constant prayer and supplication to God, one day God will answer our prayer."[41] In silence, the leaders speak only to God. Thus, silence before the earthly authorities and prayer to God became a method of resistance and struggle. Isaiah Shembe further taught that the Nazarites must lead a simple life and that every year they must walk on foot to Mt. Nhlangakazi to worship God and report all their suffering. So, whenever members of the amaNazaretha were confronted by the government or missionary Churches, all what they had to do was to ask the congregation to kneel down and have Isiguqa, which is a special prayer to God.

In light of her resistance through silence, the Church in South Africa must have the courage to accept the new "pluriformity" of the new South Africa and provide guidance in light of her many challenges.

A Summary

Could it be that the strong political leaders used too much force because they have already devalued the weak? But a disproportionate use of force against the weak equally devalues the morality of the strong. The strength of the weak is in the hope for a better future. The South African experience proves that the weak does not always need the strong, but the weak and the strong need each other in a relationship of mutual dependency.

Both the integrationist/assimilations stream of Christianity and the segregationist/apartheid stream—with their strong roots in the three-self formulae—played equally important roles in the new form that Christianity has taken in South Africa.

Those who were the followers of the integrationist ideology, called liberals, created the SACC, which became a tool for the destruction of white ecclesiastical domination. Those who were the disciples of a segregationist/apartheid ideology subsequently drove South African Christians to the three-self formulae originally encapsulated by Venn and Anderson. But this became the channel that led the way towards the full realization of the autonomy black Christians hoped for, but whose consequences the early European missionaries probably never anticipated.

The emerging Churches in South Africa—a completely unintended consequence of the missionary work—supplanted both ideologies. The most important unintended outcome of the mission work in South Africa, however, was that the Churches created by both the liberals and those of the a-partheid ideologies fell by the way side and were left behind by the black congregations who have now taken control of the life of the Church in South Africa. The brand of Churches that replaced the missionary Churches was so radical that it effectively used the Bible to wage the final assault on apartheid and on the bastions of white control in South Africa. There can be no doubt that the original missionaries to South Africa—and even a remnant of those who were sent from Europe between World Wars—would have been appalled by this unintended consequence of their efforts to "convert the heathen" in South Africa.

European Missionaries, who sets out in the 18th and 19th centuries to convert the world have become their own "first" converts in the 20th-century. They have been converted to the whole idea that "conversion to Christianity" in South Africa carried unintended consequences. Therefore, the spiritual descendants of the Protestant Christian missionaries came to the conclusion that it was not the "heathen" that had been bound by error's chains, but the whole humanity, including the missionary-producing regions of the world. This is because it is the vigor and rapid expansion of indigenous Churches in Southern Africa that has exercised the most transforming influence on the life of the African people.

The early European missionaries to South Africa, and those who worked elsewhere on the continent, took it for granted that their converts would be exactly like them. They did not anticipate that their success among Africans would lead to the formation of an entirely new brand of Christianity—a departure from their own congregational life and theology.

The African-initiated Churches began to emerge in Southern Africa in the 19th century. A century later, almost half of the black population in South Africa professed Christianity. These Christians are not only numerically powerful, but also gave rise to forces that played a key role in dismantling white control in both ecclesiastical and political matters. If the coming of European missionaries to Africa in the 18th century represented the first conversion of Africans to Christianity, the emergence of African-initiated Churches in the 19th century represented the "second conversion."

At least in part, the missionary work was the forerunner and consolidation of white control over South Africa. But an unintended consequence of the missionary activities was the mobilization of the indigenous Christians, however unorganized they have proven to be in Southern Africa, to effectively bring an end to oppression and injustice of white Christians in the twentieth century. The employment of the Christian vocabulary by South Africans to secure political freedom may be the "third conversion" experience of South Africans.

Notes

[1] The integrationists are South African Christians, predominantly Whites, who desire the integration of black and white worshippers under the same roof. They often emphasize the universal brotherhood of believers that transcends any particular race or creed. They do not often emphasize the qualities that are idiosyncratic to the indigenous people in South Africa and that Churches under the indigenous paradigm would highlight specific African idioms in liturgy and teachings. Many of the newly emerging Churches in Cape Town, such as "His People Church," and "Victory Evangelical Fellowship," could be considered Integrationist Churches.

[2] The Segregationists are South African Christians, largely Afrikaners and Blacks, that affirm the value in the particularity of a specific racial group. They believe that it would weaken their cultural identity by worshipping with other racial groups in South Africa, particularly those that do not share the view that their ethnicity is relevant in the new South Africa. The

segregationists often fail to recognize that inadvertently, their non-integrationist approach to Christianity and to worship fosters racism and apartheid ideology.

[3] Christians were initially called "the people of the way" but later, they were called "little Christs" as a pejorative term. When a band of Christ's followers entered Antioch, they were then referred to as "Christians" for the first time. The hostility between Jews and Gentiles escalated after the earthly ministry of Christ, but in the fifteen chapter of Acts, we read about the "Council at Jerusalem" where the Apostles met to resolve the problems associated with the relationship between Jewish and Gentile Christians. This particular council, however, only concentrated on matters pertaining to the salvation of the Gentiles in a Jewish religious world. See Acts 15:1–11; Ephesians 2:11–22; Galatians 3:28.

[4] E Stock, ed. *The History of the Church Missionary Society: Its Environment, Its Men and Its Works,* Vol. I (London, 1899): 59–60.

[5] Henry Venn, who retired as the secretary of the CMC in 1872, has been credited for these formulae of self-supporting, self-governing, and self-propagating, but Rufus Anderson, an American Christian leader, proposed a similar idea for missionaries sent from America in the late 1800s.

[6] This three-self formula was the vision of Henry Venn, the secretary of the Church Missionary Society based in London. Independent of Venn, Rufus Anderson, from America, developed a similar view. See G. Hewitt, *The Problems of Success: A History of the Church Missionary Society, 1910–1942* (London, 1971), 320.

[7] David Thomas, *Christ Divided: Liberalism, Ecumenism and Race in South Africa* (Pretoria: University of South Africa, 2002), 9.

[8] Ibid.

[9] Ali A. Mazrui, *The Africans: A Triple Heritage* (Boston: Little, Brown and Company), 276.

[10] International Missionary Conference, (Willingen, the Netherlands, 1952).

[11] David Thomas, *Christ Divided: Liberalism, Ecumenism and Race in South Africa* (Pretoria: University of South Africa, 2002), 54.

[12] Ibid.

[13] Ibid. 57.

[14] Ibid. 63.

[15] See E. Jacottet, "Paper on the Native Churches and their Organization." Report of the Proceedings of the First General Missionary Conference held in Johannesburg, 13–20 July 1904. (Johannesburg, 1905), 109–133.

[16] Ibid.

[17] See *The Christian Express,* Vol. 43, no. 518, (1 December 1913), 187–9

[18] J. J. (Dons) Kritzinger, "A Century of Doing Missiology in South Africa: An Overview," in *Missionalia* Vol 32 No. 2 (August 2004): 165.

[19] David Thomas, *Christ Divided,* 125.

[20] This was a turning point in the way black Church leaders see white missionaries in South Africa. For a discussion on this, see P. Walshe, *The Rise of African Nationalism in South Africa, The African National Congress, 1912–1952* (London, 1970), 418 ff.

[21] Two of the major factors that promoted traditional religions and values in South Africa in the 1930s were agrarian economy and extended family life. The urban centers promoted Industry. Population in the urban centers tended towards import and export, and this promoted the traffic of Christians and missionaries from European countries.

[22] David Thomas, *Christ Divided* (2002) is a good example. The author stated that the success of the missionaries should even be anticipated because the urban centers were too crowded, whereas the rural areas were thinly populated as a result of the demographic shift. It should be added that this shift has gone unabated since the 1930s but not only in South Africa, but also

in Africa as a whole. Some of the largest cities in the world today are located in Africa—Durban, Cape Town, both in South Africa, as well as Lagos, Nigeria and Kenyan Nairobi.

[23] See "Council Addresses Fellow Christian" in CCQ, no. 32, (March, 1952), 1.

[24] From the Report of the secretary on the Meetings he attended at Willingen, the Netherlands, 2.

[25] CCQ, no. 35, (May 1953), 4.

[26] A statement on the Present Non-European Passive Resistance Campaign in South African Outlook, vol. 82, no. 970 (March 1952), 170.

[27] See L. Kuper, *Passive Resistance in South Africa* (London, 1956).

[28] In a well-crafted book, David Thomas explored the laws of unintended consequences that missionaries in South Africa faced. See David Thomas, *Christ Divided: Liberalism, Ecumenism and Race in South Africa* (Pretoria, University of South Africa, 2002).

[29] J. Kinghorn, "Modernization and Apartheid: The Afrikaner Churches" in R. Elphick and R. Davenport, eds. *Christianity in South Africa.*135–154.

[30] CCSA Executive Committee Minute, no. 169, 7/02/63, 270.

[31] Councils in the Ecumenical Movement, 8.

[32] CCSA Executive Minute, 9/02/1966, 371–72.

[33] John W. de Gruchy and W. B. de Villers, eds, *The Message in Perspective* (Johannesburg, 1968), 35.

[34] J. M. Cronje, *Born to Witness: A Concise History of the Churches Born out of the Mission Work of the Dutch Reformed Church (Nederduitse Gereformeerde Kerk) of South Africa* (Pretoria, 1982).

[35] David Thomas, *Christ Divided,* 196.

[36] Quoted by David Thomas in *Christ Divided,* p. 203. See also, Steve Biko, "Black Consciousness and the Quest for a True Humanity," in B. Moore, ed. *Black Theology* (London, 1973), 36–47.

[37] Allan Boesak, *Civil Theology for Southern Africa,* no. 19 (June 1977): 35–43.

[38] Zion Christian Church has over 4,000,000 members. Barnabas Lekganyane founded it in Moria in 1910.

[39] See Robin M. Petersen's article "The AICs and the TRC: Resistance Redefined" in James Cochrane, John de Gruchy and Stephen Martin, eds, *Facing the Truth: South African Faith Communities and the Truth and Reconciliation Commission* (Cape Town: David Philip Publishers, 1999), 118–121

[40] Ibid.

[41] Ibid.

Chapter Five
AFRICAN THEOLOGICAL AND POLITICAL THEMES

Christianity has never departed Africa.[1] In some ways, the Church is now returning to its African roots.[2] Christianity originated in the near East, but it is not widely known that the Church was far stronger in North Africa in the first one thousand years than in Europe. The North African coast, for example, produced many apologists who have achieved theological immortality.[3] It was only after 1500 C.E. that Europe became one of Christian heartlands.

Christianity was strong in North Africa before the arrival of Muslims in the seventh century, but this was not because of the success of missionary movements only. Africans accepted Christianity as their primary religion when the Church first reached North Africa. Today, the geographical heartland of Christianity has shifted from the northern hemisphere to the southern hemisphere.[4] The center of gravity of the Christian faith has also shifted from the West to its roots in the East, and Africans continue to play important roles to guarantee this move and to make Christianity one of the traditional religions of the people.

Andrew Walls noted that the Church in tropical Africa in modern times is not exclusively a missionary creation. As early as 1792, Christianity arrived in Africa through many groups of Christians of African birth or descent who had come to faith in Christ as plantation slaves, or as soldiers in the British army during the American War of Independence, or as farmers or squatters in Nova Scotia.[5] They took to Africa their own preachers and Church leaders, and their Churches have been functioning before the arrival of modern missionaries from the Western world.[6] Therefore, what has proven to be the most enduring element in the making of Christian Africa in the 20th-century is not just what Western missionaries did (or did not do), it is also what Africans did, and what they have always done, with the Gospel.[7]

In certain parts of Africa, Christianity has been successful for many reasons, and Africans now see the Christian faith as one of their traditional religions.[8] Although many challenges face Christians in Africa, there is no reason to assume that Christianity will not continue a steady growth in Africa. Christianity is as diverse as the many cultures and ethnic groups of Africa. This is partly because the Christian identity created in Africa is meshed with diverse local cultures and beliefs. Thus, the practice of Christianity among the Zulus of South Africa is different, for example, from the Christian practice among the Yoruba people of South West Nigeria. Christianity in various parts of Africa swiftly acquired luminous local roots. Therefore, African Christians are as diverse and as sophisticated in the interpretation of the essential categories of Christianity as Christians in the West. Perhaps Christianity is now assuming an increasing significance in the creation of a modern pluralistic African society.[9]

In the early 1960s, when African nationalist leaders and politicians were fighting for political freedom from European countries and removing the last vestiges of colonialism, African Christians were also giving indigenous definition to Christianity. They defined the essential categories of the Christian faith in an indigenous religious paradigm and familiar idioms—so much so that the Christian faith in Africa today is stronger than it has ever been.[10]

Between 1960 and 1975, the Christian faith grew with rapidity. Thus, the struggle for political liberation and a Christian resurgence in many parts of Africa occurred simultaneously. Today, Africans have made Christianity a "place to feel at home." This approach is, perhaps, unequalled elsewhere in the world. Robert J. Schreiter proclaimed in 1991, for example, "Africa is the fastest growing Christian continent in the world today.[11]

Today, it is estimated that more than 386 million Christians in the world are Africans.[12] African political scientist and scholar, Ali A. Mazrui, stated: "Africa has both the oldest forms of Christianity, such as those of Egypt and Ethiopia, and some of the newest forms of Christianity, such as those of the Kimbanguists."[13]

One of the primary goals of this chapter is to consider seriously the important factors affecting Christianity in Africa today and the roles of the Church in building democratic societies in modern Africa.[14] The century we have just left behind was a century of war and conflict, which led to disasters, pain, grief, poverty, and enormous destruction in Africa. Yet it was also a century that left Africa with hope, rebirth, and opportunities to redefine Christian identity and democratic process. This chapter, therefore, also aims at reflecting upon contemporary developments of African Christianity and upon what role the Church in the West could play to foster Christian growth in contemporary Africa.

Africans are facing tremendous challenges both political and ideological.[15] To many in the non-African world, the continent is vast, poor, and far away. In practical terms, it is relatively neglected, and millions are abandoned to hunger and death, or left without shelter, protection or support. There have been despots' and military dictators' signatures beneath many of the sufferings and disasters in Africa. There have been dark days when deviant leaders dragged the societies into conflicts in the name of serving selfish ideologies. Yet the continent remains a central place in our consciousness, whether we are Africans or not. No factor has cemented Africans and the world in modern times as Christianity. Although Africans are facing many challenges, they are remarkably tenacious about their faith in God and about their awareness of the divine. One can conclude that the teaming population of Africans bustling into Churches everyday is strong. Certain factors are responsible for this growth of Christianity, but there are also factors that continue to hinder the Christian religion in Africa.

Factors Hindering Christian Growth in Africa

Some of the many factors that have hindered the growth of Christianity in Africa include the following: (1) colonialism, (2) temple democracy, (3) economic stalemate, and (4) the malaria and HIV/AIDS epidemic.

(1) One of the factors that hindered the growth of Christianity in the past century was colonialism.[16] Colonialism was an obstacle for Christian growth indirectly because it prevented believers from expressing their faith with complete freedom and cultural creativity. Tradition African drums were discarded as unimportant in Christian worship and were regarded as a mark of the past that Africans must leave behind if they were to be true believers.

Africans wanted to Africanize Christianity through the use of the talking drums, but the colonial powers prevented them in certain ways. One of the tools that European powers used was the missionary enterprise with its puritan religious identity. Africans, however, used the vernacular languages and European educational establishments to shape their Christian identity creatively. Recent studies indicate that no concrete evidence exists that the alliance between missionaries and colonialism was ever complete in Africa.[17] At best, the story of a complete alliance has been overplayed or oversimplified. Although there was a close association between missionaries and the colonial powers, which caused negative reactions to Christianity in certain areas, one must note that a non-smoker in a closed room with a group of smokers may carry the smell of tobacco. Thus, if other non-smokers met him, they would automatically assume that he too was a smoker. Such was the relationship between the Christian mission work and colonialism in Africa.

Colonialism was oppressive both culturally and socially, while Christianity fostered African religious and literary creativity.[18] This, one must note, was not the intention of early missionaries but a surprising bi-product of their missionary enterprise. Colonialism, on the other hand, created both "color and culture prejudice"[19] in Africa. Perhaps, the most devastating effect of colonialism is the psychic damage it left behind in Africa, as evidenced by the fact that most Africans often preferred European way of life and social norms to the ancient wisdom of their African ancestors. The fact that missionaries and colonial powers share the same geographical origin created a heavy burden for African Christians, who continued to struggle with this painful politico-religious hypocrisy of the West. The majority of African Christians, however, recognized that colonialism and missionary enterprise were not necessarily on the same page, but were important independent factors that paved the way for African literary connection with the Western world.

Although certain Africans continue to associate Christianity with Europe and North America, and there is a good reason to associate African-Americans with the Christian faith, while Islamic religion would be construed as Afro-Asian,[20] the majority of Africans never regarded Christianity as a "white man's" religion.[21] There are accidental similarities between Islam and African customs, such as polygyny,[22] but recent studies show that there is nothing inherently African about the institution of plural marriage. The West, on the other hand, has always had certain misgivings about marriage.

The Church in the West regards ascetic life as a higher form of religious life. The Roman Catholic Church has traditionally promoted celibacy. This is partly in preparation for God's kingdom inaugurated by Jesus. According to the Gospel of Mark, "they neither marry nor are given in marriage, but are like angels in heaven."[23] Yet the Church in the West, including the Roman Catholic, is now struggling with the problem of homosexuality and pedophilia. Africans, on the other hand, have always been committed to marriage and family life because a refusal to be married is tantamount to remaining in a state of adolescence permanently.[24] The Western society today makes divorce and remarriage easier than before. Thus, there are many forms of cohabitation that, in effect, amount to the practice and legitimization of plural marriage, without dealing with the painful inconsistencies of condemning African's open plural marriage. There is, therefore, no logical basis for associating plural marriage with Africans or Muslims, while associating monogamous relationship with the West or Christians. Not all Muslims have four wives, and not all Christians are monogamous.

Furthermore, there is no basis for the dichotomy between Islam and Christianity in Africa. Both have been successful, and devoted followers have lived together relatively more harmoniously than elsewhere in the world. One of the reasons for this uncharacteristic harmony is that religious expression in certain African societies has never been conceived as a "depository" of European culture or religious life, without Africans adding their own accent and fingerprints.[25]

Both collectively and individually, Africans have helped to soften the sharp tones of aggressive Western secularism without denying that Western secularism has profoundly and creatively affected the African Christian culture it has encountered. Christianity in many African societies is, therefore, more than a body of belief, or a cultic activity. The Christian faith is an indivisible entity unified by African believers to grasp the totality of their existence. Perhaps, this explains why Christianity is a capstone of African existence, and a cementing factor of the fabric of their societies.[26] It is in this way that Africans have moved Christianity beyond the hindrance of colonialism and affirmed the faith within their cultural and traditional religious idioms.

(2) A second source of hindrance to Christian growth in Africa is "temple democracy."[27] African political scientists have written extensively about this, arguing that because democracy has no roots in the tradition and political idioms of the common people, it has very little chances of surviving. Democracy, however, is not inherently a Western political system. For democracy to work in Africa, what is needed is an education of the public to sustain it, because democracy as a form of government is essentially the result of a creative clash of ideas.

Perhaps, one of the most destructive legacies of colonialism was the lack of respect for African indigenous political institutions. This resulted in the creation of artificial borders that are both frozen and loose.[28] The boundaries were drawn for the administrative conveniences of the colonial powers rather than reflecting any logical divisions among the over 800 ethnic groups on the continent. Therefore, the map of Africa today is practically the European map for Africans rather than the African map for Africans. Prior to colonialism, there was relatively political stability in Africa. This was based, in part, on traditional structures and pre-existing states, kingdoms, and societies. Early Europeans that colonized Africa, however, threw together groups of Africans that had little or no prior social, political, or economic ties. Few attempts were made by the European colonial powers to create a coherent sense of "national" identity among these disparate groups. In the 1960s, as nation-states began to gain political independence throughout Africa, leaders had to cope with the artificial national boundaries drawn by colonial powers. These borders did not coincide with the natural social units of the African peoples and their cultures. The continent was a whole entity before 1884-85.[29] There were conflicts,[30] but they were not resolved with machine guns; there were pains, but they were not inflicted with AK-47s. In the 1960s the broken continent was given back piece by piece to leaders who were not only foreigners to their people, but who had also formed ideological alliance with colonial warlords. Subsequently, the governments of these leaders were not the solutions but the problems, and Africans have been oppressed in all sorts of ways ever since.

The creation of democracy in Africa was also artificial.[31] African Political Scientists have written about this,[32] but what they have often overlooked is that democracy was not based on Christian faith but on the principles embodied in Christianity and in other living faiths. The principles of justice, freedom, responsibility, and love in religious teachings, for example, preceded organized religions or political institutions. They sustain religions. They were not created by organized religions. A society that is bereft of these religious teachings at its bedrock is like a house without foundation. Opportunistic politicians in Africa have failed to recognize that there is nothing inherently Christian or European or American about democracy, and in some circles of Africans there is the tendency to treat democracy merely as a Western political institution being forced upon submissive Africans. This has led to the misunderstandings of democracy itself and of Africans' painful inconsistencies about their political destiny. There is not a well-defined political philosophy in many post-colonial African nation states. What is common in Africa is an amputated specimen of European politics. For African nation states to have political prestige in the international communities in this century, there must be a new political direction, one that would take on a new form of life that is capable of taking Africans from ineffective political direction to one of dignity.

African Christians have not defined clearly their roles in bringing hope to the chaos of the dual societies one continues to see in virtually all the nation states in Africa. For example, in the twin country of Rwanda-Burundi, the permanent Hutu majority has maintained political rivalry with the permanent Watutsi minority. In Zimbabwe, the permanent Ndebele minority complains bitterly against the permanent Shona majority who has dominated them. In Nigeria, the Hausa-Fulanis Muslims in the North have threatened the political and economic stability of the Christian Yoruba-Igbo southerners by the institution of the Shari'a. These are only a few examples that make anyone wonder if the European politico-geographical map-making in Africa was not a political fraud.

The net effect of this is that multiparty systems carry the risks of disintegration or anarchy. These risks are further exacerbated where party loyalties, linguistic, regional, and religious divisions have reinforced patterns. Early leaders were sensitive to these clannish political patterns and advocated for a single-party state. The assumption was that consensus could be created through the creation of a single party system. Single party systems, however, have led to tyranny against the losers in many nation states, except in Tanzania under Julius Nyerere (c.1906–1998).

This initial unhealthy political climate affected the growth of the Christian faith. In many cases, politicians clashed with Church leaders in a bitter struggle between interest groups in which winners were not humble and losers not gracious. Winners often embezzled public money or loot the national treasury and then secure their "gains" by legislating measures to eliminate and outlaw all the losers.[33]

Kwame Nkrumah's government in Ghana, for example, used "legalized coercion" in the 1950s when it banned the Muslim Association Party, the Northern People's Party, and the Asante-dominated National Liberation Movement, ostensibly to engineer consensus in the midst of the centrifugal effects of Ghana's extreme degree of cultural pluralism. This tumultuous situation did not allow the Christian faith to flourish. The military-politicians who, through violence, took over power in Nigeria in the 1980s and 1990s, have assassinated their political rivals. When investigative journalists confronted them, they determined to prove their innocence by sabotaging the funeral processions of the political rivals they have covertly assassinated. The Church did not flourish under such rapacious political climate, where politicians become temporary managers in virtually all the nation-states on the African continent.

One can say, therefore, that African societies are defective because of both colonialism and inter-tribal wars. A full recovery from these vestiges of colonialism and the ravages of inter-tribal conflicts created by "temple democracy," therefore, is the baseline against which Africa's future political progress must be measured.

(3) Nothing hindered the growth of Christianity between 1960 and 1975 more than the economic stalemate in many parts of Africa. Neither the military regimes not the civilian governments have been successful in accelerating economic growth or spiritual development in Africa. The military regimes have been no more successful than the civilian governments in reducing ethnic conflicts created by economic woes. And the civilian governments have been no more successful than the military regimes in accommodating diverse religions, and providing order and stability necessary for Christian growth. Military *coup d'é-tat* never constituted a revolution or a change of direction from "political slavery" to prosperity in tropical

Africa, but rather has been a limited management of the existing arrangement of corruption and avarice. Since the 1960s, Africans have experienced a high frequency of military *coup d'é-tat,* and this has frustrated the growth of democracy, national unity, and religious liberty.

In the midst of economic woes are Africans that are notoriously greedy and take delight in ostentatious display of their ill-acquired wealth. There are millionaires who aspire to become multi-millionaires, and in countries like Nigeria and Central African Republic there are multi-millionaires who want to become billionaires, and billionaires who want to become multi-billionaires. Yet, hardly can anyone see musical instruments in the African Indigenous Churches that are not over a quarter of a century old. To use an African metaphor, African Christians need to remind their political leaders that, if a hunter shoots an arrow at a zebra, it hurts the zebra whether the arrow lands on the black or on the white stripe. Africans today would not debate whether or not there is God if their fellow Africans would exercise virtues that are consistent with the Christian faith—love, compassion, and justice.

Since 1970, the main characteristic of African economy has been its outward orientation. This is based on its excessive dependence on a limited number of export commodities, for which there was little domestic and diminishing external demand.[34] Also, since the 1970s, Africans have been producing what they do not consume and consuming what they cannot produce.[35] The infrastructure is not equipped to transport the agricultural products from the interior to the mainland, except in a few countries such as South Africa and Botswana. The raw material earnings continue to shrink to provide adequate education and health care for the booming African workforce. In many countries, healthcare facilities have collapsed with national economies. Yet the International Monetary Fund (IMF) and World Bank have been imposing conditions on national debts and loans that average Africans never knew why and how they got. The IMF conditionality, requiring drastic changes in domestic monetary and fiscal policies, includes the removal of agricultural subsidies, increases in the price of staple foods, the reduction of non-food imports, the freezing of wages, and the devaluation of currencies.[36]

The more than ninety-five percent devaluation of the Ghanaian cedi, for example, clearly demonstrates the extent to which the IMF has emerged as one of the most significant influences, not only on the economic and political life of many African countries, but also on their spirituality. How can African ministers of the Good News in Jesus Christ proclaim the love of God to their people, without raising a prophetic voice of protest to their oppressors? The insistence of the IMF on a free market approach, and its opposition to government intervention in the economy is tantamount to neo-colonialism.

Only Eritrea is free of IMF and of financial aid from the World Bank. Most other African nation states depend heavily on Western monetary assistance. As the President of Eritrea stated in a television interview: "it is not that Africa does not need international financial aid, but the continent does not need the corrosive dependency that comes with monetary assistance from IMF and the World Bank."[37] Monetary aid subsidizes African economic condition, but also breeds corruption and blocks innovative solutions to African economic problems, so that people do not seek out indigenous solutions and use their own resources with creativity.

Africa is oversupplied with nature. The continent produces many resources, including agricultural products. The continent also supplies diamonds, gold, manganese, natural gas, timber, uranium, petroleum, and columbium tantalite or "Col-Tan," used by many Western nations in everything from technological innovation, in aviation and space exploration, to computer chips. The United States is arguably dependent upon Africa for strategic minerals[38] used for high-tech industry and sophisticated defense projects.

African environmental conditions demand conservation and storage of certain natural resources. African political and religious leaders are responsible for teaching the significance of having reserves so that the surplus of the "seven fat years" will take care of the future "seven lean years."[39] Africans need to develop their own strategies that would enable them to maximize the economic benefits of globalization, while avoiding its perils.[40] This is because the future of the continent depends largely on the mobilized efforts of Africans and non-Africans to bring economic prosperity to all. This would involve the cooperation of elected leaders, who are pragmatic, progressive, honest, and efficient in their exercise of power. Such leaders are needed all over the continent now than ever before.

(4) In recent years, nothing has threatened the growth of Christianity as much as diseases that have been eradicated elsewhere in the world. Africa has always suffered massively from endemic diseases such as bilharzias, trachoma, and tuberculosis, to mention only a few. In recent years, however, AIDS and malaria have become the most notorious killers. One of the biggest concerns is that it is possible that more than 30 million Africans would die before 2010, unless there is a drastic measure to stop the widespread of the epidemic. The United Nations and African governments, especially Nigeria and South Africa, mobilized the world to assist them in combating HIV/AIDS in 2001. According to recent statistics, HIV infects more than five thousand Africans everyday.[41] Between 20 and 39 percent of sexually active Africans within the age bracket of 20 and 45 in major cities are infected with HIV. An African public health specialist, James J. Zaffiro, claims that, "the HIV/AIDS epidemic is crushing down on Sub-Saharan Af-

rica more virulently and at greater human social and economic cost than anywhere else in the world."[42] Unless the world takes drastic measures, the very survival of a generation of Africans is in jeopardy. In 2001, the President of Nigeria, Olusegun Obasanjo, and the Secretary-General of the UN, Kofi Annan, mobilized other world leaders to combat the spread of AIDS in Africa and in the world. Their goal was to collect between $7 to $10 billion dollars to a global fund. Former U.S. President, Bill Clinton, has also joined Nelson Mandela to combat AID/HIV in sub-Sahara Africa. These are steps in the right direction, but the goal of eradicating deadly diseases in Africa would not be realized unless more countries like the United States, Russia, France, China, Great Britain, and Germany contribute more significantly to the cause.

The words of Gerhard Hoffmann in 1970 are relevant here: "In a world characterized by the gulf between the majority of have-not nations and the minority of haves, the message of eternal salvation may lose its credibility, if it is not accompanied by concrete help to overcome earthly misery and poverty."[43] For Christians, the question is "how can we celebrate life in the midst of death?" According to Suzanne LeClerc-Madlala, a lecturer at the University of Natal, "more than anywhere else in the world, AIDS in Africa was met with apathy."[44] She continued by saying that, "the consequences of apathy is that infection soars, stigma hardens, denial hastens death, and the chasm between knowledge and behavior widens."[45] The present disaster could be dwarfed by the woes that loom if Africa's epidemic rages on. The human losses could wreck the region's frail economies, break down civil societies, and incite political instability that could lead to a decline in religious awareness.[46] Africans have a culture of sex life, but are not usually loquacious about sex education. This has not helped to arrest the epidemic in sub-Saharan Africa, and the southern cone of Africa is now notorious about the devastating effects of AIDS.

In the early 1990s, the World Bank estimated that the annual spending in sub-Saharan Africa for the prevention and treatment of HIV/AIDS was $90 million. With the exponential growth in the number of Africans with HIV since then, the financial burden on health-budgets in many African countries has become unsustainable. The World Health Organization (WHO) has estimated that there are now over 9 million AIDS orphans in Africa and that without international aid on a massive scale, there is no hope for Africans to raise resources to combat AIDS.

In August 1997, Ellen Ruppel Shell contributed an excellent article on malaria to the *Atlantic Monthly*. She stated in the article that although the Ebola outbreak in the Democratic Republic of the Congo claimed 247 lives and inspired the attention of the Hollywood in 1995, more than 20 times that many people die of malaria every day in Africa.[47] In sub-Saharan countries like Nigeria, Ghana, Togo, DRC, Kenya, and Tanzania, malaria parasites have spent centuries adapting to life in the human body, and as a result they have grown cagey.[48] The effect is so bad that it is not uncommon for a child in sub-Saharan Africa to attend school in the morning and die of malaria in the afternoon. Although HIV is horrible, particularly in Southern Africa, and Westerners are used to it ,[49] "it is malaria that keeps Africans down effectively."[50]

Factors Fostering Christian Growth in Africa

There are also factors that continue to foster Christian growth in Africa. Some of these factors include: (1) breathtaking landscapes; (2) the warmth and mutual care of the peoples; (3) the lure of African values and the communal existence of the peoples, and (4) the incomparable religious sense and joy of the people.

(1) The breathtaking landscapes and beauty of the continent are clearly seen by many Africans as a direct blessing from God. Even those who are not professing Christians recognize that the beauty cannot be accidental. This specifically promotes Godliness because it is easy to associate the breathtaking landscape with God the creator. Christians have especially drawn upon this as a reason to be grateful to God the creator of all things.

(2) Social life in Africa recognizes the dominance of personal values over those of material possessions. African society is primarily non-acquisitive, and the majority of the people have not been mainly concerned with accumulating perishable earthly possessions. Africans have faith in God who created everything, but they have few material possessions. By contrast, Christians in the West aspire to explore the moon, even when they still find it difficult to cross the street to relate to their neighbors.

The emphasis on social intercourse among Africans has been upon personal relationships, realizing that the Christian life does not only depend on the boot we wear but also on the fruits we bear. The influence of a chief, for example, may be due not to the size of his stores, but to the loyalty of his people. Therefore, in any conflict between maintaining that loyalty and retaining objective possessions, the goods will be the first to be sacrificed. In many regions of Africa, the possession of things is not as important as maintaining relationships. Therefore, personal belongings will be given up in order to strengthen the oneness of the group. This is what the people in South Africa call *Ubuntu*, and what the people in Tanzania call *ujama*, a collective consciousness of sharing and caring among the people. This transcendental and centrifugal impetus to give rather than to receive has promoted the growth of Christianity. Friendship is more important than material or monetary gains, so that even the last goat of the herd may be slaughtered to show hospitality to a friend. All possessions are held subject to the higher demands of adjusting to, or safeguarding personal relationships.

This sort of "economy" has been considered improvident or an obstruction to progress.[51] Attempts have been made, therefore, to introduce the extreme individualistic conception of private property. The result is materialism and the breakdown of personal relations.

(3) In a society that is acquisitive, there is much that is contrary to Christian living. Societies that are characterized by a strong desire to gain and acquire possessions often discover that there is no happiness in material possessions. Perhaps Africans in the rural areas understand the words of Jesus more perfectly than the Africans in the urban areas when he said "Take Care! Be on your guard against all kinds of greed; for one's life does not consist in the abundance of possessions."[52] The endless search for new thrills by the rich; the lack of friendship of many who have great wealth; the unhappy condition of one who has let accumulation of materials crowd out the search for the values of personal contacts, are all evidence of the world's need for the emphasis of Jesus to turn away from materialism. This characteristic of African life is not new. It suggests the Old Testament ideas of stewardship and is closely related to the Christian principle of being one's brother's keeper.

This is in harmony with the Christian emphasis upon the supreme value of personality. It would be a great disaster for Africans to lose this virtue, which has promoted the Christian faith all over the continent, and which is an outstanding viewpoint of the Christian conception of the beloved community. Within Africa itself, the forms of a beloved community vary widely, but all Africans have revealed a common body of social characteristics of mutual caring.

One can also see a variety of contributions in social solidarity. The chief evidence of a social solidarity is in the cohesion of the group. There is a remarkable tenacity in the ties that form any of the recognized groupings in African life. The best illustration of this is in the organization and activities of the clan, of which the Yoruba people in South West Nigeria are a good example.

The clan is a group of related people recognizing a not too remote common ancestry coming down through a single line. This group—and not a patchwork of ethnic and tribal groups inside an arbitrary colonial frontier— is perhaps, the most permanent group in African society. The relationship is eternally and externally binding and cannot be dissolved. Tribal groups like this have gone through metamorphosis that resulted in permanent Christian relationships. Lamin Sanneh's works have demonstrated that the places reflecting the most marked accession to the Christian religion and values are also those places and areas of the highest concentration of the old traditional religious and local values.[53] Therefore, John S. Mbiti argued that as Africans pass from their religio-cultural traditional values into Christianity, they do not need to go very far before walking on familiar terrain of religious consciousness.[54] The inherent values of holistic life, which has now found fulfillment in Christianity, are distant echoes of the belief that religious values in Africa predates the arrival of missionaries and that Africans have not been given what they did not possess. They internalize the truths that are now fully expressed within Christianity.

Furthermore, Africans promote Christianity through their extended family life. For example, family means those members who have died as well as those who are living and those who are not yet born. In a sense, one's family is both changing and yet permanent. It is, perhaps, through the family that African are agents of religions. This means that Africans are masters of what happens to Christianity in the process of its transmission. More importantly, they are mediators in a fluid, dynamic, and intercultural process. Thus, there is a sense of bonding between African culture and Christianity.

(4) It is likely that the most remarkable promoter of Christianity in Africa is the incomparable religious sense and exuberant joy of the people. It is in this sense that one can say with pardonable exaggeration that Christians in Africa have initiated and pointed ways to new directions in Christian thoughts and actions. Africans are gracious in the way they respond to social issues and harsh realities. Perhaps there is a unique contribution from Africans that could help believers re-enter into the Christian conversation: that Christians are not without hope and that one can deal with complexities and pitfalls with the freedom and exuberant joy of those who first encountered Jesus. Africans are hard-pressed on every side, political and economic, yet they are not crushed. One of the important lessons we can learn from this is that Africans have realized the danger and inadequacy of the contemporary Gospel of prosperity. Although most African Christians realize that following Christ will entail discomfort, there are some Christian ministers who are ensnared in making money by preaching the Gospel. But majority of Christians in Africa are convinced that accepting the Christian faith means that life would not be comfortable. Regarding the inadequacy of applying theological categories from the Western world to Africa, one must quote at length the illustration of John Mbiti about an African who studied in the Western world and then returned to be a minister to his people:

> He learned German, French, Greek, Latin, Hebrew, in addition to English, Church history, Systematic [theology], homiletics, exegesis and pastoralia, as one part of the requirements for his degree. The other part, the dissertation, he wrote on some obscure theologian of the Middle Ages. Finally, he got what he wanted: a Doctorate in Theology. It took him nine and a half years altogether, from the time

he left his home [in Africa] until he passed his orals and set off to return. He was anxious to reach home as soon as possible, so he flew, and he was glad to pay for his excess baggage which after all, consisted only of the Bible in various languages he had learned, plus Bultmann, Barth, Bonhoeffer, Brunner, Buber, Cone, Küng, Moltmann, Niebuhr, Tillich, [copies of] Christianity Today, Time Magazine....

At home relatives, neighbors, old friends...all gathered to welcome him back....Dancing, jubilation, eating, feasting—all these go on as if there were nothing else to do, because the man for whom everyone had waited has finally returned.

Suddenly there is a shriek. Someone has fallen to the ground. It is his older sister...he rushes to her. People make room for him and watch him. 'Let's take her to the hospital,' he calls urgently. They are stunned. He becomes quiet. They all look at him bending over her. Why doesn't someone respond to his advice? Finally a schoolboy says, 'sir, the nearest hospital is 50 miles away, and there are few buses that go there.'

Someone else says, 'She is possessed. Hospitals will not cure her!' The Chief says to him, 'you have been studying theology overseas for 10 years. Now help your sister. She is troubled by the spirit of her great aunt.' He looks around. Slowly he goes to get Bultmann, looks at the index, finds what he wants, [and] reads again about spirit possession in the New Testament. Of course he gets the answer: Bultmann has demythologized it. He insists that his sister is not possessed. The people shout, 'Help your sister, she is possessed!' He shouts back, 'But Bultmann has demythologized demon possession....'

Fantasy? No, for these are the realities of our time [in Africa].[55]

Until recently, the Christian Church in Africa has depended heavily on the theological categories of the Church in the Western world to sustain her ecclesiastical and doctrinal structures. Is it not time for Africans to cultivate theological categories with their own hoes? African scholars such as Efoé Julien Pénoukou, have stated that "for the Christian of the Churches of Africa it is a question of need, first, to deliver Christ from Christianity—that is, from institutions, practices, theological currents, and so forth, based on cultural monolithism, which always render him unrecognizable in other cultures. Even today, many African Christians continue to think that the West has delivered Christ to them bound hand and foot."[56]

The Roles of the Church in Post-apartheid Era

Momentous changes have taken place in African Christian thinking in the last few decades. These include matters pertaining to Church and State. The indigenous expressions of the Christian faith in the past have made Church historians and theologians in the West reassess thinking about African Christianity and about theology of politics. There has been the recognition that the Gospel is essentially holistic—directed at the whole person, physical, mental, spiritual, and psychological—and therefore requires a corresponding holistic engagement. There can be no doubt that this is one of the lessons Christians in the West have learned from their African brethren, who have renewed the Old Testament concept of corporate personality. The net result is the recognition that there is a valid cultural plurality in the ways we apprehend and express the Christian faith and that there is a room for plurality of theologies within the household of Christendom. Perhaps by the Christian actions in Africa, and reactions in the Western world, Christians have recognized that every theology, ancient or modern, wherever and whenever it is produced, is local, contextual, and, therefore, provisional rather than universal. Theology itself is also a bridge between the biblical world and one's own unique struggles with questions that were not directly addressed by the earlier followers of Jesus of Nazareth. African Christian developments, therefore, are essentially a bridge between the past and the future, or, a triangular discussion between the Bible, the African experience, and human cosmotheoandric[57] vision. Africans are obligated to allow the Gospel to encounter the reality of their time without the intermediation of those who are outside that experience. Yet Africans are also responsible for bringing their contributions to a fruitful level. In this sense, the Church in post-apartheid era must play two roles—a political role and a theological one.

Africans' religious awareness and heritage have not been at variance with biblical religions. Far from obliterating the African primal view, Christianity, in its unified nature, has, in fact, reinforced the African primal vision. In other words, it enlivens the indigenous religious idioms.

The pre-Christian religious traditions of Africans are often misunderstood as paganism by outside observers. This is partly because non-Africans have found it difficult to understand African traditional religions. There are certain psychic factors that make it difficult for non-devotees (even those with keen perception) to have adequate interpretation of African religions.[58] Yet African religious insights have real and compelling affinity with that of the biblical religions, and Christianity has no future in Africa without a meaningful cross-fertilization with African primal vision. A theology developed within the spirituality of the past will be a vindication of the oneness of God and the authenticity of traditional African spirituality. Therefore, the African past is not totally discontinuous with the new awareness illuminated by the arrival of modern Christianity.[59]

In this sense, Africans must develop a theology of the tree.[60] We must join Jesus in Africa in planting new trees of hope. In the first book of the Bible, God planted trees in the Garden of Eden. At the center of the Garden is the tree of life (Genesis 1:8). Likewise, in the last chapter of the Bible, there is the tree of life whose leaves were for the healing of the nations.[61] Therefore, believers in Jesus now have the permission to eat from the tree of life.[62] The God of Africa is the God of trees.[63]

The Psalmist begins by proclaiming that the men and women of faith are like a tree planted by the river, evergreen and strong.[64] Jesus also loves nature. On the way to Jericho, there was a tree, and Zacchaeus climbed it and was able to see Jesus. Jesus even compared faith in God to a small seed that germinated and grows to become a great tree on which the birds of the air find shelter and fruits.[65] Jesus went on to say that he was the vine and his followers were the branches, and a tree must bear the fruits of life, if it abides in him.[66] The forest has always been very important to Africans. In 1999 there was a flood in Mozambique, and a young woman climbed a tree surrounded by the raging waters. On that tree she delivered a baby. The theology of tree is probably the most relevant way of understanding the Christian faith in traditional Africa.

But the question is not whether the Church has a role to play in shaping the future of societies in Africa, but what possible promise Christianity holds for the transformation of the African societies. If Christians failed to bring hope to Africans in the midst of African political hopelessness, Christianity would have no respectable future. Likewise, without the redeeming and transforming impact of the Gospel, the political situation in Africa is doomed to failure. This is because Christianity under the indigenous paradigm is one of the few areas of life in Africa where Africans have redefined their destiny through their religious activities. The African-Initiated Churches, such as the Aladuras in West Africa and the Zionists in Southern Africa, are prime examples. They are good examples of what Africans have done to define Christianity for themselves.

Perhaps the Church can play a critical role in African societies by becoming an agent of change in the political arena. The separation of Church and State would seem to negate this possibility. However, the Church-State issues in African traditional societies are not as dramatic in their essentials as in the Western world. While the problem for many Americans, for example, is how to keep religion out of politics (hence the separation of Church from the State), the problems many Africans face is how to keep politics out of religion (hence the separation of the State from religious life). Every aspect of African life is seen from the religious viewpoint. This was played out in a rather dramatic fashion in 1992, when Frederich Chiluba declared Zambia a Christian nation.[67] He did not see the political implications of his bold declaration. This pious Zambian politician believed that one must keep politics out of religion, but not religion out of politics (and especially not Christianity out of politics).[68] Before Chiluba could make a case for his declaration, he weakened the Christian influence at home and tainted his own political reputation abroad. His cabinet ministers were not so pious, and as they embezzled public funds, the boisterous Zambians converted the acronym MMD (Mass Movement for Democracy), under which Chiluba campaigned and won, to "Make Money and Depart" or "Mass Movement for Drug Dealers."[69]

In other cases in the 1970s, the Federal Government Nigerianized most of the missionary schools so as to include Nigerian students in mission schools. South Africa did the same under apartheid, but it was to weaken the educational opportunities for the non-White South Africans. It was only recently that the governments in both countries signed into law the return of those institutions to the original proprietors—the Church. The Church in Africa can mobilize devoted Africans to see that the issues affecting them, such as a quality education for their children, do not need to come under the categories of Church and State, or the European style political institutions that have come into place following decolonization. Perhaps the greatest challenge to Africans is defining the role of the Church in relating to the central government.

In many African countries, the concept of central government is a post-colonial idea, and this has been making itself stronger in post-independent Africa. The central governments, however, have not eclipsed the traditional systems or obliterated their legitimacy in the minds of most Africans. Africans have always had a subliminal suspicion of the military and imposed civilian governments, because they have proven to be an extension of colonialism and, therefore, an illegal and illegitimate form of government. This is why military rulers as well as civilian leaders often extended their arms to embrace traditional rulers in order to win legitimacy. In the late 1950s, for example, Kwame Nkrumah of Ghana took the honorific title of Osagyefo[70] in the traditional sense, in order to win the approval of his cultured Ghanaians.

The vast majority of Africans see the central government as illegitimate.[71] In fact, it would be no exaggeration to say that in places where traditional leadership and its ritual and symbols still exert influence on Africans, the Church—because of her own closeness to the people at grassroots level—possesses a deeper and richer experience in relating to traditional rulers than to central government. Although traditional rulers are known for walking a fine line between the Church and the Mosque, it is clear that they also find it difficult to oppose what the Church has endorsed. Therefore, the Church can play critical roles, raising a voice of protest under corrupt federalism. Church leaders can also form an alliance with the traditional leaders.

A Summary

The chapter must end where it began. Christianity is permanently established in Africa, where people could still consult with oracles and talk to ancestors; where prophets ring bells in the morning on the dusty streets to call African's attention to God, as in the biblical world; where there are tonal languages such as the Koiné Greek and the Biblical Hebrew; where there are living traditions of religious dance and drama in over a thousand native tongues as on the Day of Pentecost; where, as in the days of Abraham, Isaac, Jacob, and Joseph, spirit possessions, rituals, and sacrifices are understood to have spiritual meanings; where believers see visions; where faith-healing and dreams are fundamental parts of religious sensibility, and believers understand and interpret them to be God's revelation at critical junctures for many prominent personalities, as in the days of the Prophets; where contemporary societies offer many fascinating extended family and communal life parallels to the time of Jesus; where the Bible is seen not as a book of reference but as a book of remembrance, as in the time of Saint Paul of Tarsus; and where believers wear sandals without socks to the Church, as early Christians did. African Christians, if they will look at the Christian faith with African and not with European eyes, can interpret Christianity to the world in the way that no European or American Christians can.

If we hold to the view that the Africanization of Christianity is almost complete or has been successful, it may hold promise for the Church in the West, which is now struggling and raising serious questions about how the faith can be integrated to its secular culture. In other words, is it possible for the West to receive the second conversion experience? To answer this question, Philip Jenkins once called attention to a great Medieval African Saint, Abbbot Hadrian, who, in the seventh century was sent from his North African mature Christian culture to take Christianity and Christian education to the savage pagan hordes of England. Perhaps Abbot Hadrian would be saddened to see how Christianity had shriveled in much of Europe today. Yet he would be delighted to notice the new wave of African immigrants/missionaries as they burst to Europe and North America, retracing his footsteps from Christian south to secularized North.[72] Will Europe and North America arise with Africans and be converted again for the first time? Only God knows.

In the meantime, Africa is in between times both politically and theologically. Theologically one would recall the example of the famous King's chapel in Cambridge, England. The construction started in 1446 by an endowment given by King Henry the VI of England. Another King, Henry VIII, completed the chapel almost a hundred years later. During its construction, four kings ruled England, a civil war was fought, and the culture of Christianity in England had gone through a radical metamorphosis. The stonecutters, however, kept working on the Chapel and for eighty years, they drew the plans, laid the foundation, chiseled, carved limestone, and built a magnificent Chapel. For approximately four years in those eighty, stonecutters installed some of the most beautiful fan vault ceilings of the medieval period. For four decades, windows glazers made, and installed, some of the most beautiful stained glass windows of the Middle Ages.

The Chapel was completed in 1526. But then, the Protestant Reformation had taken place and the Chapel that started as a Roman Catholic Cathedral and for the purpose of accommodating Roman Catholic worshippers, had become a Church for the Anglican worshippers. In Africa, one can begin to sense the present and the future simultaneously. One can also sense the presence of God and reflect upon what has been in the past centuries. It is almost impossible for one not to wonder about the past and the future in South Africa today. The two seem to flow together, and in and out of each other.

What England was going through in the transitional period of the construction of the King's Chapel is analogous to what South Africa is going through today—a time of transition. Africa is between times. The continent is between the past and the future. This is both a moment of danger and of a supreme opportunity for Christianity. It is a moment of danger because it is possible that African Christians themselves would be the first to reject new theological developments. It is going to be much easier for Africans to carry on with the Christian vocabularies inherited from the West. New discoveries are always intellectually and emotionally threatening, requiring the abandonment of the theological vocabularies missionaries have taught Africans about Christianity. The doctrinal certainties of the past and the acquisition of non-Western Christian idioms usually make one feel uncomfortable when one is in-between times. But this is also a moment of opportunity because for the first time, Christians will have the opportunity to scatter the seeds of Christianity within African spiritual consciousness, and the entire range of theological spectrum would be enriched.

Africans are also going through political transition, and South Africa is leading the way. One question about this political transition comes to mind. How would Africa look like in the next fifty years? By this question I have in mind whether there would be a renewed destiny in which there would be stability, orderliness, and democratic principle. Or whether the next fifty years would look like the last fifty—chaos, dependency, and decay. It is not easy to answer this question because Africa is still largely unknown and there are too many factors that will determine what Africa will look like in the next fifty years. There are at least three possibilities: (1) exposure of African fragility; (2) organic embrace, and (3) realistic Africa.

The most unlikely possibility is that the continent would totally collapse because of external and internal pressures that the people on the continent would not be able to cope with. Africa is a fragile continent both politically and economically. It would be exposed as never before to its own vulnerability in the next fifty years. Africans themselves know that in the past several decades, they have been too submissive to the agenda of non-Africans on the continent. Some political analysts have labeled post-independent leaders as essentially naïve, unduly optimistic, too moderate and cautious, and compromising. The political tactics they chose only favored the governments that once colonized then, and their preference to redress their grievances by constitutional means appeared overtly gracious to foreign governments that only aimed at exploiting them and their natural resources.

In South Africa, for example, and before the ANC resolved to confronting the apartheid government directly, the emphasis was on prudence, restraints, and a dutiful respect for the authorities God had placed over South Africans. The hope was that the apartheid government would have a change of heart. Its leaders are dignified and honorable Christians and they would see the perseverance, patience, and the justice and reasonableness of the demands of the black people in South Africa. The Sharpeville massacre of 1960 where 67 unarmed citizens died and 186 people were wounded, showed the desperation of the government. On June 12, 1976 high school students rejected the imposition of Afrikaans as the language of instruction and the government declared a state of emergency. The students understood that nothing could be more dehumanizing than to be taught to despise one's own language and embrace the language of the oppressor. The police fired into a crowd of 15,000 students in the conglomeration of African townships known as Soweto. Two students died instantly and before the end of that month, 112 students died at the hand of South African police. A total number of 176 students were killed in the surrounding areas in one month. There would be an escalation of this kind of vulnerability in the next fifty years.

In this case, the strong democratic structure that is in place since the end of apartheid in South Africa (and elsewhere on the continent) would collapse. The continent would move backward instead of forward, and many white South Africans would flee to European countries. In this scenario, there would be more violence and black on black genocide would escalate. Foreign investors would find Africa unattractive and the overall economic performance of the continent would return to its 1940s and 1950s figures. Many nation states would collapse and the disillusionment will lack visible success of democratic governments, leading countries like Nigeria, Kenya, and South Africa to consider a form of socialism with one man or woman calling all the shots. Religion fundamentalism would escalate out of desperation in places like Sudan, Nigeria, Uganda, and, possibly, Kenya, Sierra Leone and Liberia. A return to military rule would be unlikely except in places like Niger, Sierra Leone, and, possibly, Ghana and Burkina Faso. Law and order would collapse and there would be bloody political violence in urban cities fueled by high rate of unemployment and disregard for human rights. But this scenario, again, is the worse prognosis about the continent and the least likely possibility in Africa in the next fifty years.

The second possibility is also quite unlikely. There would be an organic solidarity, and African nation states would be united, proving to the world that the colonial legacy on the continent was a detachable phenomenon in the history of Africa. There would be five regional economic powers—the Economic Communities of West African States, spearheaded by Nigeria and Ghana; the East Africa Economic Cooperation, led by Kenya and Uganda; the Economic Cooperation of Southern African States, lead by South Africa and Botswana; the North African Economic Alliance, spearheaded by Egypt, Tunisia, and Libya; and Central Africa Economic Union under the leadership of the Democratic Republic of the Congo and Central African Republic.

Thus, all the regions of Africa would have an organic unity, forming alliance of economic cooperation by the year 2050. There would be both bilateral and multi-lateral co-operations and Africa would renegotiate its marriage contracts with the outside world. Countries in Africa would do this strategically, and with grace and dignity. With visionary leaders in strategic places, African political solidarity would alleviate the condition of poverty and the continent and its people would possess the will to rise again, bringing economic prosperity to the majority. In this scenario, more than three quarters of African population would begin to enjoy religious freedom, political stability, and sustainable economic growth. The rest one quarter would be under benign dictatorship, but there would be minimized corruption. What the majority of Africans would care deeply about under this scenario would be what all Africans have always cared about—their own well-beings and the well-beings of their children and grandchildren. In this scenario, African nation states will move away from the past terrible and defective political constitution to a more productive and dignified political and economic paths. Africans, in other words, will move away from the wrong side of history in the modern world.

These two scenarios are extreme. The first is an outlook of pessimism, and the second is both a positive and an ambitious outlook. The first is the worst and the second is the best outcome of the current period of transition in Africa. But the third possibility is what would most likely happen in the next fifty years.

By the year 2050 or so, Africa would have developed a mechanism of governance that would be both idiosyncratic and pragmatic. The people on the continent would realize by 2020, for example, that military administrations couldn't be the legitimate custodian of their political destiny. The militaries have not been in the last fifty, and they will not be in the next. This is good news. Therefore, the majority of African nation states will adopt viable democratic constitutions. This, however, would not be the ones they have copied from the Western world, such as the constitution of the United States. Their adopted constitutions would be based not in form but in function.

It is possible for many nation states to have their own styles of democratic governments and this has already started. For example, some countries would adopt the Tanzanian model of democracy where tribes would not matter but the political systems are, nevertheless, viable. Others would take the tribes and ethnicities seriously, and adopt a style of democracy that is more like what is currently in place in Ethiopia and Eritrea. But more states would adopt the Nigerian and South African model where tribal groups are taken seriously, but the national agenda would outweigh ethnic loyalty, and the ability of any political candidate to win would depend largely on his performance outside his own tribal or ethnic group. In the end, Africans would become more realistic about their political options, and politicians would know that they have limited choices. The Church in Africa will also possess the will to arise, and, quite possibly, lead the way forward.

A comprehension of and a sympathy for what is traditional Christianity in Africa, however, are essential for understanding the roles that the Church in Africa will play in the next fifty years. Generally, the next fifty years will be more challenging both theologically and politically for Africans than the last.

Notes

[1] Christianity entered ancient Africa through Egypt. See John Foster, *Beginning from Jerusalem: Christian Expansion through seventeen centuries.* (New York: Association press, 1956), 25–34

[2] Until recently, Christian scholars do not often focus on the contributions of Africans to the Christian faith. The reason is partly because the continent is so large and diverse that one immediately falls into the temptation of making unproductive generalizations about African Christianity. Church historians rarely take into account the accomplishments of the ancient Church of Egypt (the Coptic Church) and the Ethiopian Church whose traditions predate most of those of Western Europe when writing Church history. Philip Jenkins' recent work, *The Next Christendom* (2002) is a commendable attempt to restore this balance by affirming the old and the new of African Christianity.

[3] Hugh T. Kerr, ed. *Reading in Christian Thought,* (Nashville, Tennessee: Abingdon, 1966), 36. Examples of the North Africans who have achieved theological immortality include Tertullian of Carthage (c.160–220), Origen of Alexandria (c. 185-254), and Augustine of Hippo (354–430).

[4] See Andrew F. Walls, *The Missionary Movement in Christian History: Studies in the Transmission of Faith,* (New York: Orbis Books, 1996): 1–25.

[5] Andrew F. Walls, *The Significance of Christianity in Africa,* (Edinburgh, Scotland: The Church of Scotland, St Colm's Education Centre and College, The St Colm Lecture, 1989), 5.

[6] Ibid.

[7] Kwame Bediako, *Christianity in Africa: The Renewal of a Non-Western Religion*, (Edinburgh: Edinburgh University Press, 1995), 207

[8] John S. Mbiti, *African Religions and Philosophy*, (London: Heinemann, 1969): 229. John Mbiti stated here: "Christianity in Africa can rightly be described as an indigenous, traditional and African religion."

[9] See Paul Gifford, *African Christianity: Its Public Role*, (Bloomington, Indiana: Indiana University Press, 1998), 20.

[10] Africans have adopted the old patterns into their worship styles. Perhaps, the different forms of Christianity in Africa would make one wonder if Christianity has not totally departed from the Western form, and if these "upstairs" denominations in Africa have not moved beyond the bounds of Christianity "downstairs" itself. In Europe today, the pastors of some of the largest Churches are Africans who took Christianity that has already experienced cultural flexibility before migration to European countries. The younger generations of Christians in places like Holland and in certain parts of Switzerland, for example, only know Africanized Christianity the same way Africans only knew Europeanized form of Christianity a century ago. See Philip Jenkins, *The Next Christendom* (New York: Oxford University Press, 2002), 57.

[11] Robert J. Schreiter, (editor) *Faces of Jesus in Africa* (Maryknoll, New York: Orbis Books, 1991): vii.

[12] African Scholars have written extensively about this claim. See also my work published in 1996 by Peter Lang. Caleb Oluremi Oladipo, *The Development of the Doctrine of the Holy Spirit in the Yoruba (African) Indigenous Christian Movement,* (New York: Peter Lang Publishing Company, 1996).

[13] Ali A. Mazrui, *The Africans: A triple Heritage,* (Boston: Little, Brown and Company, 1986), 157.

[14] See Paul Gifford, *African Christianity: Its Public Role,* (Bloomington, Indiana: Indiana University Press, 1999), 1–20; 306–48.

[15] Sociologist and Cultural Anthropologists have asserted that the West does not so much have African problem as Africa has European problem. White South Africans talk about 'the native problem' but it is they who are the troublesome minority in that African country, according to South African black majority. For details, see, Paul Bohannan and Philip Curtin, *Africa & Africans,* (Prospect Heights, Illinois: Waveland Press, Inc., 1995), 14.

[16] Many European Countries, particularly Britain and France, colonized most of Africa. This is why most educated Africans today are bilingual, speaking either French or English and their mother tongues. Colonialism officially began at the Berlin Conference of 1884/5 when fourteen European powers, all European countries except Switzerland, assumed political and economic control over most of Africa. However, Britain and France took steps to control trading routes in parts of Africa before 1884. This was largely for far-reaching economic benefits since Africa produced enormous raw materials for European factories.

[17] See Lamin Sanneh, *Translating the Message: The Missionary Impact on Culture* (Maryknoll, New York: Orbis Books, 1989).

[18] Lamin Sanneh, *Encountering the West, Christianity and the Global Cultural Process: The African Dimension (*Maryknoll, New York: Orbis Books, 1993), 117–151.

[19] In Francophone Africa, the French granted full French citizenship to Africans, but suppressed their cultures. In this regards, the French were an offender of 'culture prejudice.' In Anglo-phone Africa, however, Africans were encouraged to speak their mother tongues but were not granted full British citizenship. Schools were segregated in Africa under British colonies and in this sense, the British were an offender of 'color prejudice.'

[20] See Ali A. Mazrui, *Cultural Forces in World Politics*, (London: James Currey and Nairobi, Kenya: Heinemann, 1990), 256–57.

[21] This view is contrary to the popular belief among scholars in the Western world. The steady growth of Christianity from ancient to modern time is, itself, an indication that Christianity stands on its own axis in Africa. Even missionaries have always depended on indigenous agencies for supports, and indigenous Christian leaders have sustained Christianity for centuries.

[22] Some scholars and writers often mistakenly equate polygyny in Africa with a low social status for women. Most African women, however, have inalienable rights to farms as daughters, mothers or wives. Although many African women do not hold political offices in most places, in the old kingdoms of traditional political structures special offices for women existed and were integral part of the traditional form of government. Today, some of these women are the Queen mothers of the Asanti Kingdom in the Ghana Empire and they continue to play important political roles. See Paul Bohannan and Philip Curtin, *Africa and Africans* (Prospect Height, Illinois: Waveland Press, 1998), 64–69.

[23] Mark 12:25.

[24] See Kwame Bediako, *Christianity in Africa,* 183.

[25] An important exception would be Nigeria where opportunistic politicians have poisoned the existing harmony between Christians and Muslims. Although ideological differences remain between Christians and Muslims, most Christians and Muslims in Nigeria see family ties as stronger than ideological and religious differences and politicians continue to tantalize devotees to wage war against each other.

[26] An important exception to this is Uganda where it is more important to be either Roman Catholic or Anglican. Christianity in Uganda does not promote social harmony because of an unhealthy rivalry and hostility created by tension between the Roman Catholic and the Anglican. See Paul Gifford, *African Christianity: Its Public Roles* (Bloomington: Indiana University Press, 1998).

[27] They are temple democracy because they are based on faith rather than rational calculation or clearly defined political philosophy of the common people.

[28] The boundaries were frozen geographically because the international communities recognize these nation states and the federal systems associated with them. Therefore, the indigenous political institutions are often ignored by foreign powers in favor of the temple democratic systems. The borders are loose culturally because nothing prevents relatives who have been artificially divided from crossing the borders to attend to domestic needs characteristic of African traditional life and agrarian concerns. There are approximately 100,000 Maasai in Kenya and close to that number in Tanzania. But the legitimacy that the world accorded these two countries does not prevent the Maasai from going from Kenya to Tanzania as warrior or herdsmen without paper documentation. One can say the same thing about the Hausa and Fulanis of Nigeria and Niger.

[29] Although British and French showed interests to control Africa before late 19th century, November 1884 marked the beginning of former control when 14 European powers met in Berlin, Germany to fight for a control of Africa for trading and political gains. Switzerland was the only country that did not send representatives. Not a single African participated at this conference that has changed the identity of Africa forever.

[30] One should not have a romantic view that Africa was perfect before colonialism. There were ethnic conflicts in the many African Empires, and the traditional leaders were not completely blameless for the misery of their people before and after Colonialism.

[31] Military elites in Nigeria often make this claim as justification for their control of the government. The promise to return the government to civilian rule during coup d'é-tat announcement, however, often indicates their illegitimacy in power and that military seizure of power was illegal.

[32] See, Ali Mazrui, *The Africans: A Triple Heritage* (Boston, Little, Brown and Company, 1986), 179–237.

[33] See Kwame Bediako, *Christianity in Africa: The Renewal of a non-Western Religion*, (Edinburgh: Orbis Books, Edinburgh University Press, 1995), 237.

[34] See Adebayo Adedeji, "The Shaping of African Economics" Paper Delivered at the Africa at 40 conference in London, October 1997.

[35] Colin Legum, *Africa since Independence* (Bloomington, Indiana: Indiana University Press, 1999), 48.

[36] Ibid. 66.

[37] See also Colin Legum, *Africa Since Independence* (Bloomington, Indiana: Indiana University Press, 1999).

[38] Nigeria is a major supplier of crude oil to the United States and the Democratic Republic of the Congo supplies Col–Tan.

[39] Colin Legum, *Africa Since Independence* (Bloomington, Indiana: Indiana University Press, 1999).

[40] International Monetary Fund Survey 26, no. 23 (15 December 1997).

[41] Colin Legum, *Africa since Independence*, (Bloomington, Indiana: Indiana University Press, 1999), 96.

[42] Ibid.

[43] Gerhard Hoffmann, "The Crisis in World Mission: An Issue of death or of life," trans. W. J. Hollenweger (Berlin, Germany: German Evangelical Missionary Council, 1970): 40.

[44] Quoted in Johanna McGeary's article "Death Stalks a Continent" in *Time Magazine* (February 12, 2001), 53.

[45] Ibid.

[46] Ibid.

[47] Ellen Ruppel Shell, "Resurgence of a Deadly Disease" in *The Atlantic Monthly* (August, 1997), 45.

[48] Ibid. 47.

[49] It seems as if many countries in the West consider malaria a necessary evil in Africa and maintains an attitude of apathy to keep African perpetually down. See Ellen Ruppel Shell, *The Atlantic Monthly* (August, 1997). Malaria can damage the brain, cause heart failure, respiratory distress, kidney failure, internal bleeding, disorder, and a number of other systemic breakdowns.

[50] Ellen Ruppel Shell, *The Atlantic Monthly* (August, 1997). Other than Denmark, Sweden and Canada, population control, not disease control, is the central mission of most Western countries in Africa. Many Westerners assume that infectious diseases like malaria, tuberculosis, and HIV/AIDS are simply the price to the devil the third world must pay for their overpopulation problems. To the contrary, recent medical research shows that poor health actually exacerbates overpopulation because higher mortality rates leads to higher birth rates as Kenya has demonstrated. The birthrate becomes stable and infant mortality goes down when parents do not need to have many children in order to keep some alive.

[51] See Colin Legum, *Africa since Independence*, 71–98

[52] Luke 12:15.

[53] See Lamin Sanneh, *West African Christianity: The Religious Impact,* (London: C. Hurst, 1983), 227–41.

[54] John Mbiti, "Christianity and East African Culture and religion," *Dini na Mila,* vol. 3. no. 1 (May 1968), 4.

[55] John Mbiti, 'Theological Impotence and the Universality of the Church,' in *Lutheran World* Vol. 21, no. 3, 1974; See also Gerald H.Anderson and Thomas F. Stransky, C. S. P. (eds.)

Mission Trends No. 3: Third World Theologies, (New York: Paulist Press and Grand Rapids: Eerdmans, 1976), 6–8.

[56] Efoé Julien Pénoukou, "Christology in the Village: in *Faces of Jesus in Africa,* Robert J. Schreiter, ed. (Maryknoll, New York: Orbis Books, 1991), 47.

[57] Charles Nyamiti, from Tanzania, East Africa, used this term to refer to the symbiotic relationship in which the world, God and humanity are united. See "African Christologies Today" in *Faces of Jesus in Africa,* Robert J. Schreiter, ed. (Maryknoll, New York: Orbis Books, 1991): 3–23. See also his *Christ as our Ancestor: Christology from an African Perspective,* (Gweru, Zimbabwe: Mambo Press, 1984).

[58] There are certain African scholars, however, who have advocated for a complete departure from the pre-Western Christian religious traditions of Africans in order to become Christians. Such scholars see it as a theological pitfall to embrace the past in order to interpret the new. They wanted a complete replacement of the pre-Christian religious traditions with Christianity. For details, see Byang H. Kato, *Theological Pitfalls in Africa,* (Nairobi, Kenya: Evangel Publishing House, 1974).

[59] See Kwesi A. Dickson and Paul Ellingworth (eds.) *Biblical Revelation and African Beliefs,* (Maryknoll, New York: Orbis Books, 1969): vii, and 16 ff.

[60] Kenyan theologian, Douglas W. Waruta, has written about new theological thinking using the tree metaphor. See "Who is Jesus Christ for Africans Today? Priest, Prophet, Potentate" in Robert J. Schreiter, ed. *The Faces of Jesus in Africa* (Maryknoll, New York: Orbis Books, 1991), 52–69.

[61] Revelation, 22:2.

[62] Revelation, 2:7.

[63] In November 2000, there was an all Africa Baptist Theological Educators' Conference at Ibadan, Nigeria. Douglas Waruta, Kenyan scholar, presented a paper in which he articulated this theology of trees. See Douglas W. Waruta "Celebrating Christ: The Hope of Africa" in *All Africa Baptist Theological Educators' Conference: African Baptist Theology and Identity.* (Ibadan, Nigeria: Oritamefa Baptist Church and Africa Exchange Resource Center), 21–31.

[64] Psalms, 1.

[65] Matthew, 13:13.

[66] John, 15.

[67] See Paul Gifford, *African Christianity: Its Public Role* (Bloomington: Indiana University Press, 1998).

[68] For a detail account of this declaration, see Paul Gifford, *African Christianity: Its Public Role,* (Bloomington: Indiana University Press, 1998), 181-245. See also, Niels Kastfelt, *Religion and Politics in Nigeria: A Study in Middle Belt Christianity,* (London: British Academic Press, 1994).

[69] See Paul Gifford, *African Christianity: Its Public Roles,* 206

[70] The title means Messiah or redeemer or savior, but not in the Christian sense but in the sense of saving the Ghanaians from the shackles of colonialism and foreign oppression.

[71] This is partly because most Africans still live in the rural areas. More than seventy per cent of all Africans still live traditional lives and most still confine themselves to agrarian economy according to recent statistics.

[72] See Philip Jenkins, *Hidden Gospels: How the Search for Jesus lost its Ways,* (Oxford: Oxford University Press, 2000).

Chapter Six

RELIGIOUS TOLERANCE
AND THE CRISIS OF FAITH

How does religion as a motivating force in its various forms act as a gateway for understanding the new life in post-apartheid South Africa? The overriding concern of this chapter is not to defend the Christian faith or any other religious path South Africans have followed but to reflect upon the sufferings of religious intolerance during apartheid years and how this intolerance collapsed with the dismantling of apartheid.

The chapter also focuses on why Protestant missionaries are faced with challenges as they continue to proclaim the gospel and share the distinctive truths of Christianity in the modern world. Two of these challenges need immediate attention according to scholars of Christian missions. The first challenge revolves around how to be faithful to the fundamental teachings of the missionary-producing communities in a pluralistic age. According to S. Mark Heim, this involves witnessing to the decisive and distinctive power of relationship to God in Christ.[1] This witness can be both explicit and participatory—a testimony that, through Christ, humanity encounters possibilities that are open in no other way and a testimony of their faith through service, prayer, and rituals. The second, a more subliminal challenge, is especially daunting and affects missionaries directly. How does one honor the truth, virtue, and substantial integrity of believers of other living faiths and religious traditions? In defining other religious traditions, Protestant missionaries have been clinging tenaciously to the pre-modern Christian categories, despite the uncomfortable suspicion that these categories would soon break down (as they have in our own era). There has been enough exposure to the reality and goodness of other living faiths.[2] How does one reconcile the relationship between Christianity and such faiths? In this chapter, We will explore this question and the two challenges associated with it.

Missions and the Quest for Relating to Other Faiths

Certain evangelical missionaries affirm all religions as versions of the same truth, transcendence, and God's goodness. Such abstraction, however, betrays a benign contempt for the concrete aims and actual practice of the religions.[3]

The exclusivist assumptions of Christian superiority are now shaken in the thick forest of religious diversity worldwide. Taking other religions seriously and on their own terms is now a part of human culture. Huston Smith put it best when he wrote:

> To claim salvation as the monopoly of any one religion is like claiming that God can be found in this room but not the next, in this attire but not another. Normally, people will follow the path that rises from the plains of their own civilization; those who circle the mountain, trying to bring others around to their paths, are not climbing.[4]

But this also shakes the pluralistic assumptions about religions' interchangeability. Heim affirms, for example, that: "there is too much particularity in the wisdom, truth, and human transformation in the differing religious paths, seamlessly woven into the concrete, unique textures of these traditions, to ignore."[5] Thus, a pluralistic model does not provide the final answer.

Before the dismantling of apartheid in April 1994, devotees of non-Christian religions in South Africa united with Christians for a common cause and to develop a common plan for action. Thus, Allan Boesak, the celebrated anti-apartheid theologian, who was not permitted by his own Dutch Reformed Church to preach in white congregations, was received warmly by Muslims to preach at their mosques in Cape Town. Whether this open cross-fertilization among the people of different religions was a mark of the future is still difficult to predict. There is no question, however, that it was an indication that the past could not be carried to the future in the South African context.

In the West today, it is increasingly hard for Protestant missionaries to believe that the Dalai Lama's virtue and wisdom are unrelated to the specific Buddhist convictions he holds. These virtues and wisdom are not directly connected to the missionary's own particular virtue and wisdom. This problem of finding echoes of Christianity in Buddhism, however, cannot be dealt with by the text of general revelation alone. There is substance in the Buddhist religious tradition on its own. In other words, "The religion has validity not despite its difference from Christianity, but because of its difference."[6] On the other hand, one cannot explain the tradition's power by simply appealing to the common truth behind the specific religious teachings. The specific convictions the believers take to define the truth of their religions are crucial. For example, one does not come to the Presbyterian, Baptist, Methodist, Lutheran, or the Aladura Christian traditions and accidentally get the full measure or benefit of Tibetan Buddhism. The explicit "exclusivity" of the tradition is crucial to its validity. The Protestant missionaries who find much that is appealing in other religious traditions raise conscientious doubts about the need for a universal Christian witness and about the uniqueness of Christianity. The pluralistic Christians that find the goodness and virtue of the various religions too stubbornly particular raise doubts about the dogma that religions all have the same aim. He is of the view that there is something unique in every religion.

Heim's remarks are important. He affirmed that while exclusivists struggle with the idea that what is contrary couldn't be true, pluralists struggle with the importance of differences in religious traditions. How important is the difference between Christianity and a traditional African religion? Exclusivist Protestant missionaries interpret the importance of difference in the various religions in terms of contradictions, which to them means a falsehood. On the other hand, Pluralist Protestants interpret the contradictions between the various religious traditions in terms of their differences, which to them indicate a truth: religious truth claims can have conflicts only on matters of secondary significance. In other words, what one religion could be wrong about, and another right about, must not have significance in matters pertaining to human salvation.

An Epistemological Defense of Religious Tolerance

John Stuart Mill, the nineteenth-century English philosopher, first introduced the fact of religious diversity in our world and the epistemological implications of that fact.[7] In his essay entitled *On Liberty,* Mills noted that most individuals never consider that "mere accident" decided which religious view they adopt and that the same causes that made them a Christian "in London would have made them a Buddhist or Confucian in Peking."[8] John Hick poses the problem more sharply: "It is evident that in…ninety-nine percent of cases, the religion…to which [one] adheres depends upon the accident of birth."[9] In other words, the place of one's birth has a decisive effect upon the culture and religion one would likely adopt or favor. A person born in England in the nineteenth-century was more likely to be a member of the Anglican Church than a person born in China, India, or South Africa in the same period.

One of the reasons for accepting the reliability of the experience of transcendence in one's particular religious tradition is because one's experience is internal to the tradition itself. Therefore, we have no justification for rejecting the epistemological reliability of the experience of transcendence in other religious traditions. In the South African context, for example, early missionaries assumed the epistemological reliability of the Gospel and claimed the epistemological unreliability of traditional African religions. Consequently, it was assumed that the indigenous South African religions were inferior to Christianity. It is quite possible, however, that early European observers were not conversant about the religious traditions of the indigenous peoples of South Africa.

Another reason for accepting the reliability of the experience of transcendence in one's particular religious tradition is that there is an adequate epistemological explanation of the diverse accounts of ultimate reality that emerge in the various religious traditions. N. Ross Reat and Edmund F. Perry have affirmed that one of the things that the religions of the world attempt to do is to give "structure and evocative power to the universal notion of that which is ultimately desirable for all human kind."[10] They do this by proposing ultimate referents that can serve to integrate and render reasonable non-material human values. In doing so they "affirm and guide the universal human urge to affirm meaning and purpose in one's life."[11]

When adherents of a religion concede that their religion's ultimate referent is relative to a more ultimate reality, they become more honest, and their religion becomes more universally credible. But when devotees of a religion insist that the ultimate referent in their religion symbolizes an even more ultimate reality, they effectively negate the exclusive and proprietary claims on the ultimate. This admission renders plausible the possibility that the ultimate referents in other religions authentically symbolize distinctive dimensions of ultimate reality. When a religion surrenders exclusive and proprietary claims on ultimate reality—by granting that the ultimate referent of the religion is a symbol—it validates itself by making credible, in a forum of universal discourse, the claim that its ultimate referent presents an authentic dimension of ultimate reality.[12]

When there is a conflict between two religions, an exclusivist would maintain that only one could be correct. Wishing to affirm Christianity, Protestant missionaries in South Africa sought out conflicts associated with non-Christian religions, and in each case affirmed the error of the differing African traditions. In other words, if one religion differs from another, one religion is wrong from a logical stance in the view of an exclusivist.

The Pluralists, on the other hand—wishing not to attribute error to one religion against another—recognize differences among religions but do not equate the differences with religious validity. Where religions differ, the differences are only apparent because of the metaphorical and symbolic character of religious language. The differences are real but irrelevant in attaining the one true end of religion—salvation. There is a common bond beyond the apparent differences of the religions of the world. This common bond is to overcome the scattered desire of the flesh and crack the shell that has imprisoned faith in God and in our fellow human beings. If one thinks that his religion is a real alternative to someone else's religion, the second religion is often regarded as wrong. Similarly, if a Muslim thinks that his religion is a real alternative to Christianity, Christianity must be wrong from his point of view.[13]

In order to move beyond these two inflexible perspectives, one must reconsider the presuppositions of religious pluralism. Scholars that pay a passing attention to inter-religious dialogue and the inflexible perspectives of religious pluralists within it, would be familiar with the argument. The major question surrounding both the pluralist and exclusivist position is whether devoted followers of a particular religion can recognize other ways to religious fulfillment other than their own, and if so, how?[14]

The common typology of views, such as exclusivist, inclusivist, and pluralist, presumes there is only one religious fulfillment, or, what Christians call "salvation."[15] This typology has been developed with painstaking thoroughness within the Christian theology but applied analogously to other faiths. Christian exclusivists believe the Christian tradition is in sole possession of effective religious truth and offers the only path to salvation. Christian inclusivists affirm that salvation is available through other religious traditions because the God most decisively acting and most fully revealed in Christ is also redemptive and available within or through those traditions, although the devotees do not realize it. Christian pluralists maintain that various religious traditions are independently valid paths to salvation and Christ is irrelevant to those in other traditions, though for Christians he serves as a means to the same end.[16]

This typology, according to Heim, "divides people according to their convictions about the means that are effective to attain this single end. Exclusivists contend that their tradition alone provides those means; inclusivists argue that faiths other than their own may prove functionally effective as implicit channels for the truth and reality most adequately manifest in the inclusivist's tradition; pluralists maintain that each religious tradition provides its own separate and independent means to attain the one religious end."[17]

The presumption of a single religious fulfillment is usually not a tentative claim but an axiom. There could be no reason for one's devotion to a particular religion other than one's salvation. The axiom challenges believers to recognize that those of other faiths actually are seeking, being shaped by, and eventually realizing the same religious end.

One must not leave this presumption without a challenge. Can there be other reasons besides salvation for one's devotion to a particular religion? Christian Protestant missionaries have spent a great deal of time considering whether there are varying ways to salvation, and their collective answer has been in the negative. They have spent little time considering, however, whether there are different, real religious ends being sought that are not related to salvation at all.

One argument is based on what one can call the principle of "epistemological reciprocity." The stimulus for this idea is John Rawls' criterion of reciprocity in the political realm and William Alston's detailed reflections on religious knowledge. Rawls' criterion suggests that reasonable individuals will advance fundamental political principles that they truly believe others will also see as fair to them. The principle of epistemological reciprocity suggests that the kinds of internal arguments advanced by one religious tradition in defense of its claims should be granted to other religious traditions. John Hick puts this way; "if it is rational for the Christian to believe in God on the basis of his or her distinctively Christian experience, it must by the same argument be rational for the Muslim…for the Hindu and the Buddhist…on the basis of their own distinctive forms of experience."[18] In other words, the principle of epistemological reciprocity suggests that, since devotees of other living faiths also advance the same kinds of internal reasons that Christians advance for their beliefs, the Christian has no grounds for claiming epistemological advantage. In fact, there are positive reasons to believe in the epistemological veracity of other religious traditions. Keith Ward puts it this way; "if one asks the question, 'can people find resources to help them love others and find meaning in life more or less equally in many traditions?' the answer is obviously in the affirmative."[19] Consequently, if religious experiences were interpreted as encountering "the God of Abraham, Isaac, and Jacob, creator of heaven and earth, Father of our Lord Jesus Christ," we seem to be on an epistemological par with the one who, in another context, chants "there is no God but God and Muhammad is his prophet."[20] What then follows this concerning one's own religious commitments? If we cannot prove that Christian perspective is epistemologically superior to the truth claims of other religious traditions, should we abandon the claims to religious truth? In connection to this question, William Alston stated that, even if we have no non-circular proof of the reliability of our religious beliefs, it does not follow that it would be irrational for us to continue to pursue our practice if our practice is proving itself by its fruits. Therefore, in the absence of any external reason for supposing that one of the competing practices is more accurate than my own, the only rational course for me to take, according to Alston, is to sit tight with the practice of which I am a master and that serves me well in guiding my activity in the world.

One must add to Alston's comments that the rational course for Muslims or Jews or Buddhists to take, is to sit tight with the practice of which they are masters and that serves them well in guiding their activities. This is because "the basic claims of at least all of the major world religions are more or less an accurate description of the same transcendent reality."[21]

One obvious objection to the advancement of this thesis is that religious tolerance means an endorsement of religious pluralism and that incompatible beliefs are essentially descriptions of the same reality. But, it does not naturally follow that the Christian beliefs about the transcendent entail the falsehood of incompatible beliefs about God affirmed by a Muslim or followers of other living religious traditions. It is certainly not the case that the apparent incompatibility of the respectively held beliefs necessitates thinking "that somehow the other person has made a mistake, or has a blind spot, or hasn't been wholly attentive, or hasn't received some grace...or is in some way epistemologically less fortunate."[22]

The truths about God that appear incompatible are also of the same essence. One can imagine an individual who is raised in a certain culture chanting, "the God of Abraham, Isaac and Jacob" experiencing only one claim of God. One can also imagine an individual who is raised in the Middle Eastern culture chanting, "there is no God but God" experiencing only the God claim in an Islamic context. Moreover, there are no independent reasons for viewing God one way or the other. Both interpretations are appropriate responses to that which is independently real.

Therefore, we may affirm that transcendent reality is being differently conceived, and responded to from within our different religio-cultural ways of being human.[23]

If we have no problem recognizing that radically different Christian interpretations of God are nevertheless responding to the same ultimate reality, why should we have difficulty recognizing that different religious traditions are also responding to the same ultimate reality? Our interpretation of the transcendent is so underdetermined by our experience of the transcendent that we should in fact anticipate radically different views.

If we can now return to the hardest question, we would see more clearly the justification for defending religious tolerance. This question deals specifically with the radical conceptual dichotomy between those religions that view ultimate reality as a personal being, and those that view ultimate reality in terms of a non-personal principle. Those who experience the transcendent as impersonal may have focused on the unchangeable moral perfection that characterizes the transcendent, while those who experience the transcendent as personal may have focused on the relational character of God.

In *The Divine Relativity,* Charles Hartshorne argues that "the idea of the Supreme Being connotes absoluteness; it connotes, therefore, external relations; it also connotes relativity, internal relations."[24]

In effect, this means that God is both changing and unchanging. There are dimensions of God properly described by these predicates. So, those who experience the transcendent as personal and those who experience the transcendent as impersonal are simply experiencing different dimensions of the same reality, and each can learn from the other.

It is in learning from others that the early history of God became the exclusive property of ancient Israel. This is one of the major arguments of Mark S. Smith in *The Early History of God.*[25] According to Smith, Israelites and Canaanites were culturally identical and mutually dependent. Israelite monolatry was a development through conflicts and compromise between the cults and Yahweh and other deities.[26]

It is quite possible that one of the greatest barriers to the cross-fertilization of Christianity with other living faiths is not so much a lack of understanding of Christianity's historic doctrinal truth. The barrier to cross-fertilization has been partly a lack of genuine listening among Christians and non-Christians. A lack of cross-fertilization between Christianity and non-Christian religions in Africa has made it difficult for Africans to dwell solidly in the Christian life experience, even when scholarship shows that the African worldview is much closer to the biblical worldview. To cross-fertilize with other religions is quite consistent with the historic Christianity. Early Christianity drew heavily from Judaism and was able to re-conceptualize the truth it borrowed from its Jewish religious environment so radically that subsequent believers recognized the primarily borrowed elements to be in sharp contrast with the larger religious environment from which Christianity had emerged.

The New Testament Church traditions did not evolve in an isolated cultural and religious vacuum but rather in the religious and cultural milieu of the ancient Near East, which was as complex as ours today. Full participation and endorsement of Christian principle in the world will be possible when Christians of the current generation allow non-Christians to lead them in the interpretation of the essential categories of their faith.

Salvation: Overcoming fear of Religious Institutions

Theologian S. Mark Heim pointed out that those in hell have achieved the fulfillment of their desires. It is not a matter of external punishment. That is to say that if one knew and felt then what one does now, one would have behaved and thought differently and so avoided this retribution. For example, if someone overate and consequently had a stomachache, it is entirely his or her fault. But in this case, the situation is partly the product of his or her choice, and the distress follows directly from the choice, rather than being "enforced" by someone else. Paradoxically, the person who overate wanted the overindulgence but not the suffering of overeating. However, the suffering is already factored in during the overeating. In a way, the one who overate did not really regret the behavior.

The person who overate also chooses proleptically the consequences of overindulgence. Therefore he or she chooses both the act and the consequence, desiring both, consciously or unconsciously. The stomachache itself becomes part of the end sought and realized. If there is any regret, it is decisively focused elsewhere. It becomes, for instance, a reason to reproach God for mixing this vexing concomitant—the pleasure of overindulgence, and the reproach that accompanies overeating.

Those in hell, according to Heim, insist on not substituting any others' lives or wills for their own. In a striking symmetry, those people in paradise have no desire to substitute others' lives or wills for their own (even if that might be on some scale "better"), nor do they have any desire to substitute their will for that of another. It is in this respect that their purposes harmonize with God's will. It is not the case that God chose for them ahead of time what they did not desire. It is not a passive acceptance of God's autocratic decree, but a free concurrence with God's decision to give and honor radical freedom in creatures. To take away that freedom from the lost, Heim continues, would be the last, absolute destruction of their worth and dignity.

What makes people in heaven or hell unique endures in the free and continuing choice of their circumstance.

In an eschatological allegory eloquently presented in *The Great Divorce* (1946), C. S. Lewis points out the way in which a certain attitude evaporates in the air of heaven. He gives an illustration of a bus excursion that brings residents of hell to the outer limits of heaven, where they visit with people they had known in their earthly lives. The visitors suspiciously deflect invitations to stay longer. They insist on the superiority of their current accommodations in hell and cast aspersions on the little mindedness or cruelty of those who extend to them the offer of a change of address. They observed (correctly, we may suppose) that walking closer to heaven was difficult and painful. Some even complained that the grass was hurting their feet. Most of them eventually took the bus back to hell.

The protagonist in this piece was told that the bus ran regularly between hell and heaven and that anyone who wished could take it at any time. In the end, there are only two kinds of people: (1) those who say to God "Thy will be done" and (2) those to whom God says in the end, "thy will be done."

Thus, in matters pertaining to human salvation, dichotomy is not created between the freedom of the human will and the determinism of God.

The person in hell who has no wish to be elsewhere—but wants others to feel guilty or anguished on his account—gets no cooperation from his acquaintances in heaven. Anyone who manifests even the slightest wavering in his desires, some openness to a different life or relation, always finds the most profound care and responsiveness from God. Neither heaven's nor hell's occupants desired to exchange places. From heaven, there is no delight at pain associated with the condition in hell. So in hell, where pain of the sense exists, it has been appropriated as part of the end most deeply and effectively desired.

Jesus and Religious Tolerance

Another question remains about religious tolerance. "What is the view of Jesus on religious toleration?" Jesus did not leave his followers without giving some idea about this question.

In the gospels, there are two passages that come closest to addressing this question: "Whoever is not against us is for us"[27] and "Whoever is not with me is against me, and whoever does not gather with me, scatters."[28] In the first passage, the Gospel of Mark recorded that it was John who said to Jesus: "Teacher, we saw someone casting out demons in your name, and we tried to stop him, because he was not following us." But Jesus said: "Do not stop him; for no one who does a deed of power in my name will be able soon afterward to speak evil of me. Whoever is not against us is for us."[29]

These passages are striking because both statements occur in the context of a discussion about casting out demons. There is no doubt that casting out demons is an important religious activity.[30] The incident in Mark's gospel involved a person who does not belong to the group of followers of Jesus, but is casting out demons in the name of Jesus. The name of the person is not known, but the effect of what he did reverberates among the disciples. This unknown exorcist is using the name of Jesus religiously but does not join him directly as a disciple. In Matthew's gospel, it is the exorcism of demons by Jesus that was challenged by people who claimed that he did "this work" by the power of the devil.

When we take these two passages together, it appears that in a case where someone associates the true works of the spirit with Jesus' name (though with no explicit contact with or authorization from Jesus), the principle is "whoever is not against us is for us." This is the case in the situation recorded in the Gospel of Mark.

In the case of someone who attributed the actual acts of Jesus and the presence of the Holy Spirit to Satan, as in the Gospel of Matthew, the principle is "whoever is not for us is against us." Heim observed the difference with great insight: "What is most severely rejected is any claim that the spirit and power of God are not associated with Christ."[31] In Mark's gospel, the tone was positive, but in Matthew's gospel it is negative. Jesus exercised a broad religious tolerance for the "unauthorized" association of his name with real works of God's spirit. In the gospel account, and in these two examples specifically, what is at issue is the way those of "other religions" treat Jesus, the person. Neither text, for example, really addresses the question of religious practice that simply ignores Jesus. What the passages affirm and illustrate very well is the integrative tolerance of religious principle.

Jesus made important points in these passages that are crucial about religious tolerance. First, Jesus cautioned the principles that there is far more than one way to cast out demons. Alfred Lord Tennyson extended this to mean that there is far more than one way to God and that God can be fulfilled in many ways.[32] Thus, "many are the roads by which God carries his own to heaven and all roads, if we pursue them long enough and far enough, lead to God."[33] Tennyson continued: "It is a fearful thing for any man or any Church to think that he or she has a monopoly of salvation." In other words, human beings would reach their lowest level of religious arrogance when one person thinks that other human beings could not merit God's favor because they do not believe in God the same way he does.

Furthermore, religious thinkers are often too quick to name what they do not understand. The disciples were too quick to pass a judgment on the exorcist, excluding the acts of exorcism. By so doing, the disciples cast a shadow on the common ground for religious dialogue—the act of exorcism.

The enemy is not another religion. The enemy, rather, is the devil to be cast out. Jesus is not jealous, and he is happy when the community gets the essence of his message no matter how they get it, and whether they are Jews or Gentiles, Hindus or Christians, Muslims or non-Muslims.

Early Europeans lumped together the vast and amorphous mass of new and old religious cults, customs, and practices of the people of India and called them Hinduism. Its adherents never named it Hinduism. They knew it as *Sanatana Dharma*, Eternal Teaching, or Eternal Law. *Sanatana Dharma* is very broad, drawing on the term "Dharma" that signifies "truth," "practice," "duty," and "way of life." The European term "Hinduism" has diminished the original meaning of *Sanatana Dharma*.[34]

But we should not infer a pluralistic comfort or a triumph of religious pluralism from the criticism invoked by the statement of Jesus. There was no specific reference to a non-Jewish faith by Jesus and he remained faithful to Judaism although disappointed by it and by its religious leaders. He was much more interested in the people than in their religions. Thus, there are standards in religions although they are not the standards we are using.

Second, it is important to note that religious truth is always more elaborate than any human's grasp of it, making established theology or doctrines constantly out of date because of the inability of the mind to catch up with religious experience. No man or woman can possibly grasp all truths of religious experience. The basis of tolerance is the feeling that there can be assurance of our experience. In other words, the basis of tolerance is simply the realization of the magnitude of the sphere of truth about God. "Tolerance," John Morley wrote, "means reverence for all the [religious] possibilities of truth, it means acknowledgment that truth dwells in diverse mansions, and wears vesture of many colors, and speaks in strange tongues."[35] It means frank respect for freedom of indwelling conscience against mechanical forms, official conventions, and social force. It means the charity that is greater than faith and hope.[36] Intolerance, on the other hand, is a sign of both arrogance and ignorance; for it is a sign that a man or woman believes that there is no truth beyond the circles of truth he or she sees.

Third, Jesus reminded the disciples to be genuinely open to others in an attitude of questioning and searching. As he transcended the boundaries of his particular religious tradition, he desired the same for his followers. Though Jesus belonged to a particular spiritual tradition, which he also assumed, it was through this tradition that he opened himself to the traditions of all other human beings and, indeed, to the tradition of the various peoples of the earth.

Christians must always be ready and willing to change and move from where they are, and they must make the attempt to enter into others' worlds as thoroughly as possible. With such attitudes and efforts in cross-fertilization, a "shaky common ground" can begin to take shape. Even though at first it will be fragile and thin, even though it will always be "breaking down" and be "re-examined," it will provide a sufficient footing on which both Protestant missionaries and devotees of other religions can stand and genuinely hear, and learn from others. The question that will constantly be raised is not whether we believe in God, but whether God can believe in us.

Ludwig Wittgenstein alluded to this by maintaining that every language is distinct and can be judged only by the rules of its own "game." The problem with so many "efforts to carry on cross-cultural discourse or global [religious] conversation [until recently], is that one language game is always hearing and judging the other according to its own rules."[37] Commenting on Wittgenstein, Paul F. Knitter stated, "As we are not trapped in our languages, we are not trapped in our cultures and religions. Bridges of communication can be built over the chasms of diversity.[38]

A Summary

As the world grows smaller and the interactions with those of different traditions become greater, a positive appreciation for the insights of other religious views will be more in evidence. Religious tolerance will increasingly become the most widely held alternative to that which is antithetical to the gospel of faith and reconciliation.

Christians of every epoch have seen Jesus as a reality to help them in their existential condition. This is what Protestant missionaries must also do today. Interpreting the message of Jesus and the categories of Christianity requires working under new conditions. A critical analysis of the Christian tradition will prepare believers to see beyond the documents, and the pressure of religious diversity will prepare Christians in the modern era. Even Christian leaders and their writings have pointed to new directions. In studying the sources, one need allow the image to take form within us with original freshness.

Like the disciples of the previous epochs, we may look at the reality directly. This is what the earliest disciples did. They looked at the reality within their own context independently of a defined faith. The new way we look at the Christian faith in Christ will demand a certain kind of preparation. Once gained, the new vision will have all its original freshness just as it did for the earliest disciples. But the Church alone cannot arrive at the new vision. This does not mean that the Church is incapable of preparing the way. Otherwise, the new way would be merely a guide to criticism. In order to encourage a risk-forming picture of the reality before us, we must join our critical doubt with a feeling for the tradition. It is then that we will have a sustained and substantiated story of Jesus for our time, and our knowledge of the past and the light through which we see Jesus will be uniquely our own. Some of our forefathers saw Jesus in the realistic daylight. To others, Jesus was a transfigured messiah, like a magician. To still others, his message was atypical. He walked soberly in the light of this world.

The original view of him has disappeared from our theological and communal view—and rightly so, for what matters is not the beginning but the process. Our sense of reality rejects such a thesis. There is unity in the polarity, and a person can hold two views that appear to be contradictory ideas. But there is always a sense of greatness in the range of the contradictions that are held together.

I am convinced that a true religious tolerance may be achieved through the proposed method of cross-fertilization. It is only by following this pattern that the original intentions of those who first called Jesus "Lord" will take on greater clarity. In it we find the ground for their possibility. And such an investigation will help us to refute the false criticism that takes the deviations for the thing itself. We must bear in mind that no image of Christianity can be absolutely valid for all time and in all circumstances. Christians 37 years after the resurrection of Jesus would probably think that believers today are not true Christians. We do not make animal sacrifices as a part of our Christian life the way they did, and so would we them if we were to meet them. Above all, the cross-fertilization method of interpretation, as easy as it is to enunciate, can never be fully applied.

Without this cross-fertilization with other living faiths, our experience in the world would be limited, and we would be ignoring all the spiritual contents that minds can acquire only by entering into the world of religious tolerance. We would have eyes for only a small range of human suffering, faith, joy, love, and spirituality. Furthermore, there would be no development of the human nature through the fulfillment of the world, or through the shaping of experiences in the world, or through the mind of Jesus Christ. For we would be saying that all the essential knowledge is already attained. The possibilities of life in the world would be lost by our indifference to the confluence of religious knowledge. Meanwhile, this method of cross-fertilization is consistent with the mind of Jesus Christ, who, with unlimited radicalism, broke through all worldly orders. Without denying the world, he subjects all things to the condition of the kingdom that will come at the end of the world. In this light he assays their eternal value as good or evil, true or false. In rebellion, looking to the end of the world, Jesus established an unconditional ethos in harmony with God's will.

Religion in the sense of Church dogma is not essential to Jesus. Religion, rather, is a stimulus to resistance by which the one resisting first gained self-awareness. We must stand with Jesus in the current existential condition we find ourselves in the world. Jesus is now a question addressed to us that leaves us no peace. He is the beacon by which we can gain an orientation to God's kingdom. He is not only a model for us to imitate. Although the contents of his thinking cannot be ours, the manner of his thinking can show us the way forward.

I do not think I am over dramatizing or romanticizing when I express my views that, as humanity steps further into this new millennium, the religious traditions of the world will find themselves at a turning point. Up until now, religious communities have not adopted a cross-fertilization approach but have understood themselves from within the circle of their own experience and tradition. We are being challenged at this age of religious confluence to expand our ways of knowing whose (God's) we are by allowing our circles to touch and overlap with the religious circles of others. That is how I have understood my own Christian identity and story. Both the nature of our intercommunicative world and the crisis this world faces offer and require such a cross-fertilization of religious self-understanding. This is partly because we are still interdependent, and if we are to survive on this planet, we will have to embrace one another in the celebration of our common existence. That we cannot do it without one another is a mark of our common humanity. We can hear this spirit of cross-fertilization speak with a voice that transcends our religious differences and calls us to join hands as we affirm our own particularities and deny them at the same time, opening ourselves to the particularities of others in an effort to remove the suffering that humanity is facing.

But to announce a universal spirit that makes tolerance possible is not to announce a universal foundation that all the participants can sight and affirm. The spirit of cross-fertilization is not the bringer of absolute, universal truths.

In proposing a cross-fertilization method for understanding our religious life, I am not proposing a single truth that we can all finally come to or a universal foundation on which we can all build a new religion world order. Rather, I am suggesting a process—a way of being and of being together by which a community of religious thinkers can be initiated and maintained, but never completed. I am proposing a process in which we respond to our common religious problems or to concerns we can all identify as universal. These will then provide us with the inspiration and the data to form a greater community in which we can act and talk together; our circles and religious heritage will then truly overlap.

Thus, the truth we will discover along the way will not be only a propositional statement that we will all affirm; rather, it will be a way of being, in which we will find that we can indeed move between each other's worlds in an effort to enhance the well being of one another both individually and collectively. In the words of David Krieger, "Truth in this sense is less something that we know than something that we do. Truth is thus to be ascribed less to a proposition, no matter how greater the consensus supporting it, than to a form of life, which we may characterize as 'cosmotheandric solidarity.'"[39]

Following the footsteps of S. Mark Heim, it is appropriate to conclude this chapter's summary by reflecting on the words of Paul in Romans 11:33–36.

> O the depth of the riches and wisdom and knowledge of God! How unsearchable are his judgments and how inscrutable his ways! "For who has known the mind of the Lord? Or who has been his counselor? Or who has given a gift to him, or re-

ceive a gift in return?" For from him and through him and to him are all things. To him be the glory forever. Amen.

Notes

[1] S. Mark Heim, *The Depth of the Riches: A Trinitarian Theology of Religions Ends,* (Grand Rapids, MI: William B. Eerdmans, 2001), 1.

[2] Ibid.

[3] Ibid.

[4] Huston Smith, *The World's Religions* (New York: HarperCollins, 1991), 73. This edition is a completely revised and updated edition of Smith's *The Religions of Man.*

[5] Heim, *Depth of the Riches,* 2.

[6] Ibid.

[7] John Stuart Mill (1806–1873) was a philosopher, economist, and administrator. He was one of the most influential philosophers in the English-speaking world during the nineteenth-century and is generally held today to be one of the most profound and effective spokespersons for the liberal view of man and society.

[8] Mill, *On Liberty,* (Garden City, New York: Dolphin Books, 1961), 495 ff.

[9] John Hick, *An Interpretation of Religion* (New Haven: Yale University Press, 1989), 2.

[10] N. Ross Reat and Edmund F. Perry, *A World Theology: The Central Spirituality of Humankind,* (Cambridge: Cambridge University Press, 1991), 21.

[11] Ibid.

[12] Ibid. 23.

[13] Heim, *Depth of Riches,* 2-3

[14] Ibid. 3.

[15] This widely accepted typology of approaches to religious pluralism includes three categories: (1) the exclusivist paradigm is represented in the tradition of the Protestant missionary scholar of phenomenology, Hendrik Kraemer. Kraemer was professor of the history of religions at the University of Leiden in Holland and he set forth this position with unparalleled eloquence and responsible scholarship in his 1938 work, *The Christian Message in a Non-Christian World,* published for the International Missionary Council; (2) the inclusivist typology is represented in the tradition of Karl Rahner through the proclamation that devotees of other religious traditions may be called "anonymous Christians" because the grace of God is present and universal in all people. Therefore, God is present through, not despite the non-Christian religions; (3) the pluralist model can be traced to many founders including the brilliant historian and philosopher Ernst Troeltsch. In modern times, however, John Hick is the most celebrated representative according to Paul Knitter, possibly because of Hick's publication of *God and the Universe of Faith* in 1973. Hick called for a "Copernican revolution" in theology and a move from a theology that is Christ-centered to one that is God-centered. For more details, see Gavin D'Costa, *Theology and Religious Pluralism,* (Oxford: Basil Blackwell, 1986); Alan Race, *Christian and Religious Pluralism: Patterns in the Christian Theology of Religions* (London: SCM Press, 1993).

[16] See Heim, *The Depth of Riches,* 3ff.

[17] Ibid. 3.

[18] John Hick, *Problems of Religious Pluralism* (London: McMillan, 1985), 103.

[19] Keith Ward, "Truth and Diversity of Religions," *Religious Studies.* vol. 26. 1 (March 1990): 4.

[20] In an unpublished work, "The Epistemological Defense of Religious Pluralism," (2001) Robert Baird of Baylor University advances this argument.

[21] Ibid.

[22] Ibid.

[23] John Hick, "Religious Pluralism and Salvation," *Faith and Philosophy* vol. 5. 4 (October 1988): 370.

[24] Charles Hartshorne, *The Divine Relativity: A Social Conception of God* (New Haven: Yale University Press, 1948), 94.

[25] Mark S. Smith, *The Early History of God: Yahweh and the Other Deities in Ancient Israel* (New York: HarperCollins, 1990).

[26] Mark S. Smith, *The Early History of God,* xxiii–xxiv.

[27] Mark 9:40 (New Revised Standard Version)

[28] Matthew 12:30

[29] Mark 9:38–40.

[30] Heim, *The Depth of Riches,* 80.

[31] Ibid. 81.

[32] Quoted by William Barclay, *The Gospel of Mark* rev. ed. (Philadelphia, Westminster Press, 1975), 226.

[33] Ibid.

[34] See "Hinduism: Myriad Paths to Salvation," in John L. Esposito, Darrell J. Fasching, and Todd Lewis, eds. *World Religions Today* (New York: Oxford University Press, 2000), 273–351. See also, Margaret Stutley, *Shamanism: An Introduction* (New York: Routledge, 2003), 3.

[35] Margaret Stutley, 3–5.

[36] Ibid.

[37] Quoted in Paul F. Knitter, *One Earth Many Religions* (Maryknoll, NY: Orbis Books, 1995), 76.

[38] Ibid.

[39] David Krieger, "Conversion: On the Possibility of Global Thinking in an Age of Particularism." *Journal of the American Academy of Religion* 58 (1990): 231.

❊ Chapter Seven
NELSON MANDELA AND THE RESURRECTION

Christians in the West have certain theological fixed points about the resurrection of Jesus Christ. In the Western Christian faith tradition, one question towers about all others—is there a life after death? Although this question is not unique to Christianity, it is definitive for Christians in the West and in Africa alike because both believe in the resurrection of Jesus Christ. When grandmothers die and aunts pass away, or when uncles are infected with deadly diseases such as HIV/AIDS, or grandfathers are ill with cancer, or when spouses or children experience accidental deaths, the words of comfort on the lips of every close family member are always related to afterlife. When we face treacherous medical paths, we often think about life beyond death. Facing death in a real and practical sense has created certain feelings of anxiety about the false illusion that human beings are somehow incapable of defeat. Despite medical advancements and modern technological innovations to prolong life, the incontrovertible evidence that death is certain but life is not, reminds us of our mortality and vulnerability.

The pain of losing those we love through death has not been assuaged since the beginning of time. It is only Christianity, however, that has theological fixed points about the question of death because of the transparent solution that Christ provided through his own death and resurrection. A person does not have to believe in the resurrection to note that it has always been the highest point of the Christian proclamation. The resurrection of Jesus Christ demonstrated concretely what happened to death, and it released the anxiety about death's power, which has gripped humanity since the beginning of existence. Even if one holds to the view that the resurrection is not the only piece that points to the uniqueness of Christianity—that there are interrelated categories that make Christianity a unique religion—one would still have to hold the resurrection to be a central piece of Christian essential categories. This is because the resurrection represents an unrepeatable triumph over humans' greatest fear—death. In the Christian tradition, the resurrection of Jesus Christ remains the only answer to human fundamental need. But more importantly, the resurrection of Jesus Christ remains the only explanation for having faith in God and it is the only explanation for giving God the glory in heaven and on earth.

South Africans, both individually and collectively, have experienced great losses of human lives under apartheid and during the sustained struggles that dismantled it in the early 1990s. In a well-crafted post-apartheid study, Tristan Anne Borer stated: "The number of deaths during the first years of the decade was staggering: between February 1990 and October 1992, almost 8,000 died, and in the period between September 1992 and the 1994 elections, South Africa suffered an average of 300 deaths a month."[1] This is quite higher than the average rate of deaths that South Africans have suffered. There is no doubt that the question about life after death continues to be relevant after the dismantling of apartheid. As time goes on, this question, as well as the fear that sustains its theological relevance and significance, often grows darker. Is there a resurrection of the dead? This question, however, is not as immediate as the much older question of Job: "If mortals die, will they live again?"[2]

In a modern drama, there is a remarkable scene about life after death. A teacher was discussing the problem of death with his students. After a long silence, one of his students reluctantly says that death, in his view, is something like the birth of a newborn. Before birth, he explains, the fetus is totally surrounded by its mother and gets all its nutrients and life from the mother, but it does not yet see its mother. The experience of birth, the small boy thought, must have been something like a shock to the fetus. It is only after birth that it will be able to see its mother. Thus, the boy continued, in our life on Earth we are totally surrounded by and are getting our lives from God, but God remains invisible. It is only after the shock of death that we shall see God.

While resurrection is central to Christianity, life after death is an essential teaching of major world religions. In 1984, a Jewish scholar, Pinchus Lapide, argued that the resurrection of Jesus Christ was a part of Judaism, claiming "the resurrection of Jesus on that Easter Sunday and his appearance in the following days were purely Jewish faith experiences. Not one Gentile saw him after Good Friday. Everything that [the] Gentile Church heard about the resurrection came only from Jewish sources because he appeared after Easter Sunday as the Risen One exclusively to Jews."[3] It is equally important to note that it was through Judaism that the voices of the Great

Prophets such as Samuel, Elijah, Jeremiah, Ezekiel, and Isaiah were heard, and their censure of the immorality and injustice of the rulers and the people, contained a universal ethical message that was destined to ring throughout the world. For Christians, if Christ were not raised, if he was not more than a Jewish rabbi of Nazareth and one more leader in the long line of religion teachers, then there is no need to get excited about him, either as a man, or as the incarnation of God. Jesus performed many mighty deeds during his ministry. But these activities were not sufficient to establish him as the Messiah because there were many miracle workers in his days. Although he performed mighty deeds by the "hands of God," it was his resurrection that secured for him the status of the Messiah. Even Christians would not have held him as the exalted Messiah without the resurrection. Thus, Christianity lives or dies at the point of the resurrection of Jesus Christ.

One could respect him as we respected Moses or Socrates, but it would be nonsense to give him the exalted position that he has had in the Christian Church. It would be nonsense to acclaim him as Savior and Lord, and it would be nonsense to say a prayer to God through him. The Lord's Supper would be nonsense and so would any discussions about the Christian faith. The cornerstone would be pulled out, and the Christian structure as we know it would collapse.

Resurrection continues to be the most powerful symbol for the Christian faith. But Christianity is more than primarily a matter of believing in the personages and events of the resurrection recorded in the Scriptures. A person could believe in the resurrection of Jesus without necessarily living a Christian life. Therefore, and more importantly, Christians are to find the meaning of existence in terms of this basic scriptural symbol of life beyond death. Yet, finding such meaning in this symbol is also a mystery because the event itself was a mystery. Hence, John Macquarrie wrote: "The idea of resurrection, implying as it does the mysterious interaction of the material and the spiritual, yes, even of the human and the divine, lies at the uttermost edge of what our finite mind can grasp, and it would be foolish and arrogant to suggest that we can have any clear or complete understanding."[4]

Resurrection of Jesus: A Quest for Existential Hope

One question that gets to the core of Christianity in Africa is that of the existential meaning of resurrection. Other questions remain to be asked, and Christians and non-Christians have raised them. These questions focus on what it means to be raised from the dead, and on what kind of body is a resurrected body. These questions, however, are superficial and speculative.

They do not really address the issues of human suffering and what resurrection means in this life.

In a collection of his sermons given between 1976 and 1993, Archbishop Desmond Tutu repeatedly stated that one cannot preach a blissful life beyond death when "the rainbow people of God" are suffering here on Earth. In order to establish peace, justice, and prosperity, all of the people of South Africa—black, whites, Coloured, and Indians—would have to join hands together.[5] Just as a rainbow will not be a rainbow without the colors, the many "races" of people in South Africa make the country what she is. For the "rainbow people of God," the resurrection of Jesus Christ means that God can always bring forth the new and that the human conditions of suffering are not permanent. This constitutes a true meaning of the resurrection of Jesus Christ for South Africa. While the cross speaks of God standing with us in our suffering and in the flux of events, the resurrection is about God. Human faith in God and in the resurrection is analogous to putting clothes on the nature of the Divine. The resurrection speaks of God as being always ahead of human events, and resurrection is, therefore, the great ground of hope for the oppressed and marginalized. This means that it is the resurrection that takes African Christians very far in understanding the future hope not yet realized. In other words, what resurrection promised to the people of South Africa that suffered under the yoke of apartheid was the restoration of hope in the midst of hopelessness for the majority.

In the South African experience, it is the suffering of the people that gave birth to the hope that was experienced among the people. Suffering does not annihilate hope but makes people more determined as the case of the Civil Rights movements in the United States also demonstrated. In other words, the apartheid system put the majority of South Africans in the ditch of suffering. In order for the majority to remain in the ditch, however, the government must also stay in the ditch with the people, who were anticipating freedom. A belief in the resurrection was not necessarily a prerequisite for the hope yet to come for South Africans. It was the suffering and injustice they experienced in the hands of a "Christian" government that made "the rainbow people of God" hopeful. This hope also gave South Africans, White and Black, Indian and Coloured, the boldness to confront the injustice they suffered.

To scholars[6] who maintained that the resurrection was the result of the proclamation of the disciples and a belief already arrived at as a result of meditation on the Scripture, Lapide has the following question: "But how can we explain the boldness of the disciples after the resurrection?"[7] The claim that the resurrection is the result of the belief that the Church arrived at, and that the Church herself is his risen body was proposed in the late 1800s by German theologians; Rudolf Bultman, for example, claimed "the resurrection is the proclamation of the Church that Christ lives on and his word still summons men and women to decision of faith."[8] Nothing gave the disciples such confidence in rabbinic literature as the resurrection. The frightened band of apostles was just about to throw away everything in order to flee to Galilee in despair. They had betrayed and denied their master and then failed him miserably, but they were suddenly changed into a confident mission society, convinced of salvation and able to work with much more success after Easter than before Easter. No vision or hallucination is sufficient to explain such a revolutionary transformation.[9] Yet this belief did not pave the way for the Jewish people to see Jesus as the Messiah—the anointed one of God. Clemens Thomas, for example, states:

> For Jewish scholars, the testimony of the resurrection was no proof for the messiahship of Jesus because for them the concept of resurrection is not connected with messianic expectation of salvation. At the time of Jesus, Judaism was expecting the resurrection of various figures—of Enoch, of Moses, of Elijah, of Jeremiah…but not the resurrection of the Messiah.[10]

Despite the lack of association of the resurrection with Messiahship, it is important to note that Jewish scholarship affirms the resurrection of Jesus Christ. While only a handful of the disciples became convinced that the risen Jesus was in fact the Messiah, there was uniformity in the assertion that Jesus of Nazareth who was crucified was later seen alive. Jewish disciples further supported this claim by stating that nothing else could have emboldened them to proclaim the activity of God in the world.

The experience of the resurrection as the foundation act of the Church, which carried the faith in the God of Israel into the Western world, also belongs to God's plan of salvation for Africans and for the people in the non-Western world. The belief in the existential resurrection of Jesus is vital to the existential redemption of Africans. This is partly because many believers see Jesus as the embodiment of victory over death, and injustice, and suffering in this life.

Douglas Waruta, a Kenyan scholar, expressed this more poignantly when he stated:

> Africans are not interested in suffering through their problems now while waiting for the bliss of heaven. This is the type of Christianity evangelistic missionary Christianity to a large extent communicated to the African people. Africans want a leader who shows them the way to liberation now—liberation from disease, oppression, hunger, fear, and death. This type of Jesus is the one presented in the Gospels. African identify very much with [Jesus]. He is the prophet who exhorts them to a better and more hopeful living. He is a priest who mediates between them and the external powers of the living God. He is the king who leads his people to victory over the overwhelming threats of life."[11]

The existential victory over death and suffering is vital to the credibility of Christianity for Africans in the post-apartheid era. But Africans are not entirely unaware of the scholarship about the resurrection of Jesus in the West. For example, the propositions that the disciples were either mistaken or that they knowingly perpetrated a myth intended for a symbol, or that the eleven disciples conceived a "Passover plot," spirited the body of Christ out of the tomb, and disposed of it neatly—and to their dying breaths maintained conspiratorial silence—are not unfamiliar to ordinary Christians in Africa. These criticisms are on shaky grounds, however, because existentially, the event was so mind-boggling that it could not have gone as a secret without someone from the eleven disciples uncovering it. The argument that the resurrection was a cover-up cannot be maintained from a psychological or an existential point of view. Resurrection cannot be some event that people were going to be vague or indecisive about. The Scripture noted quite honestly that the disciples themselves were so unprepared and so staggered by the re-appearance of Jesus that at least one of them, Thomas, demanded for a tangible proof of fingering the wounds in the hands of Jesus and on his sides.[12] How can the disciples be surprised when they were also coached in advance that the event of the resurrection was inauthentic but that they should maintain the cover-up?

Furthermore, the post-resurrection appearances to the disciples were numerous, and were for over a period of more than forty days, according to the Gospel of Luke.[13] The variety of witnesses to the account of the resurrection makes it firm in the minds of the disciples that Jesus was raised from the dead. According to Charles Colson, "the records of the event, written independently by various eyewitness reporters, belie the possibility that the disciples were mistaken."[14]

Until the nineteenth century, New Testament scholars did not specifically the resurrection or regard the resurrection event as a myth. Many first-century religious truths were conveyed through symbols, and it was assumed that the resurrection of Jesus was within the broad domain of a Christian symbol. The suggestion of a myth to explain the resurrection of Jesus was articulated by Rudolf Bultman, who first articulated the view that the life of Jesus himself was clouded in myth and in need of demythologization.[15] It is relatively easy to move from symbolic expression to mythological expression when one discusses the resurrection of Jesus. Contemporary New Testament scholars, however, have categorically rejected demythologization, claiming that it is the reader that must be re-mythologized into the New Testament world for a proper understanding of its religious categories. Certainly African scholars who have studied the post-resurrection account have serious doubt about the myths of the resurrection. Thus, there is no uniformity of opinion that the resurrection of Jesus was a myth. The argument is quite comprehensive, in the sense that when the disciples reported the resurrection, they were certain that they were not using a symbolic device. Their testimony was straightforward. This is one of the reasons that Paul wrote to the Corinthian Church that if Jesus was not actually resurrected, Christianity was a sham. There is no doubt that Paul was not talking about the resurrection of Jesus as a symbol but as a verifiable historical event. Thus, the myth theory cannot be sustained because a cover-up by the eleven men, with the complicity of up to five hundred others, cannot be humanly sustained over a long period of time. In other words, if the resurrection of Jesus were a myth, what Christianity is saying amounts to stating that men and women in the world are capable of being ostracized by friends and family, living in daily fear of death, enduring prisons, living penniless lives and in hunger, sacrificing the love of their family, being subject to torture without mercy, and ultimately dying, all because the disciples wanted to cover up what they themselves did not believe was true. On the contrary, the band of the disciples clung tenaciously to their enormously offensive story that the resurrection of Jesus was a historically verifiable event and that their Lord was alive. It seems contradictory to human nature to die willingly for what one believes to be a cover-up. In Charles Colson's book, *Loving God* (1982) this point was made in the chapter that he aptly called "Watergate and the Resurrection." If the resurrection of Jesus was a cover-up, and nobody was willing to reveal the lie in order to be free, then there is something fundamentally wrong with the psychological condition of the human nature.

One could be willing to die for a noble cause and for what is true. Only a person with a low mental and moral capacity would be willing to lay down his or her life for what he or she knows to be a cover up. Therefore, it is not likely that a plot to perpetuate a myth about the resurrection of Jesus could have survived the violent persecution of the apostles, the scrutiny of the early Church councils, and the horrendous purge of the first-century believers who were cast by the thousands to the lions for refusing to renounce the Lordship of Christ and his resurrection. Is it not probable that at least one of the apostles would have renounced Christ before being beheaded or stoned or tortured? It would make more sense that one of the conspirators would have made a deal with the authorities and denounced the resurrection as a cover-up so that he could save his life.

Blaise Pascal, the extraordinary mathematician, scientist, inventor, and logician of the seventeenth century, was convinced of the truth of Christ (and of the resurrection) by a thorough examination of the historical record. In his classic work *Pensees*, Pascal wrote:

> The hypothesis that the apostles were knaves is quite absurd. Follow it out to the end and imagine these twelve (sic) men meeting after Jesus' death and conspiring to say that he had risen from the dead. This means attacking all the powers that be.

The human heart is singularly susceptible to fickleness, to change, to promises, to bribery. One of them had only to deny his story under these inducements, or still more because of possible imprisonment, torture and death, and they would all have been lost.[16]

One of the disciples whose life went through a radical transformation after the resurrection was Simon Peter. In order to save his life from the torture of the wicked government, Simon Peter renounced Jesus before the resurrection. After the resurrection, however, he was willing to die rather than deny what he experienced. Ultimately, Peter died a violent death by choice. But what is more significant for Christianity today, in South Africa and elsewhere, is the existential interpretation of the resurrection of Jesus of Nazareth.

Hope and Resurrection in Post-apartheid Era

How does one interpret the resurrection for Christians today? The bitterness of death is a constant theme in the Old Testament. I Samuel 15:32 states this bitterness, and Psalm 115:17 echoes its bitterness when the writer states: "The dead do not praise the Lord." Prophet Isaiah states in 38:18, "For Sheol cannot praise you, death cannot praise you; those who go down to the Pit cannot hope for your faithfulness; The living, the living, they thank you...." In Judaism, there is no psychic projection of human longing for bliss after life. The people live here and now for God, and it is exactly here that one finds a people that lives with God in an extraordinary intensity, without any idea of an eternal life which would one day solve all the problems that remain unsolved on Earth.

The Old Testament depicts the lives of the people in the existential moment. The people in the Old Testament obeyed God—and obeyed God in the wholeness of life without any expectation of a reward in a future life. This is quite instructive as one looks at Africans in the post-apartheid era. Their suffering and sense of hope propel them to their perspective about living a post-resurrection life here and now. The perceptions of Africans and that of the religion of Judaism are a shared understanding of the resurrection. Thus, as in Israel, and as described in the Old Testament, our eyes become open to what a belief in the resurrection entails by living a resurrected life here and now.

Ancient Israel warns against any cheap concept of the resurrection that might prove to be nothing else than a dream of a perfection that is lacking on Earth. As they experienced God in the existential moment, believers are not to entertain any dreams of another world and another time. According to the theologies of the Old Testament, we should not project our wishes onto heaven as a kind of super-life that we expect from the future. As Israel lived with her God on this Earth, in the history of her time, in an existence limited by birth and death and rebirth, so too are we empowered to live a post-resurrected life.

In I Samuel 2:6–8, Hannah's song reads:

> The Lord kills and brings to life; he brings down to Sheol and raises up. The Lord makes poor and makes rich; he brings low, he also exalts; He raises up the poor from the dust; he lifts the needy from the ash heap, to make them sit with princess and inherit a seat of honor.

There is a clear indication that the people of the Old Testament did not create a dichotomy between this life and the post-resurrection life. As Hannah's song indicated, there is life to be lived in post-resurrection time. This is probably because death was not so much a problem for them as it is for believers today. Resurrection is an experience within the earthly life. God has the power to let one die and to let another be born, and the grey theological areas we face about life beyond death are necessary for the depth of our knowledge about the resurrection. God's power leads to wealth and to poverty; God's power honors and also humiliates. It is in the existential condition of human beings that one sees the hope promised in the resurrected life. In the experience of the ups and the downs of human lives, God's power of resurrection is manifested. Yet the end of the passage shows that there is more to this post-resurrection. The author of the song knew that all this is not simply blind fate but that there is the one who is Lord over the ups and the downs. The power and the activities of this Lord show a clear trend. The Lord raises up the poor and the needy from the dust. Apparently, the person who first created the hymn had experienced the power of his God when he himself was lying in the dust and in the pit.

This Lord is, first of all, present with his power, and his help is steady when human beings are totally at the end of their own power and when they see no help. There is a definite theme in the history of Israel and in the nation's experience with God—the trend towards help out of need, salvation out of danger, and life out of death. Destruction by killing, bringing down, or making poor, is not God's true aim. God wants to raise the poor from the dust and lift the needy from the ashes. And this is exactly what Israel has experienced time after time. This life after "death" is a constant theme in the life of the people of God. Whenever they were at their end, whenever all their hopes had collapsed, God was always ready, more so than ever, to lift them up and see them through.

For South Africans who lived under apartheid, resurrection is also a depiction of a triumph over death and a symbol that death and suffering would not have the last word among God's people and those created in the image of

God. In this sense, South African Christians do not see themselves as walking toward a triumph over oppression, but as emerging from such a triumph because of Christ's resurrection. The victory of Christ over physical suffering and death becomes a pre-figuration of their own suffering and death inflicted by an oppressive system of apartheid. It also means that good and evil were both present and that God was triumphant. The apartheid government represented existential evil and death, but God sent courageous liberators, including such leaders as Allan Boesak, Frank Chikane, Chris Hani, Nelson Mandela, Beyers Naudé, and Desmond Tutu. These courageous South African leaders did not lead every fellow citizen through the narrow and crooked paths of life. They could not have carried every citizen on their shoulders through life's twisted turns. What they did, however, was to teach South Africans to start believing in themselves. Nelson Mandela taught his fellow South Africans that it was important to believe in God, but more important that God could believe in them to bring universal justice to the people against the evil of apartheid. This could only happen when South Africans could believe in God and believe in themselves simultaneously, and create a just society in which God could be proud.

Desmond Tutu has stated repeatedly that the end of apartheid in South Africa was a miracle.[17] In a characteristic statement, Tutu has also pointed out that it was not because South Africans were fewer or more in number than any other people that the Lord loves during the moment of crisis, but simply because the Lord loves South Africans and that God could still perform miracles in our time. The challenge ahead in South Africa remains whether the citizens could continue what God in Jesus Christ did through their courageous leaders to promote social and political justice. Thus, the Christian life is not only about whether we believe in God or not, but also about whether God can believe in us to carry on and implement the just society inaugurated through the life and resurrection of Jesus Christ. These leaders put South Africans on the path of righteousness that God can believe in South Africans to carry on what God in Jesus Christ started. What is quite revolutionary in South African Christian experience is that it is when God can trust us that we are truly saved, not whether we believe in God or not. Indeed the devil, too, believes in God.

This means that the Christian message in Africa is consistent with the resurrection's message of hope. The God who was always ready whenever man was low in his life would be ready even more when man was at the lowest point of all—in death. One is reminded here of the vision of Ezekiel in the Old Testament.

During the Exile, Prophet Ezekiel had a vision. He saw a valley full of dry bones. Then the Lord God spoke to the bones, a noise arose and a rattling, and the bones came together, bone to bone. Tendons grew, and then the flesh and the skin. Finally, the spirit of God came like a breath upon them and the bones lived and stood up. Ezekiel 37:1–10 has been an important subject for biblical interpretation among scholars. The resurrection in the vision of Ezekiel cannot be proven, but from the existential condition of Africans, and from a theological point of view, the vision was a hope ringing out in the midst of hopelessness. The vision told Ezekiel and the whole exiled people of God about the future restitution of Israel, a restitution that would occur within the earthly history of the nation.

The chapter does not contain the message of an individual life of a man after his physical death. The vision was a prophesy of change in the destiny of Israel as a whole, through new historical developments. Yet this text is also about the meaning of resurrection. The imagery that forces itself upon the prophet's mind is that of a God whose power is not at its end, even if he finds nothing but dry bones. Thus, the idea of something like a resurrection of the dead enters the thinking of Israel first, on the occasion of an experience of God's help in world's history. It was not yet the answer to the question of human destiny after death. This problem, the eternal wish of humankind for eternity, is still far away from Prophet Ezekiel's preaching. What he wanted to proclaim—and this is where Africans can resonate with Ezekiel's prophesy and its force of perception about God—is the character of the God of all creation. The limitless power of this God manifests itself in this vision. God's character is to redeem and to make whole by bringing life out of death, and order in the midst of chaos.

Prophet Isaiah goes even further. The prophet states: "[God] will swallow up death forever. Then the Lord God will wipe away the tears from all faces, and the disgrace of his people he will take away from all the earth, for the Lord has spoken."[18] This prophesy of Isaiah was not the proclamation or a proof of resurrection, but the hope for a coming time in which those who will then be living will no longer endure death. In a real sense, the prophecy was about God, not about humanity or his condition. It is a testimony about the final victory of God over death and oppression. Isaiah did not reckon with the possibility that he himself would be a part of this world to come, an indication that the prophecy was not a personal wish for an eternal life. In other word, Isaiah did not simply project into a belief in resurrection. It was rather the praise of God's power, which cannot be annihilated—not even by the fact of death. Nothing is said about the problems and wishes of the individual believers. It is enough for him to know that this is the God into whose hands his life is committed. Life and death are not mere chance, and God is triumphant over both.

Both Ezekiel and Isaiah recognized that God has been involved in the earthly life of the people, and in the earthly history of the whole people.

They did not raise the question about what this means for them as individual prophets.

Jesus and the Resurrection Question

According to the Gospel of Mark,[19] the Sadducees asked Jesus what it would be like at the resurrection if a wife had been married successively to seven brothers in an arrangement one can call a levirate marriage common among Africans. The answer of Jesus was rather startling: "And as for the dead being raised, have you not read in the book of Moses…how God said to him, 'I am the God of Abraham, and the God of Isaac, and the God of Jacob?' He is not God of the dead, but of the living."

The answer to the human question about resurrection comes to this: God is more interested in people living for God than in dying for God. In the same manner, God does not want believers to keep the words in the Scriptures, but to fulfill them in active existence. Jesus does not speak to human beings, or to their souls, nor their ability to transcend themselves, nor their dreams, nor their longings for final justice. Jesus speaks of the living God, and that God is not the God of the dead but the God of life.

That God is alive and in charge of those who are living is one of the prominent features of the theologies of the New Testament. God is alive, and humanity is alive because of God. Human beings will always live in the tension of that relationship. This is the trend in God's acting that Israel has learned to see. God's aim is to help, to save, to bring to life, to support those in danger, and to bring suffering to an end in this life. Therefore, human beings are to live a post-resurrection life that is characteristic of justice, love and compassion. This is what vindicates the cross of Jesus Christ; it is the reason why he died.

There is something more, however, in the answer of Jesus about the resurrection. Jesus quoted from the Old Testament that God is the God of Abraham, Isaac, and Jacob. This means, perhaps, that God is not a God in general, or a generic God. God is the God who gives to humanity, even to this and to that specific man or woman.

This interpretation is most appealing to African Christians under apartheid. If it is true that God was close to Abraham, to Isaac, and to Jacob, then God does not do so only as long as these individual Patriarchs are strong and good. It must also be true when they are weak or abused or oppressed by the accidental circumstances of history. It will be even more so in death, when God's presence would be manifest, than in times of strength and supcriority. Is there any weakness or lowliness that could become stronger than the faithfulness of this Lord? If God is really the God of the living and not of the dead, does this mean that God ceases to be the God of Abraham when Abraham dies? No! God does not abandon Abraham in the moment of his greatest weakness, his death—not because Abraham or a part of Abraham is eternal, but because God's "yes" to Abraham cannot fail whether Abraham was alive or dead. This means that when God gives to a person, it means permanently, eternally, and finally. It means life—not death.

Death and Immortality in African Cosmology

A Catholic Missionary to Kenya, Michael C. Kirwen, wrote *The Missionary and the Diviner* (1986) and shared his experience about African cosmological vision. What is fascinating about the book is not only the dialogical approach Kirwen used to convey African's religious ideas but also the range of his coverage of indigenous African worldviews.[20] In the last chapter of the book, "Everlasting Life: Remembrance or Resurrection," Kirwen maintained that one must look closely at death in African worldview because Africans believe that physical death is not the cessation of existence and because Africans make provision for life after death through cognitive and dialogical remembrance.[21] Among Africans, there is a common socio-religious relationship between life and death. Life is seen as a continuum incorporating both physical and non-physical existence. One of the roots of this relationship is the conception that religion is a process of total immersion into one's community. John S. Mbiti expressed it poignantly when he stated:

> In traditional society there are no irreligious people. To be human is to belong to the whole community, and to do so involves participating in the beliefs, ceremonies, rituals and festivals of that community. A person cannot detach himself from the religion of his group [because] to do so is to be severed from his roots, his foundation, his context of security, his kinships and the entire group of those who make him aware of his existence. To be without one of these corporate elements of life is to be out of the whole picture. Therefore, to be without religion amounts to a self-excommunication from the entire life of society, and African peoples do not know how to exist without religion.[22]

Africans have an important idea of life after death that is not only secured through religion or spirituality but also through a realized existential condition of hope. While the Christian conception of immortality is a gateway to emerging perceptions of life after death among African Christians, one would note that, rather than being converted to the Western missionary idea of immortality, Africans have taken the missionary ideas of life after death and converted them into their own realized existential immortality. They have done so with creativity—and with such consistency that their conception of life after death, borne out of their traditional religious views, has often been deemed a wholly Christian conception.

In African understanding, to die is tantamount to changing one's address from one realm or location of existence to another. Hence, the dialogue partner in Michael Kirwen's work stated: "You see, [God] created only one world wherein humankind lives, dies, and is reborn through names."[23] Death, therefore, is not only a biological cessation of life but also the first stage of a shift to another realm of existence. Cessation of life occurs when no one remembers the person who died. Therefore, to secure one's immortality it is important to have as many children as possible, for they will preserve one's memory through remembrance. Kirwen's dialogical partner continues:

> However, if people die without children, no one will name their children after them. Such people quickly enter into the realm of the unknown ancestors where their names are lost forever. So it appears that the final state of a person depends on fertility.[24]

Thus, "life" is a continuum with two aspects—one visible and physical, the other invisible and beyond human control. In his commentary about the conversation with the Diviner, Riana, Kirwen affirmed: "Life for Riana is a continuum embracing the dead, the unborn, and the living."[25] Therefore, human existence is never restricted to immediate family members but embraces an extended family of the dead, the living, and the members who are yet to be born. In other words, this view means that the human community "encompasses the whole of human life whether ancestral, contemporary, or potential."[26] Taking to its logical conclusion, salvation could also be extended to the here and now as well as beyond death. Accordingly, the dialogue concluded rather forcefully that "salvation must be in terms of the here and now."[27] Kirwen further commented:

> Death itself is so silent and final that there is no concrete evidence for either personal resurrection or nominal reincarnation. However, if one sees in the faces and lives of one's children the images and lives of the ancestors, then Riana seems to have the more plausible belief, and the Christian belief in the resurrection of the body is seen to be more extraordinary.[28]

The Resurrection of Jesus and Existential Reality

In the modern era, at least one scholar embraces the existential reality of the resurrection of Jesus in his works and sermons. Thomas H. Troeger, the former Vice President and Dean of Academic Affairs at the Iliff School of Theology in Denver, Colorado[29] and now at Yale Divinity School, has poignantly and eloquently maintained that the resurrection of Jesus was not only a celebration of life after death but also a terror that should challenge believers to a life of transformation in the way that would show the true meaning of resurrection here and now. The resurrection of Jesus should shake and awaken Christians to a new life that would bring death to injustice, racism, and sexism. It is by taking the biblical meaning of resurrection seriously as an event, that Christian has the challenge to realize here and now that Christians can truly and profoundly enliven Christian hope for the human existence.

According to Troeger, an earthquake occurred at the resurrection of Jesus. The earthquake in biblical language is more than a "geophysical phenomenon"[30] or the shaking of a mountain. Drawing from the works of Paul J. Achtemeier, a biblical scholar and theologian, Troeger stated: "On virtually every occasion that an earthquake appears in the Bible, it has a figurative dimensions of God's intervention."[31] At the death of Jesus, the gospel account was also clear that there was an earthquake, and the Gospel of Matthew specifically states:

> At that moment the curtain of the temple was torn in two, from top to bottom. The earth shook, and the rocks were split. The tombs also were opened, and many bodies of the saints who had fallen asleep were raised. After his resurrection they came out of the tombs and entered the holy city and appeared to many. Now when the centurion and those with him, who were keeping watch over Jesus saw the earthquake and what took place, they were terrified and said, "Truly this man was God's son!"[32]

Troeger's commented: "Biblical earthquakes portend the disruption of the ordered world of meaning by which we normally interpret life. An earthquake is the death of the illusion that we are in [control] of our existence. An earthquake in the Bible is the fragmentation of those certitudes that we thought would be fixed in place forever."[33] Modern scholars have suppressed the true meaning of the resurrection by embracing exclusively the joy of the resurrection to the neglect of its terror and true significance. Resurrection ought to take Christians with boldness to the "dark and uncharted land where solid meanings fold."[34] Thus, Christians in the modern era must not base their exuberant celebration of Easter on the Alleluia song of the resurrection if they grasped its profound meaning. Easter is diminished to a momentary delight if we celebrated the joy at the expense of the terror it brings to our sense of comfort. As agents of healing and reconciliation in a fractured world, Christians are not to linger in comfort, but are to proclaim the hope the event of the resurrection of Jesus demonstrates.

According to Troeger, the earliest gospel account of the resurrection ends not in joy but in terror. But so deeply wounded was the early Church that an augment to this terrible end was necessary to encode the resurrection of Jesus with a triumph. The original ending to the Gospel of Mark was 16:8 which reads: "So they went out and fled from the tomb, for terror and amazement had seized them; and they said nothing to anyone, for they were afraid." New Testament scholars in the modern era have affirmed consistently that Mark ended without a triumphant note. One of the patristic fathers in the fourth century also affirmed this view of the end of Mark.[35] It is not an unreasonable speculation to assume that early believers were not happy with the original ending of Mark. The terror of the resurrection was therefore replaced with the triumphant celebration that Jesus was alive so that believers went out and proclaimed the good news of the resurrection to everyone. Thus, believers were led to render the addition to Mark's Gospel. This new ending, according to Troeger, "transforms the story of resurrection so that it moves from terror to good news, from saying nothing to anyone because of fear, to spreading the word everywhere."[36]

The first ending and the addition to the ending were radical opposites. What is common to both endings is that death is no longer an absolute category of human existence. Death cannot have the final word. If death cannot have the final word, one can project that neither can human suffering, injustice, apartheid, racism and sexism. Troeger maintained that if death is overcome, if the one indestructible certitude that marks existence is shattered, then reality is wide open, and there is hope in the midst of every situation of hopelessness.[37] Thus, pessimism has not known the power of the resurrection. If death is overcome, all the pessimistic certitudes—which claim there would always be wars, there would always be oppression, there would always be apartheid, there would always be racism, and there would always be tribalism—come crumbling down. Resurrection is a terror to every oppressive assumption that debilitates our energies to establish a just and compassionate world. If death is overcome by the resurrection of Jesus Christ, then all forces of death such as fear, prejudice, hatred, violence, and abuse, will also meet the terror of the resurrection. Therefore, taking resurrection seriously means that Christians no longer have moral excuses for not making the world a better place that God intended, by raising Jesus from the dead.

In South Africa, the oppression of apartheid came into full force in 1948, when the National Party took into power under the Christian banner. Thus, the regimented power of politics became united with religious convictions. Nothing is as deadly as when religion is wedded to military might. In South Africa, the National Party did not want resurrection to take place, and in order to seal the tomb, the apartheid leaders fused together sword and controversial Calvinistic doctrines of predestination. This union of sword and creed became the most potent force for oppression for the majority of black South Africans. This unhealthy and diabolical marriage of politics and religious fervor gave birth to bigotry, racism, and the unjust laws of apartheid. The

South African parliament in the 1950s passed more laws to restrict the freedom and economic progress of the indigenous population than in any other decade of the apartheid years. The 1950s could also be seen as a period of transition and political ambiguity in South Africa. Most of the legislators were avowed Christians and members of the Dutch Reformed Church. The fear of the "resurrection" of the blacks in South Africa created a dark hole in the minority white politicians' Christian perception. Suddenly, however, there was a great earthquake in South Africa, for an angel of the Lord, descending from heaven, came and rolled back the stone that prevented resurrection, and sat upon it. The appearance of the angel was like lightning and his clothing white as snow. He feared no man. For the fear of him, however, the guards of apartheid shook and became dead.[38] Thus, the living guard of the tomb who would have kept the dead buried in the ground became dead. The dead who were supposed to stay dead became suddenly alive.

As the resurrection of Jesus crushed the power of death, the potency of apartheid was brought to an end when Nelson Mandela was elected Democratic President in 1994, and new life surfaced again for all the peoples of South Africa. Thus, the end of apartheid, just like the resurrection of Jesus, paralyzed the very powers that the religious and political establishments depended upon to maintain the oppressive and unjust rule. Furthermore, the resurrection of Jesus destabilized the power center in Jerusalem and disrupted the courts and the temples, for the terror of resurrection could not be ignored. Likewise, South Africa could not ignore the dismantling of apartheid, and the wave of this "South African resurrection" and its "terror" for the minority political leaders was felt worldwide. The historical event of Mandela's election in April 1994 symbolized the demise of apartheid. Resurrection brings terror to death. It means that death is dead. Likewise, the demise of apartheid brings terror to the system of injustice everywhere. It means that the cause of death for the majority in South Africa is dead. Perhaps the architect of apartheid, such as Hendrik Verwoerd, could not have imagined that apartheid structure would die. When it was in place, it brought certitude to the minds that had framed it, as if it was fixed in place forever. Its demise means death to the illusion that the National Party would always control South Africa. The National Party banned ANC in 1960, as if it would never rise again to bring hope and a new life to the majority of South Africans. The ANC was dead and went underground in a symbolic burial. But the African National Congress could not stay buried forever because there is the God of resurrection and of life.

In *God's Wrathful Children: Political Oppression and Christian Ethics* (1995) Willa Boesak argued that God's anger against oppression and the evil system of apartheid was carried out vicariously through the children of God in South Africa. While the black South Africans should not seek or demand revenge for their oppression, the oppressors are responsible for appeasing the majority of South Africans. This, however, is with the understanding that nothing could ameliorate the harm and injuries the oppressors have inflicted on the oppressed. Boesak maintained in the study that the oppressed and oppressors cannot be in a state of healthy relationship unless the oppressed are appeased by the retribution of the oppressors in a constructive reconciliatory ethic.[39]

Nelson Mandela and the Resurrection

If the end of apartheid brought a true re-birth to the peoples of South Africa, what does the resurrection of Jesus mean in the new context? The process of moving from terror to good news would not be complete until Christians of every age recognize the significance of the paradoxical dimension of the Christian religion. The Christian faith is not only about the good news. It is also about the bad news, and the terror that takes believers away from the good news from time to time and brings them to the moments of creative doubts and of accepting their responsibilities in the world. Christians are responsible, therefore, for being the embodiment of the good news through fear and trembling. Staying in the mode of fear and terror, however, is a sign of hopelessness, the opposite of faith. Therefore, the good news will be complete only when it is balanced with the paradox of terror.

If Christians were to proclaim the message of the resurrection without considering the terror it unleashed in a society that feels comfortable with worldly power and possessions, it would mean that the Christian proclamation is in vain and that our preaching is devoid of eternal value. When there is a wedded paradoxical dimension of resurrection and terror, then reality in the Christian world will be rearranged, and Christians will regain a sense of renewal and of faith and identity. When apartheid crumbled, all the Dutch Reformed Church's excuses for not acting quickly to bring about social transformation in South Africa also crumbled.

The Church today, both in South Africa and beyond, needs to make a painful confession, because every page in the history of the Church is wet with her leaders' compromises and inaction in the face of oppression and injustice. It is as if the book of James was never a part of the canon.[40] The Church, though claiming and proclaiming the resurrection, is guilty of suppressing the fruits of the resurrection. Thomas Troeger put it this way: "Although claiming to believe in the resurrection, [the Church] has often been the first to post a guard of soldiers at the corner of the heart to make sure there would be no resurrection, no disturbance of the ground of solid meaning."[41] There are numerous examples of the Church, preventing the emergence of the new life through resurrection, and four examples are particularly obvious.

First, the Ptolemaic astronomers saw the earth at the center of the universe and explained the movement of planets by postulating "epicycles." By the time of the flowering of the Ptolemaic view, the growing number of epicycles started to render the Ptolemaic view less and less plausible. But the Roman Catholic Church held tenaciously to the Ptolemaic view, even when scientific evidence indicated otherwise. It was Nicolas Copernicus (1473–1543), the Polish astronomer, who first challenged the Medieval Roman Catholic Church and her world-view with the theory that the universe was centered on the sun—and not the earth. According to him, "in the middle of all sits the sun on his throne, as upon a royal dais ruling his children [the planets] which circle about him." Galileo Galilei (1564–1642), the Italian astronomer and physicist, followed Copernicus. By observation, he argued that the planets revolve around the sun. This assertion evoked a conflict between Galileo and the Church, securing for him a conflict with the Pope himself. Coming under fire with the inquisition for writing in favor of the Copernicus' theory, Pope Urban VIII placed Galileo under house arrest in 1638. Contemporary scholars of the Inquisition have maintained that Galileo's own obstreperous personality was partly to blame for his humiliating treatment by the Church. They have maintained that Galileo could not have been acquitted without undermining the integrity of the Roman Inquisition. One continues to wonder, however, why it took centuries before the Church finally exonerated Galileo. His books were banned, and he became broken-hearted and went blind. He died at Florence in 1642. In 1992, 350 years after Galileo's death, the Roman Catholic Church made a statement that Galileo was right in his views, and that the theory that the sun was indeed at the center of the universe (not the earth) was credible. Thus, the Church finally abrogated the Ptolemaic cosmology and Galileo was vindicated. But the Church held to the Ptolemaic erroneous view for over a thousand years.[42] When the Copernicus' view was initially confirmed by Galileo Galilei's theory in the early 1600s, the Church's opposition was vehement and venomous. Hence, Faith and Science started to see each other as enemies in the mirror. Faith started seeing Science as sinking in ignorance, lust, and violence with the heart of Lucifer. Science began to see Faith, on the other hand, as defective because it underestimated the scientific capacity to interpret the world created by God. There is a long tradition of atavistic hatred between Science and the Christendom in the West, but there is no place here to follow the twisted paths of the animosity between them without underestimating the intractable web of problems associated with their relationships.

What is more relevant to this study, however, is that the Church has frequently closed the gateway for progress in the spirit of the resurrection. The

Church often posted guards of soldiers, rolling the Scriptures like a stone over the human heart in an attempt to stop the power of the resurrection and the new life of scientific inquiry.

Second, from the 17th through the 19th century, over eleven million Africans (predominantly from West and Central Africa) were transported to the Western world as slaves. It is estimated that for every slave that crossed the Atlantic Ocean successfully, another died in transit.[43] Although slavery has been an integral part of countless societies, from ancient Greece to the American South of a little over a century ago, slavery continued for so long because of the silence of the Church. A systematic subjugation and exploitation of human beings by other human beings, slavery was particularly endorsed in the country that was regarded as the heartland of Christianity— England. But the Abolitionist Movement also started in England beginning in the 18th century.[44] Although Africans had known slavery and slave trading before the coming of Europeans, the scale and finality of an export trade across the Atlantic was something new, causing humiliation for blacks and a recollection of veiled or acknowledged sin for whites. The ideological elements that sustained slavery were not only the philosophy of Aristotle and economic dictates but also religion. The Christian interpretation of certain passages of the New Testament that seem to support slavery paved the way for the justification of slavery. Societies that did not accept the Abolitionist Movements were not limited to the Arabs in East Africa; they also included the Christian Belgian and the Southerners of the United States, who struggled to preserve their dominant position through bloody confrontations in American Civil war.

The success of Christianity for each generation depends not only on the eloquent believers stating their convictions, but also on how ordinary Christians conceive and translate Christianity into the human existential condition or daily lives. In other words, the most important manifestation of Christianity will not be only in words, but also in deeds.

When the abolitionists pushed for an end to slavery in the United States, there were preachers in the South who posted a guard of soldiers, as it were, rolling the Bible as the Church did during the Copernican revolution to block the power of resurrection. The Church wanted to block the power of a new life that was stirring people to claim the God-given right of freedom and dignity for the black people.[45] During the Civil Rights Movements, and in anticipation that black people could be free and Public Schools desegregated, many private Christian schools started to emerge in the South. There is no doubt that the intention was to keep black students out of these private institutions, with the claim that, as private schools, they reserved the rights of entrance for students.

Third, the Holocaust has defined the Jewish history of modern era the way slavery defined the black people. When Jewish people needed help to survive during World War II, very few Christians came to their rescue.

The Church in Rome cited the "Jewish problem" as an excuse, namely, the question of why God permitted Jews to continue to exist despite the fact that, as Christians saw it, Christians had replaced the Jews as God's chosen people. From the sixth century on, the popes had turned to the negative witness theory. This theory was developed originally by Saint Augustine of Hippo (354–430 C.E.), who suggested that it was God's will that Jews wander the Earth without a home, their impoverished existence functioning as a negative witness that proved the superiority and the truth of Christianity.[46] Scholars have maintained that this "negative witness theory" became the operative papal strategy for dealing with the "Jewish problem" in medieval Christendom.[47] Before Vatican II (1962–1965), the popes followed a paradoxical policy of preaching that God had rejected the Jews and simultaneously acting as Jews' legal protectors and guardians, insisting that they not be physically harmed. Thus, discriminating against the Jews and nurturing them at the same time was seen as part of God's will. Just as the Church kept silence during the plight of the Jews during World War II, the Church is now silent about the plight of the Palestinians, who have replaced the Jewish people as a displaced people in the Middle East. Few post-Holocaust Jewish and Christian scholars are critical of the Zionist Movement in its measure against the Palestinian people. Marc Ellis is one of the few Jewish scholars whose vision has transcended the present pain and agony of both the Palestinians and the Jews in the Holy Land. He has argued consistently that the suffering of the Jews during the Holocaust must never be an excuse for the oppression of their Palestinian and Christian neighbors.[48] Jews must remember that the covenant relationship with God, and with the land, is consistent with a demand for justice and compassion toward the stranger.[49] Therefore, Jews must not only accept each other in their diversity, they must also accept their Christian and Muslim Palestinian neighbors in "Jerusalem" in a way that promotes justice and peace for all. Such a task would not be easy, but it is consistent with the demands of life that has experienced resurrection.[50] If the Jews and the Palestinians failed to practice justice, and if neither had no peace, it is because they have neglected that they belong to each other.

There have been Christians in the Middle East who have posted guard of soldiers, as in the era of slavery, rolling the word of God like a stone over the human hearts in an attempt to block the power of resurrection, and the power of a new life that demanded the recognition of dignity for both Jews and Palestinians.

Finally, there was the apartheid in South Africa. While the hidden curse of Christianity in the nineteenth century was slavery, and while the hidden curse of Christianity during World War II was the Holocaust, the hidden curse of Christianity in the twentieth century was apartheid under the banner of the cross.

The Afrikaners are a unique people in South Africa. Their language of Afrikaans evolved over 200 years and is based on the high Dutch spoken by the early settlers in the Cape. They gradually moved inland and established themselves as farmers.[51] The Dutch Reformed Church, to which most Afrikaners belong and which preaches Predestination, a part of Calvinistic Christianity based on the Old Testament teachings, has long been removed from the majority of the world's Protestant communities. The Afrikaners, however, structured South Africa on the basis of race, although the preparatory roads included the colonization of South Africa by the British. The word apartheid is coined from two French words—*à part* and *heid*. The two words together mean apartness or separateness. The Zulus, the Swazi, the Xhosa and the Themba, collectively known as the Uguni people, were to be separated from the white settlers. The argument for the separation was based on the illusion that it was the Afrikaners who first settled in the Southern cone of the continent of Africa, that it was they who fought for the land and farmed it, and that it was they who initiated the huge developments that made South Africa prosperous.[52]

What made the segregation firm, however, was the religious tone infused into the subjugation. These ambitious Christians believed that they were God's chosen people. In 1857, there was an important decision of the synod of the DRC. The synod went public and stated:

> The synod considers it desirable and according to the Holy Scripture that our "heathen" members be accepted and initiated into our congregations wherever it is possible; but where this measure, as a result of the weakness of some, would stand in the way of promoting the work of Christ among the heathen people, then congregations set up among the heathen or still to be set up, should enjoy their Christian privileges in a separate building or institution.[53]

These segregationist Christians believed that they were God's chosen people and that God had ordained South Africa to be their land. The incursion of Afrikaners at the battle of Blood River in 1838 and their victory on the 16th of December that year secured their confidence that God was with them. They did not see their victory as a result of a sudden attack against the ill prepared Zulus and a demonstration of their military strategy at the *Ncome River;* instead, they wrapped the victory in an aura of divine approval.

The culmination of their bravery came in 1976 (over a century after the synod of the DRC) when Afrikaners attempted, but ultimately failed, to impose their language on the rest of the population. Pushing the indigenous population too far became the beginning of the end for these soldiers of God on the African soil. But the scale of callousness and oppression in South Africa was intergenerational. The wedding of the political might with religion on such a scale did not last. The Christ that cannot be sealed in the grave cannot be sealed in the book, even the Bible. That the same book that gives witness to the living Christ could be misused to try to keep the indigenous population of South Africans buried in injustice should not be a surprise. What is rather baffling is that the Bible was conscripted to sustain apartheid for so long.

Although the Bible is an important book of instruction for Christian living, Christians are not to employ it as a definitive answer to all human sickness and quandaries. Even the *sola scriptura* proclaimed by Martin Luther (1483–1546) could not be properly translated "scripture alone, because structurally and practically, it means scriptures preeminently in matters of faith and practice. If the scriptures were to be final, then God is limited to and contained within the Bible. The prevailing assumption among scholars, however, is that even the Bible is an account and record of believers who encountered God through their experience.[54] Thus, the Bible was misused in South Africa and became like a stone to keep the risen Christ, as it were, away from the existential condition of the people. This way, the risen Lord was to be prevented from disrupting the world created by apartheid. The words of David Buttrick are straight to the point:

> Frequently biblical preaching has told a biblical story replete with oodles of biblical background, a "holy history," but has not permitted God to step out of the biblical world into human history. The God of biblical preaching has been a past tense God of past-tense events whose past-tense truth may be applied to the world, while God remains hidden within a gilt-edged book.[55]

Thomas H. Troeger reiterated this point by stating that Christians today must ask the difficult question of where Christ, the resurrected Lord, is in the life of the Church. How can the Church move beyond the Jesus of yesterday to the Living Lord of today?[56] How can Christians recognize Christ today and renew their faith and identity?

One of the ways to interpret the resurrection for believers and non-believers alike is to see the resurrection of Jesus as a provision of new possibility for those who are not trained as Christians to bring Christ to the Church through the back door. In other words, certain anonymous Christians who have never been to Church are not necessarily incapable of meeting Christ and bringing him to the Christendom. In this case, the modern history of South African has shown that there have been several people who have been discarded by the Church but who have interpreted Christianity for our generation. Nelson Mandela, for example, has exercised a superior sense of forgiveness that seems almost humanly impossible. But this is consistent with the resurrection story in the New Testament, where those who ate with Jesus and talked with him failed to recognize him. Those who have merely heard of him but were not disciples believed Jesus and acknowledged him. Three examples of the post-resurrection appearances illustrate this interpretation.

In Luke's gospel, the women went to the tomb. The narrative is very clear:

> The women were terrified and bowed their faces to the ground, but the men said to them, "Why do you look for the living among the dead? He is not here, but has risen. Remember how he told you, while he was still in Galilee, that the Son of Man must be handed over to sinners, and be crucified, and on the third day rise again." Then they remembered his words, and returning from the tomb, they told all this to the eleven and to all the rest.[57]

Luke continued that, on the way to Emmaus, the Lord himself appeared to the disciples, but they did not recognize him. They then narrated the story of his crucifixion, and it was only when he broke bread with them that they realized who he was. So those who assumed that they knew the Savior failed to recognize him, and it was left to a "stranger" to make him known again for the first time.

In another instance in Luke, Jesus was in the midst of the disciples, and they were talking about what happened to him, but they all failed to recognize him. Then Jesus said: "Peace be with you."[58] Then they were startled and terrified, and thought that they were seeing a ghost.

In John's account, he appeared to Mary, but she did not recognize him because she was consumed by sorrow. Mary took Jesus to be a gardener, and Jesus said to her: "Woman, why are you weeping?" It was after Jesus called her by name that she heard the familiar voice and finally recognized Jesus.

Another account of the appearance occurred on the Sabbath and the doors where the disciples gathered were closed. But again, the disciples did not immediately recognize him until he said to them: "Peace be with you."[59]

In most of the accounts of the post-resurrection appearances, the followers of Jesus did not immediately recognize him. Lost in despair, anger, helplessness about the brutal injustice of the political and religious power systems, they became blinded. Thus, those who were the closest to Jesus became the farthest from him in the post-resurrection appearances, and they needed to be reintroduced to Jesus again by the Lord who posed to them as a stranger. Could it be that every generation of believers of Christ often needed to be reintroduced to the Lord by someone outside the sphere of the Christian influence? Perhaps Nelson Mandela served this purpose to South Africans. Members of the Christian Church, especially the Dutch Reformed

Church, that was purportedly closer to Jesus and was supposedly the ambassador of God in the society, supported the unjust system of apartheid and many determined to extinguish the light of the hope in the resurrection of the majority. The political leaders in the country, who were nurtured by the Church, defended the oppression of the majority on religious grounds. It was Nelson Mandela, who was not necessarily an insider of the Dutch Reformed Church, who pointed the attention of the Christians in South Africa (and in the world) to the true meaning and existential significance of the resurrection. In a concrete way, Mandela joined the disciples in a spirit that forgives them and pointed their way to the meaning of Christian humanism. Likewise, Christians have been called to be peacemakers in a culture of wars, destruction, and death, to bring reconciliation, healing, and resurrection.

Thomas H. Troeger's interpretation of the post-resurrection appearances pointed to a new direction when he stated: "the stranger always speaks first."[60] In the case of the two walking on the way to Emmaus in Luke, it was the stranger who approached them and said: "What are you discussing with each other while you walk along? They stood still, looking sad. Then one of them, whose name was Cleopas, answered him, 'Are you the only *stranger* in Jerusalem who does not know the things that have taken place there in these days?'"[61] In the case of the appearance to Mary, recorded in John's Gospel, it was the stranger who asked: "Woman, why are you weeping? Who are you looking for?"[62] And in the case of the disciples meeting when the door was closed, as recorded in Luke, it was the stranger who came and stood among them and said: "Peace be with you."[63]

A Summary

Jesus appeared when he was least expected. In South Africa, the resurrection of Jesus could be translated existentially to mean that when Christians least expected their liberation, God demonstrated his power of resurrection. Thus, empowerment replaced hopelessness for South African majority population, and the pain of grief, suffering, and death was replaced by a spiritual transformation. Perhaps the resurrection of Jesus Christ and the emancipation of the people of South Africa from the shackles of apartheid have ethical and theological implications for the Church of the twenty-first century. Three aspects of this implication can be enumerated:

First, God has the ability to empower those that are not within the Church tradition to reintroduce to the Church the true meaning of certain aspects of the Christian faith. Therefore, the dichotomy the Church has created between ecclesiology (the doctrine of the Church) and pneumatology (the doctrine of the Holy Spirit leading God's creation to new transformation) is a false dichotomy.

Second, the Church is at her best when there is recognition that the truth of God is not localized within the walls of the Church alone. When the Church becomes territorial, she loses her influence in the world. There are "strangers" outside the Church that are empowered to proclaim the message of Christ, and the Church would be judicious to listen to their proclamation. These "strangers" could include Muslims and Jews, Buddhists, and Hindus, Christians and secularists. Thus, the Church must read beyond the Bible, but not against it. While the Church could go beyond the Bible, it should not go beyond the kerygma or the proclamation of the Scriptures.

Finally, there will always be hope in Christ and in his resurrection. The Christian faith, therefore, is not only a religion of faith and love. Ultimately, it is also a religion of hope in the midst of hopelessness. Hence, Christians are summoned to be as courageous as lions in a hostile world. Although believers should not always expect to receive justice in this world, they should never stop practicing justice, compassion, love, and forgiveness. Perhaps the greatest lesson of Nelson Mandela is the last. It is a new way of being human. Christians in South Africa did not take Christ to Nelson Mandela, but Mandela took Christ to them. This is because of his extraordinary spirit of forgiveness towards those who imprisoned and wounded him and those that he loved.

It would be arrogant for the Church of the intergenerational faith to think that she possesses the truth or can control Christ. Instead, the Church would regain its vitality when believers begin to see the need to be open to strangers, not just to tolerate them. Sometimes the strangers might just turn out to be the risen Christ that the Church needs for renewal and recapitulation of her identity in the world. It would be arrogant for believers to say that they have found Christ in the practice of their religions. Christ found believers and he wanted them to live for him in their day-to-day lives. Thus, believers would become energized and irrepressible witnesses of Christ in this era. It is in this way that the resurrection of Jesus would start to become a living story rather than a past event.

From what we know of Christianity in Africa, it is not a religion of speculation but of a living remembrance. Christianity in Africa has regained it vitality and enthusiasm because of the hope that the resurrection of Jesus has provided in South Africans' existence. Nothing demonstrates this more eloquently than in their songs and in their stories. The Evangelical Christians in Ghana composed and spiritedly sing a song about their new identity; the song has been translated from Ewe and has entered many Christian hymnbooks in the West:

Je-su, Je-su, fill us with your love, show us how to serve
the neighbors we have from you.

(1) Kneels at the feet of his friends, silently washes their feet,
Master who acts as a slave to them.

(2) Neighbors are rich and poor, varied in color and race,
Neighbors are near and far away

(3) These are the ones we should serve; these are the ones we should love;
all these are neighbors to us and you.

(4) Loving puts us on our knees, serving as though we are slaves,
this is the way we should live with you.

(5) Kneel at the feet of our friends, silently washing their feet,
this is the way we should live with you.

Je-su, Je-su, fill us with your love, show us how to serve
the neighbors we have from you.[64]

Notes

[1] Tristan Anne Borer. *Challenging the State: Churches as Political Actors in South Africa 1980–1994.* (Indiana: University of Notre Dame Press, 1998), 171.

[2] See Job 14:14.

[3] Pinchus Lapide, *The Resurrection of Jesus: A Jewish Perspective* (S.P.C.K., 1984), 124.

[4] John Macquarrie, "The Keystone of Christian Faith" in *If Christ be not risen: Essays in Resurrection and Survival,* eds. John Greenhalgh and Elizabeth Russell. (San Francisco, California: Collins Liturgical, 1986), 10.

[5] Desmond Tutu, *The Rainbow People of God: South Africa's Victory Over apartheid.* (New York: Doubleday, 1994).

[6] Rudolf Bultman, for example, claimed that "the resurrection was the proclamation of the Church that Christ lives on and his words still summon men and women to decision of faith." For the details, see Rudolf Bultman, *Jesus Christ and Mythology* (1966). See also, John Macquarrie, "The Keystone of Christian Faith (1986), pp. 19ff. More recently, John Shelby Spong in *Resurrection: Myth or Reality* (1995) raised a similar issue but maintained the significance of the resurrection while re-interpreting its categories for modern Christians. Spong claims the true meaning of Easter is beyond a bodily resurrection. For the details, see John Shelby Spong, *Resurrection Myth or Reality: A Bishop's Search for the Origins of Christianity.* (San Francisco: Harper Collins Publishers, 1995).

[7] Pinchus Lapide, *The Resurrection of Jesus: A Jewish Perspective* (S.P.C.K., 1984), 125.

[8] Pinchus Lapide, *The Resurrection of Jesus: A Jewish Perspective* (S.P.C.K., 1984), 19. See also Rudolf Bultman, *Jesus Christ and Mythology* (1966).

[9] Pinchus Lapide, *The Resurrection of Jesus: A Jewish Perspective* (S.P.C.K., 1984), 125.

[10] Pinchus Lapide, *The Resurrection of Jesus: A Jewish Perspective* (S.P.C.K., 1984), 125.

[11] Douglas W. Waruta, "Who is Jesus Christ for Africans Today? Prophet, Priest, Potentate" in *Faces of Jesus in Africa*, Robert J. Schreiter, ed. (Maryknoll, New York: Orbis Books, 1991), 62.

[12] John 20:24–26. See also Charles Colson, *Loving God* (1982), 68.

[13] See Luke 23 and 24.

[14] Charles Colson, Loving God, 68.

[15] See, Rudolf Bultman, *Jesus Christ and Mythology* (New York: Clark Publishing, 1969).

[16] Blaise Pascal, *Pensees*, translated by A. J. Krailsheimer (New York: Penguin Classic, 1966), 125.

[17] In 1999, the author collaborated with administrative officials at Baylor University to invite the Archbishop of Cape Town, the Most Reverend Desmond Tutu, to the University. Tutu gave an inaugural lecture of the Presidential Forum on September 13 and, in the presence of an enthusiastic audience, Tutu stated that the end of apartheid without a civil war in South Africa was a modern miracle in his Country's modern history. Four years before Tutu's lecture at the University (1995), the first "full democracy" President of South Africa, Nelson Mandela, appointed Tutu to serve as the chairman of the Truth and Reconciliation Commission (TRC). The commission became a model in the world for looking into the past atrocities committed on political grounds and was empowered to grant amnesty if the perpetrators were to come forward and confess to the political crimes they committed, and face the victims or their families. The full report was given to President Thabo Mbeki in 2003, who succeeded Nelson Mandela in 1999 as the President of South Africa.

[18] Isaiah 25:8.

[19] Mark 12:18–27.

[20] Michael C. Kirwen, *The Missionary and the Diviner* (Maryknoll, New York: Orbis Books, 1986).

[21] Ibid. 107–131.

[22] John S. Mbiti, *African Religions and Philosophy* (New York: Praeger, 1969), 1–5, 15. See also James L. Sibley and D. Westermann, *Liberia Old and New* (London: James Clark, 1928), 187–88; Willie Abraham, *The Mind of Africa* (Chicago: University of Chicago Press, 1962), p. 52; Robert T. Parsons, *Religion in an African Society* (Leiden: E. J. Brill, 1964), p. 173–76, 179, 183–85; Geoffrey Parrinder, *Religion in Africa* (Middlesex, England: Penguin, 1969), chapters 2–6; Placinde Temples, *Bantu Philosophy,* translated from French by Colin King (Paris: Presence Africaine, 1959); and Margaret Washington Creel "Gullah Attitudes Toward Life and Death" in ed. Joseph E. Holloway, *Africanisms in American Culture* (Bloomington, Indiana: Indiana University Press, 1990), 69–97.

[23] Michael C. Kirwen, *The Missionary and the Diviner,* 112.

[24] Ibid.

[25] Michael C. Kirwen, *The Missionary and the Diviner,* 128.

[26] Michael C. Kirwen, *The Missionary and the Diviner,* 122.

[27] Ibid. 128.

[28] Ibid. 129.

[29] Thomas H. Troeger has argued consistently that the resurrection of Jesus needs fresh interpretation for modern Christians. A faithful and respected scholar of the Bible, his interpretation is closer to the views that I have articulated about the resurrection although we worked independently of each other. It was my honor to finally meet him when he came to the Baptist Theological Seminary at Richmond as the Keynote speaker at our annual preaching conference in April 2004. I depend heavily on his ideas of the resurrection of Jesus because of his robust ideas and his giftedness. See for example, his work: *Borrowed Light: Hymn texts, prayers, and poems* (New York: Oxford University Press, 1994).

[30] Thomas H. Troeger, "Solid Meanings Fold: The Terror of Resurrection." *Keynote address at the 2004 Worship and Preaching Conference* (Baptist Theological Seminary at Richmond, 2004).

[31] See Paul J. Achtemeier, *Harper's Bible Dictionary,* (HarperSanFrancisco, 1985), 232–33.

[32] Matthew 27:51–54.

[33] Thomas Troeger, "Solid Meanings Fold: The Terror of Resurrection," unpaginated.

[34] Ibid.

[35] James L. Mays also stated that Eusebius and Jerome "held that Mark ended at 16:8." See James L. Mays, General Editor, *Harper's Bible Commentary,* (HarperSanFrancisco, 1988), 985.

[36] Thomas H. Troeger, "Solid Meanings Fold: The Terror of Resurrection," unpaginated.

[37] Ibid.

[38] See Matthew 28:2–4. In this passage, the Gospel describes the resurrection of Jesus Christ and it is adopted here because of its similarities with apartheid and its end in South Africa.

[39] Willa Boesak, *God's Wrathful Children: Political Oppression and Christian Ethics* (William B. Eerdmans Publishing Company, 1995).

[40] The Book of James is regarded as one of the most practical books of the New Testament about Christian living. It exudes faith balanced by good works as a way of proclaiming gratitude to God for redemption. It is the only book in the New Testament that challenges believers (1:22) to be doers of the word, and not merely hearers who deceive themselves. The letter defined religion that is pure and undefiled before God the Father as a religion that cares for orphans and widows in their distress, and that assists one to keep oneself unstained by the world. In 2:17 we read: "So faith by itself, if it has no works, is dead." In a rhetorical statement the writer of the letter stated in 2:18: "But someone will say, 'You have faith and I have works.' Show me your faith apart from your works, and I by my works will show you my faith."

[41] Thomas H. Troeger, "Solid Meanings Fold: The Terror of Resurrection." Keynote Address at the Worship and Preaching Conference at the Baptist Theological Seminary at Richmond (April, 2004), unpaginated.

[42] See Gavin D'Costa, *Theology and Religious Pluralism* (Blackwell, 1986), 22–51. Thomas S. Kuhn wrote a more comprehensive treatment of this in *The Copernican Revolution: Planetary Astronomy in the Development of Western Thought,* (Cambridge, Massachusetts: Harvard University Press, 1957, renewed in 1985).

[43] See Joseph E. Holloway, "The Origins of African-American Culture," in Joseph E. Holloway, ed. *Africanisms in American Culture* (Bloomington, Indiana: Indiana University Press, 1990): 1–18.

[44] Philip D. Curtin's work on Slavery has documented the statistics of Trans-Atlantic Slavery. See Philip D. Curtin, *The Atlantic Slave Trade: A Census* (Madison: University of Wisconsin Press, 1969). See also Susanne Everett, *History of Slavery* (Secaucus, New Jersey: Chartwell Books, Inc., 1991); and Basil Davidson, *The African Slave Trade* (Atlantic-Little Brown, 1961).

[45] Thomas H. Troeger, "Solid Meanings Fold: The Terror of Resurrection." unpaginated.

[46] See John L. Esposito, Darrell J. Fasching and Todd Lewis, *World Religions Today* (New York: Oxford University Press, 2002), 145.

[47] Ibid.

[48] See Marc H. Ellis, *Unholy Alliance: Religion and Atrocity in our Time* (Minneapolis, Minnesota: Fortress Press, 1997). See also *Revolutionary Forgiveness: Essays on Judaism, Christianity, and the Future of Religious Life* (Waco, Texas: Baylor University Press, 2000). In his more recent work, *Out of the Ashes: The Search for Jewish Identity in the Twenty-First Century* (London: Pluto Press, 2002), Ellis challenged the Jewish faith by affirming that it is con-

sistent with the covenant the Jewish people made with God to be magnanimous towards those who do not share their beliefs and religious values.

[49] See Marc H. Ellis, *O, Jerusalem! The Contested Future of the Jewish Covenant* (Minneapolis, Minnesota: Fortress Press, 1999).

[50] See Marc H. Ellis, *Practicing Exile: The Religious Odyssey of an American Jew* (Minneapolis, Minnesota: Fortress Press, 2002). See also, Paul Johnson, *A History of the Jews* (New York: Harper and Row, 1987), and Jacob Neusner, *Self-Fulfilling Prophecy: Exile and Return in the History of Judaism* (Boston: Beacon Press, 1987).

[51] See Leonard Thompson, *A History of South Africa* (New Haven, Connecticut: Yale University Press, 1995), 31–153.

[52] Leonard Thompson, *A History of South Africa,* (New Haven, Connecticut: Yale University Press, 1995), 70–153.

[53] H. Russell Botman, "The Offender and the Church" in James Cochrane, John de Gruchy, and Stephen Martin, eds. *Facing the Truth: South African Faith Communities and the Truth and Reconciliation Commission* (Cape Town: David Philip Publishers, 1999), 137.

[54] This interpretation is at variance, if not at odd, against modern interpreters. See John 21:25.

[55] David Buttrick, Homiletic: Moves and Structures (Philadelphia: Fortress Press, 1987), 18.

[56] Thomas H. Troeger, "Solid Meanings Fold: The Terror of Resurrection," unpaginated.

[57] Luke 24:5–9.

[58] Luke 24:36b.

[59] John 20:19.

[60] See Thomas H. Troeger, "True Meanings Fold: The Terror of the Resurrection," unpaginated.

[61] Luke 24:17–18.

[62] John 20:15.

[63] Luke 24:36.

[64] CHEREPONI. Words: Tom Colvin, 1969; Music: Ghana Folk song; arranged by Tom Colvin, 1969; harmony—Charles H. Webb, 1988. (Hope Publishing Co., 1989).

CONCLUSION

There are many things in life that are close to human hearts and no doubt religion is one of them. We have come to the conclusion of this study to find out that neither "Religion," the noun, nor "religious," the adjective, occurs in the Bible frequently in the real sense. The equivalent word does not appear frequently either, and this should not be surprising to scholars of the Bible. Perhaps one can say that religion is partly a body of beliefs associated with human beings in an attempt to be reconnection with the spiritual. The spiritual world is enshrined within the inner strength and vitality of human religious consciousness. Therefore, most human beings desire to be connected with the spirit. However, the Bible affirms again and again that it is how we are that matters most to God, not our affirmation of a particular religion.

Although the biblical world was interested in the spiritual world, most of the authors of the Bible were not specifically interested in religious systems or religious ideas. The fact that the word "religion" does not appear in the Bible frequently may also mean that the religious world of the biblical times was rather uniform in outlook and intention, despite local differences. What then was the people's interest in the Bible as a canonical text?

The Bible has always been more interested in humanity and his relationship with God and fellow human beings than in his religions; that is, human beings on earth are the major focus of the canonical Bible. The word "religion" is abstract, but religious people are concrete. Therefore, religion can only be real in religious people. There can be no religion without humanity because "being religious is part of being human."[1] It is difficult to find a human being without religion. Even atheism can be a form of religious expression—that one does not believe in a deity or a higher spiritual being to guide one's life does not mean that one does not believe in believing. On the other hand, Huston Smiths pointed in another direction when he stated: "a nation can assume that the phrase 'under God' in its Pledge of Allegiance shows that its citizens believe in God when all it really shows is that they believe in believing in God."[2]

It seems that true theoretical atheists may exist, but there cannot be many practical atheists. Yet certain elements of both exist in varying degrees in many religious thinkers. Whether one is a theoretical or a practical atheist, a human being without a "religion" or "religious notion" is a contradiction in terms.

One of the changes Christians have to make today, however, is a clear distinction between religion and the God of all humanity. In May 2002, scholars from all over the world gathered at the University of Aarhus, Denmark, to discuss this question. Their ideas and reflections on this question were published.[3] There is little doubt that the current map of our perception of God is inadequate, and this is reflected in the contributions of many theologians and some of the most exalted minds of our time that gathered at this conference in Denmark. In his concluding remarks, Viggo Mortensen, the leader of the conference, stated that Christians' mental pictures of God need a radical change. The Christian conception of God ought to be more elastic to make room for the people that traditional Western missionaries have deprived of natural spiritual basis through proselytizing. This would be consistent with the methods of early Christians who, after 70 C.E., determined that it was no longer conceivable to meet in the Temple. Mortensen stated: "After 70 it became clear to them that they would never again continue to meet together in the temple. They would never again hear the psalms of David sung in Hebrew in the right way. They would soon disobey the ritual rules of clean and unclean and start eating pork as the most natural thing in the world. Yes, the candlestick had indeed been moved.[4]

In one of his most quoted works, *Translating The Message: The Missionary Impact on Culture* (1989), Lamin Sanneh also insisted that the vernacular translation of the Bible is consistent with the nature of the Christian faith, and that, with every translation of the Bible by missionaries in Africa (with the cooperation of the indigenous people), God is given a new name.[5] Thus, the process of biblical translation has given validity to the indigenous spirituality. Through translation, the name for God in every culture is resurrected. Mortensen reiterated this significance by stating that the process of translation is a stage in the serial story of God, and that by the very fact that God is given many new names, there is a transformation of Christianity.[6]

The Christian faith has entered a new phase of its history. The new context of multi-culturalism and multi-religiosity requires a change in its interpretation of God and of the Christian intellectual map. This interpretation would include embracing an image of God who is not just present on Sundays, who does not only look after the hereafter, who is not just concerned about our salvation, but an almighty God who is with us, who is present in space, in the weather, in the clouds, in the fields, in people, and in all events in everyday life.[7] This is an age of spiritual questioning unmatched in the history of Christianity. Perhaps the Christian faith and its conception of God has now become like a small boat in danger of sinking. In certain unexpected places, this new and more inclusive intellectual map has already started to take shape, and African Christians are at the forefront.

One of the indirect consequences of apartheid in South Africa, for example, was the resurrection of the indigenous conception of God. Segregation by race was not only complete in apartheid years, but also made the indigenous people protective of their cultural norms and identity, as well as the eloquence of the local customs, including the perception of God. Protestant missionaries professed God and articulated the categories of Christianity as a religion. New faith in God, however, is a new dimension borne out of experience in South Africa, and the difference can be seen as follows:

Classical Christianity	*Modern Faith*
Emphasis on the transcendent God as King	Emphasis on the God with and within us as Friend
Jesus is on the right hand of God Above	Jesus is a close companion
Creation is sinful and estranged	Creation is fractured and wounded
Sin is individual lapses from religious paths	Sin is both personal and institutional
Public Prayer is promoted	Personal Meditation is encouraged
Body-Soul Dichotomized	Organic theme of the whole person
A dipolar worldview (this life and the next)	Life is a continuum (this life is a stage)
There is a need for forgiveness	There is a need to address systemic oppression
There is a religious duty to fulfill	There is a self-awareness of God in us
God is a Ruler and a Judge	God suffers in our struggles and pain
Focuses on understanding the Gospel	Focuses on experiencing God
Faith is presented as truth	Faith is presented as trust
Doubt is the opposite of Faith	Fear is the Opposite of Faith
Believers go through the narrow Gate	Believers embrace the wide mystery
Heaven is the reward	Living for God is rewarding
Believers possess the Truth now	Believers are being possessed by the truth

Goal oriented Religion	Process oriented Religiosity
Sin in the world is catastrophic	Sin in the world is educative
Human nature is tainted with corruption	Human nature is good
The world is heading in the wrong direction	The world has the capacity for progress
The world is an evil theater	The world is an opportunity to be good
Accent on Religious Propositions	Feeling God in the Existential reality
Authority comes through Religious institutions	Authority comes through loyalty to God
Gender role spiritual apportionment	No gender-specific roles in spirituality
Guidance of spiritual borders	Openers of spiritual borders
Mission is to win souls	Mission is for the whole person
Mission entails going to a new place	Mission entails going out of one-self
The Church is an Ecclesiastical structure	The Church is a Revolutionary Movement
Conservative in tradition	Progressive and dialogical in tradition
Passive in receiving	Active in receiving
Active in giving	Passive in giving
Consolidate the Past	Nurtures the Future
Anxious to take risks	Willingness to take Risks
Guards Doctrinal boundaries	Crosses Doctrinal boundaries
Concerned about protecting doctrines	Concerned about protecting life
Concealment of human vulnerability	Exposure of human vulnerability
Compulsively time oriented	Less time conscious
Competitions among religions	Co-operations among religions
Tendency to manipulate the environment	Adaptation to the Environment
Emphasis on doing	Emphasis on being
Salvation is individualistic	Salvation is personal
God's calling is for a task	God's calling is for discipleship
Dichotomistic thinking	Holistic thinking
Opposition is perceived as "Liberals"	Opposition is perceived as Uninformed

Emphasizes obedience to God	Emphasizes Relationships with God
By God's grace, God is on our side	By God's grace we are on God's side
Salvation Question: Do I believe in God?	God's Quest: Will God believe in me?
Places values on appearance	Places values on Substance[8]

A test of this generation will be whether Christians can develop a new concept of God that would embrace the column on the right above and satisfy modern spiritual direction and the curiosity about the divine. This means having "God who is present in all events in everyday life. Not until the gospel gains a foothold in all events in everyday life has the religious change been accomplished."[9]

Humanity and a New Perception of God

Human religious awareness gives an account of humanity's relation to God. Human religions are partly a projection upon the real or pretended revelation of God. In the modern era, with the process of globalization becoming intense, people in the West are more and more adopting the religions of the East, a sophisticated indication that human beings are "incurably religious." Relationship with the divine belongs to the very essence of humanity, and human beings can only be human in relation to God.

In the two volumes of the *Nature and Destiny of Man,* originally given as Gifford Lectures, the pastor-theologian Reinhold Niebuhr devoted scholarly attention to man as a creature; like all other creatures, he is completely dependent upon his creator, yet man is entirely different from all other creatures.[10] Thus, human beings are both at the top of the creation pyramid and a creation *sui generis,* bearing a secret that is only their secret.

Humans' secret is that we are created after the likeness of God. This expression means *a parte Dei,* meaning that human beings are a reflection of God.[11] If human beings are a mirror or *speculum Dei* (follower of God), and *a parte hominis* (called to have dominion over every living creature), it means that humanity is both a part of God's creation and humanity transcends creation at the same time. This relationship with God qualifies and strengthens human dignity. These two qualities of humanity assume a cosmotheandric[12] vision.

In terms of eschatology, this means that, from the outset, God has given to human beings what they are and will definitively become at the end, and this is their destiny.[13] They will actually or efficaciously become in the resurrected life what they have made of their destiny in the physical world of human habitation. This means that what God intended for human beings as their destiny becomes efficacious and dependent upon what they make of their destiny here below, in their relationship with God and with the cosmos. Stated another way, it means that human's relationship with God is incomplete apart from his relationship with his fellow human beings, and his relationship with the world. But as a creature, humanity can only bear and maintain his humanity in relationship with God. It is not up to humanity to ultimately cut off "the *imago Dei,* or the image of God imputed in him as if he could be God's creature apart from being in God's image." This also means that human beings cannot ultimately claim independence when they are completely dependent upon God. It is a part of human's responsibilities to recognize his dependence on God, and human religions are signs and confessions of the undeniable fact that humanity is dignified and renewed only in relation to God.

A Different Kind of Christianity

In the modern world, a believer is challenged to be a different kind of Christian. The views of non-Christians about Christ and human condition of suffering have the potential to enlarge the Christian's visions of his faith. Followers of other living faiths could influence Christians to be more reflective in their own spirituality in a way that was not clothed in ancient realities but consistent with the Gospel of hope.

One of the reasons why Christianity is strong in Africa is not because African Christians have a better understanding of the ways of Christ than non-Africans, but because they have creatively integrated their Africanness with their faith in the ways that only they can do. At the same time, they are thoroughly respectful of the Christian faith as articulated by their brothers and sisters in the Western world. Drawing from the rich resources of faith has made African Christians both secure and irrepressible in their proclamation. Drawing from the rich African cosmological vision as a way of enriching their understanding of God, is not a weakness but a new reality of our age. Excessive religious authority borne out of a concrete knowledge of the truth of Christianity, on the other hand, could freeze Christian progress and expansion—and thus would be the gateway to religious tyranny or anarchy.

It does not suffice to clothe Christianity in Western metaphors or in African metaphors, for this would indicate that one culture could be a gatekeeper of God's revelation, while other cultures could be outside of God's kingdom. One lesson that Christians in the modern era need to learn is that God had preceded the Evangelists, the pastors, the ministers and also, the missionaries. God is everywhere, and there will always be diverse ways of looking and interpreting the Christian faith. This is the nature of the Christian story itself.

Therefore, believers in the 21st-century will continue to see Christianity differently. They will graduate from yesterday's illusion of certainty—that the teachings of Christianity can be translated into other religious spheres without ambiguity or variation—to the understanding that many positions we have held about Christianity are less certain and that we need to learn more. Therefore, believers will renew their faith by seeing God's beauty in complexity. The ambiguity is of necessity for a greater depth of our knowledge of God and of the world.

The Christian faith has always been easier to share than to prove, and public certitude about religious teachings would continue to generate more heat than light. This is, in part, because epistemological criteria of right and wrong vision about our religions are soft and tender. It is more important as an epistemological criterion to be possessed by the truth of the mystery of God. Inner certitude of our faith is not impossible without a public proclamation or profession. The Christian faith at its most profound level is both a liberator and a burden. It is a liberator because of the new life in Christ, but it is also a burden because of the lingering human nature that has created oppression and religion fanatics.

Thus, Christians in the Western world as well as in the non-Western world can indeed learn from each other and draw from their criticisms of each other to enliven a perception of God and of the world. Religious expression is different from one region of the world to another, and so is the proclamation. We see echoes of Asian religions in Judaism, Christianity, and Islam—what a glorious overlaps. Yet, these religions are not the same.

Perhaps Christians are called to be ministers to this generation and to see that the missionary-sending West has not ceased to be a mission field itself, and that there are important lessons we could learn from those who do not believe in God the way we do. It would not be enough to castigate the non-Western world as a mission field, because Christians in Africa, Asia, and South America have become missionaries to the northern hemisphere, teaching many Christians in the West those ancient Christian values of modesty and of Christian living not characterized by a strong desire to gain and possess. As they plant immigrant Churches in the northern hemisphere and define Christianity through a different idiom, their language of faith and their irrepressible zeal would continue to show that Jesus is the transparent embodiment of God's vision for humanity. For them and for all Christians, the coming of Jesus into the world was not like an airplane trying to find a place for a perfect landing. Rather, the coming of Christ into the world was like a bomb that has created its own landing place in the hearts of humanity.

Yet Christian conversations cannot set limits to the universal saving power of God, as many Christians have done over the centuries. Their humble boldness, based on an encounter with suffering in the world—often at the hands of those who have professed the same faith as they do—has created a need for the renewal of the Christian identity. Unlike many Christians in the Western world who have the ideological notion that whatever is good for them is good for Christians elsewhere in the world, these new "missionaries" to the Western world take with them a new proposition that suggests that "whatever is good for other Christians in the world, is also good for Christians in the West."

The new immigrant Churches that are now a reflection of the two-third world Christian identity in the West are utterly different from the traditional Christian Protestantism. Among other characteristics, their liturgical liveliness sets them apart. But what has been so new to us in the West, that Christians of different historical and cultural backgrounds have brought from the non-Western world, has the potential to engage Christians in the West, and hold forth the promise of enriching and transforming our own Christian identity in a positive way. Thus, the circles of our Christian identity and story would be enhanced when they overlap with the circles of others, so that both could be transformed. These immigrant Churches represent a reformation in our era.

Christianity interpreted this way would be threatening to the concept of what it is to be a missionary. This is partly because missionaries will cease to have geographical, linguistic, or cultural boundaries. This will also bring transformation because God has not established that a particular region, or language or culture is effectively a gatekeeper of the kingdom. The Church that was founded by Jesus of Nazareth was a community of persons and individuals, old and young, schooled and unschooled, each one called as he really is, each one ordained a missionary to give to the world what he or she really has. Christians are not to learn someone else's skills, or to project a personality they do not have, or to say words that are not their words, or to do anything at all that is fundamentally alien to who and what they are.

It is no enmity to our Christian heritage to believe that the past did not exhaust God. And there is no disloyalty to the Christians of antiquity for modern Christians to believe that the best days of Christianity are ahead. Unless it prepared the way for a better Christian future, the past was not a helpful past, and only those Christian values of love, freedom of the oppressed, forgiveness, compassion, and mercy, can make ready for better things to come.

Christians could exercise a disloyalty to the past—by believing that all the great events of Christianity were in the past. Perhaps the worst disloyalty to the past is to say that the past was also the future, as if God were no longer active in communicating what is divinity to humanity. Very great and glorious that past might have been, if it binds believers forever in the chains of its institutional forms and ecclesiastical traditions, it would have failed to teach Christians its lessons, and it would have failed to fulfill its mission in the will of God. Furthermore, if the past Christian tradition binds believers forever in its doctrines, it would have failed by not making them ready for a larger and a more complete truth, leading to such a unity as Christ himself.

Offered here, therefore, are only my thoughts on this important topic, which I hope, nevertheless, point to a more comprehensive and coherent understanding of the Christian faith in our time. As suggested, the positions on some of the issues discussed in this volume are not final. They are tentative.

I am fascinated by religious diversity, and this is the point of my departure as the study comes to a close. The way I understand the Christian faith is different from the way early believers understood it. Most early Christians had no idea about trinity before Tertullian of Carthage. The truth of the Gospel cannot be spoken of in abstraction from the tradition of the communities, which communicates it. Even the Bible itself is the testimony and witness of the early Christian communities and their encounter with God. There can be no revelation without someone experiencing, remembering, and transmitting it.

Revelation takes place within a social and historical context. The claim that Christ is decisive for all human life is powerful. But this claim would not be meaningful unless it is interpreted in the life of the community that lives by the tradition of the apostolic testimony. There cannot, therefore, be a total disjunction between the Gospel and Christianity.

To be raised in a Christian or a Jewish or a Buddhist or a traditional African religious community is to be raised in an interpretive community that has already set the boundaries for understanding ultimate reality. This is as basic as the fact that we learn words from our community, words like God, Allah, Tao, Brahma, or Olodumare. Even the naming process is culturally contingent. The pluralistic view calls religious thinkers to abandon religious exclusivism and encourages us to move from Christocentricism to theocentricism, claiming that God is at the center of our religious consciousness, not Christ. But how is this possible for Christians? After all, the very essence of the Christian proclamation is Christ himself.

Since accepting the reliability of the experience of transcendence in our own religious tradition is internal to the tradition itself, we have no justification for rejecting the epistemological reliability of the experience of transcendence in other living faiths and religious traditions. What are we to make of this powerful battery of theological and phenomenological arguments? How can we move from Christocentricism to theocentricism without damaging the central claim of the uniqueness of Christ as God's revelation?

These are nagging questions that I am capable of raising but not prepared to answer.

There are two other fundamental questions I want to raise at the conclusion of this study. The first concerns what the basis is for the belief in the universal salvific will of God at the center of the universe of faiths? The second concerns the normative theocentric center. This is the notion that an all-loving God accommodates only some forms of theistic religion. What of certain strands of Hinduism or Buddhism where belief in a personal God is absent or denied?

The chief engineer of the paradigm of inclusivism is Karl Rahner, the Roman Catholic theologian. Its roots, however, go back to the Protestant missionary, John Farquhar. The point of inclusivism is to show that God is present through, not despite, the non-Christian religions. Furthermore, non-Christian religions contain both natural and supernatural elements arising out of grace. Therefore, we can be "Christians" without knowing it. Christ may not be known objectively. But how can it be possible for a person to accept the God that is historically and definitively revealed in Christ, if he has failed to recognize Christ objectively? This is also problematic on another level because a Muslim in Saudi Arabia could claim that a Christian in England is an anonymous Muslim if he follows the precepts of Allah as revealed to Prophet Muhammad in the Holy Qu'ran.

At the conclusion of this study, readers would probably think that I have gone off the field and now wandering without a destination, or that I have left the central focus of the study—South Africa. This is because in the final analysis, I am interested in the big picture. The paradigm that I want to defend is that of cross-fertilization. My stimulus for this model is based on my experience as an African Christian. Let me comment on this notion of religious experience again because it is a notoriously elusive notion.

Transcendent reality is conceived differently and, therefore, is experienced differently. This is why we also respond differently to God from within our different religio-cultural ways of being human. This is the way I understand my faith and spiritual journey as an African.

In chapter one, I argued for a model of transformation rather than conversion. This is also real in my own life. I have seen that when Africans interacted with Christianity, they have responded in several ways. Some followers of African Traditional Religions have responded by retreating along traditional lines, or to some point that they considered safer. This response, I argued, is not borne out of faith. Followers of African Traditional Religions have also responded by arguing against Christianity and have even tried to show that the truth and goodness in the Christian faith are entirely false insofar as they differed from what they found in African Traditional Religions. This also does not express faith in my view. The devotees of African Traditional Religions have also opened up themselves and learned from Christianity. But if they are impressed by what they learned in Christianity and no longer impressed by African Traditional Religions, they have responded by converting to Christianity. But this response, I also maintained, shows a lack of faith. If in learning from Christianity, Africans like me simply add new information to the old, leaving the old unchanged, that is still not a demonstration of faith. Faith is a cross-fertilization of the old with the new. This is why I would not be asking my Muslim family members in Nigeria or my Muslim friends in South Africa to convert to Christianity. My life as a Christian is relevant to their transformation of Islam as theirs my transformation of Christianity. My Christian life is more important than my tongue to point their ways toward God. Also, my own Christian experience has been shaped by their particular Islamic experience to the extent that my faith would be diminished without a meaningful interaction with their particular Islamic experience. Likewise, their Islamic experience will be incomplete without a meaningful cross-fertilization with my own Christian experience. Authentic faith does not abrogate previous religious experiences but enlivens them. Likewise, conversion does not erase the past but embraces new religious possibilities. Christians in our own time would be served well by realizing that what the Protestant Reformation of the sixteenth century is to the Middle ages Christianity, calling the Church back to her ancient faith and fervor, is what Islamic religion is to Christianity and Judaism in our time. It is regrettable that Christianity in the West is so distant from the Muslim world. I do not mean a geographical, linguistic or political distance alone, but also a distance of spiritual awareness. The dogmatic division between Christians and Muslims is largely because of arrogance and one wishes that the lives of Muslims and Christians today would be more intertwined and characterized by mutual understanding. I hold the view that dogmatic differences will continue to exist between Muslims and Christians, leading possibly to the repetition of the controversies of the past. But dogmatic controversies are of relatively little value when they take us away from the spiritual realities into a platform of conflicts and wars. We have more in common if we would only listen more, travel more, and place ourselves in the realm of spiritual consciousness of the others. Furthermore, religion dogma is infinitely fraught with complexities and often beyond resolution and dogma shows more about humanity than about God. It is important to understand the beliefs of others, but more important to be patient with one another.

We communicate our faiths not by what say alone. We are created to complement, not to dominate, each other. Our cultural and religious differences tend to diminish in importance in an atmosphere of genuine personal exchange that involves authentic spirituality. Our words are often interpreted by who we are and how we live. How we treat other people will show them the God we worship in closed doors when the people we have interactions with in ordinary day-to-day life are not looking.

In my judgment, I am not at all abandoning the Christian witness contained in Scripture and tradition, but rather understanding it more deeply and thus preserving it by the anthropological method of cross-fertilization. These are the roots and the branches of the study in this book. Perhaps theologians and philosophers would see the method of cross-fertilization as more valuable than that of a polemic or apologetic approach.

The concept of religions is a modern invention[14] that scholars in the West have exported to the rest of the world, leading men and women of faith everywhere to think of themselves as members of one exclusive salvation-offering society against all others. I am not sure if the notion of a religion as a particular system of belief embodied in a bounded community was known before the modern era.

Even the New Testament has no word that is equivalent to our modern concept of religions. The New Testament speaks of such living matters as faith, obedience, and disobedience, piety, worship, the truth, and the way, but not of religions as communally embodied systems of belief. Nor within the European tradition did the Latin word *religio* mean a religion in our modern sense. The title of St. Augustine's *De Vera Religione*, for example, should not be translated as scholars in the West have done, as "On the true Religion" (i.e. Christianity in contrast to other religions), but as "On True Religiousness" or better still, on "True Piety" of Christianity.[15] The same is true of Zwingli's *Vera et Falsa Religione*, written a thousand years after Augustine; the subject was not Christianity as the true religion in contrast to false religion, but rather the true or false *religio*, i.e. "piety" of Christians. Again, John Calvin's *Religionis Institutio* is not properly translated as "The Institute of the Christian Religion," but as "the foundations" or, perhaps, "the structures of the Christian piety." Religion, as a system of doctrine, was effectively formed later in the West.[16]

Lastly, I do not think I am over-dramatizing or romanticizing when I express my conviction, as other scholars have done, that as humanity steps further into this millennium, the religious traditions of the world will find themselves at a turning point. Up until now, religious communities have not adopted a cross-fertilization approach, but have understood themselves from within the circle of their own experience and tradition. They are good tradition and are needed.[17] The challenge at the age of religious confluence is to expand our ways of knowing who we are by allowing our circles to touch and overlap with the religious circles of others. That is how I have understood my own Christian identity and story as an African. I have come to know more clearly and meaningfully who I am by talking to my Muslim family members and with other religious persons. Both the nature of our intercommunicative world and of the crises this world faces offer and require such a cross-fertilization, and a correlational manner of religious self-understanding.

Paul F. Knitter put it best when he stated that if we are to survive on this planet, we will somehow have to embrace one another in the celebration of life—those who worship differently, those who eat differently, those who look differently; that we cannot do without one another is a mark of the common humanity we share.[18] This is one of the greatest lessons one can learn from the post TRC South Africa.

We have come to the terminus of our study but not to the end. Therefore, this closing remarks that I have been bold to call conclusion can only be tentative or, if we like, the end of one journey and the beginning of another. Therefore, I trust that no reader will take the title "conclusion" too seriously because I have not. In my formulation of the materials and the research that stood behind the materials, the matters before us are too serious to have any finality. But not only can there not be a conclusion, there must not be a final conclusion. Human spiritual journey in Africa, and elsewhere, is not yet complete. Western missionaries might have added another religious dimension to African spirituality; but it can only be an historical contribution. There is an ongoing dimension we are yet to comprehend, and there are new territories yet unknown. The only traditions that are complete are the ones that are extinct.[19] Religious traditions are always in transition. Therefore, we would be unwise to predict the future. Our cumulative spiritual traditions in Africa are manifestly in perpetual development; we have not yet reached the peak of the mountain.

The Christian Church traditions in Africa are still in process—so are the Islamic traditions, and the Jewish traditions and the Buddhist traditions as well as the Hindu's. Therefore, if there was any comfortable point in our theological and anthropological inquiry, it is this: religion under a theological inquiry, I hope, will always let us down because we are only able to see a little of it. Perhaps we have been able to see that human intelligent and creative efforts to elucidate his religious awareness can only marginally be a way the universe is trying to rediscover itself. I do not know what Christianity is, and I find it more and more difficult to define Islam or Judaism or any other religion for that matter. But I know God. Our religious traditions evolve primarily out of our existential conditions. Therefore, human faiths vary, and so are human religions, but God endures. I believe that to know God is far more superior than explaining all the paraphernalia surrounding our beliefs. Perhaps, when we know God fully, all religions will—as they should—cease to exist.[20] In God, before God, through God, and within God, everything else evaporates. I see God as the kernel and our religious paraphernalia as the husks and cloaks. Sometimes, they have led us astray but in some cases, they have led us to the Promised Land. But I am no longer concerned about religion as a path that leads to God. I am now fully aware that religions have led many astray and, possibly, away from God. This occurs also even in our unrelenting efforts to find God in our anthropological and religious quest.

I have written from within the Christian Church experience in South Africa. The study, however, is an indirect call to Christians everywhere, especially in the non-African world, in the hopes that it might contribute something to our doing justice intellectually both to what we know of God as Christ has revealed God to us, and what we now know of the world around us.

Written in the context of the African Church from the culture of a respected Churchly institution, it is my hope that fellow scholars might find it an important contribution to their search for the ultimate that cannot be taken away or destroyed. For we are no fools if we let go of our religious paraphernalia, which we cannot ultimately keep, so that we may gain the relational quality within God that we would never lose.

As for the non-African Church and the religious culture of the Western tradition, it is my hope that we can be challenged to see that the windows through which the Church has always seen the world are not only dusty but are broken and they need to be replaced. Through the broken windows, what we have been able to see are the patterns of the religious concepts we have inherited. But these concepts are so crooked now that they have prevented us from seeing the world outside of ourselves. But replacing these windows would not be easy. It is always difficult to give up a structure that we have inherited. Within the missionary context especially, it would require abandoning the essential categories of the Christian faith and our doctrinal certainties.

It is my hope that, through our skills and vulnerability, our fears and our joys, we would be able to present to the world an alternative to the rich religious history of humanity, not by holding on to our essentials but by giving them up so that we can cling to God, who is the ultimate. Our attempt to understanding and conceptualize our own faith and the religious traditions of Africans has yielded a little more than a fatal result of apartheid. The vitality of a personal faith and progress for understanding the religious traditions of other people are seriously weakened if not totally blocked by our imagination. This is because ultimately, it is their window as it is their faith. The missionary imposition of a different window has been acquired, but it has not spoken to the wellsprings of many Africans and their religious consciousness. Yet, it is believed that after apartheid, it would be difficult to see Christianity in quite the same way in South Africa.

A Post Resurrection text: The Model of Jesus

Chapter twenty-one is a part of an epilogue to the Gospel of John, and it must have been printed forever on the mind of Peter, the most vocal disciple of Jesus. For after a long night of fishing and catching nothing, Jesus changed the subject of their conversation from fishing to shepherding. During this important conversation, Jesus reinstructed Peter and called his attention to what it means to renew one's identity as a follower of God. In a three-fold affirmation, Jesus associated Peter in the closest possible way with his own ministry. Perhaps Jesus wanted to re-habilitate Peter after he denied him three times and the passage itself leads naturally to making this assumption.

The text is also an occasion for Jesus to call the attention of Peter to what he was commissioned to do now that his faith is renewed. It is exactly here that I see a message for Christians in our religiously pluralistic time.

First, the text makes it clear here that the foundation of Christian ministry is our love and devotion to Jesus Christ. According to the question that Jesus asked Peter: "Simon, son of John, do you love me more than these?" Jesus affirmed that the motivation for a renewal of Christian identity begins out of one's love and devotion to Jesus Christ. Humanity often fails, and Church members and religious leaders often disappoint, but they are not the primary focus of Christian vocation. What would energize Christians and put them on the path to a renewal is their devotion to and love for their Lord. Jesus stated: "Simon, son of John, do you love me?" By these words, Christ means that no Christian of each era can faithfully and diligently prepare for the Christian ministry and execute his or her responsibilities as faithful servants of the Church and of God's creation, and sustain the task of his or her ministry, unless he or she looks beyond the members of the congregation. Peter's preparation for the ministry was laborious and troublesome, for nothing was more difficult than for him to abandon everything in order to follow Jesus. If Christians were going to discharge their responsibilities and faithfully persevere in good and bad times, their motivation would be the love for Christ. Unless he reigns in each heart and mind, and unless believers love him above all things, they would not be totally devoted to the shepherding business to which he had invited them.

There is a second instruction for Peter that could help believers today on their path toward a renewal of faith and identity. Jesus asked Peter: "Simon, son of John, do you love me?" and Peter replied simply, "yes Lord, I love you." Then Jesus instructed Peter, "Feed my lambs."

Greek words are often used interchangeably in the New Testament. The word used in verse 15 of the Gospel of John chapter 21 has been translated "feed" but it is different from the word used in verse 16 that the English language has also rendered "feed." Modern translations have corrected that by rendering the Greek word in verse 16 as "take care of my sheep" or like the New Revised Standard Version suggested "tend my sheep."

The methods of Christian proclamation for the Church of this generation are unlimited. The preparation for Christian ministry is broad. Likewise, the ministry of healing and reconciliation is broad. Christian ministry has several dimensions, and taking care or tending the sheep may include many Church-related responsibilities—including feeding, clothing, watching, preaching, praying, listening, visiting, protecting, scolding, and admonishing.

The Christian proclamation is elaborate and so must be the Christian preparation for our time. It means that Christians have to take care of the human family in the name of Jesus Christ in a variety of ways and whether the sheep identifies himself as a Christian or non-Christian, a Muslim or non-Muslim, an atheist, or non-atheist. In this century, it is becoming increasingly clear that the mission of the Church will have to be the mission of the whole Church, with the whole Gospel, for the whole person, in the whole of society, and for the whole world.

What is more important in the Bible—and this is equally instructive for Christians in this age—is the challenge Jesus presented by using Peter's word in verse 17. "Simon, son of John, do you love me? And Peter was grieved because he said to him the third time, "Do you love me." Lord, you know all things, and you know that I love you, and Jesus said to him, "Feed my sheep." In this third exchange between Jesus and Peter, Jesus did not insist on his own vocabulary. Jesus used Peter's word, *Phileo*. In verse 15, Jesus used *agape*, do you *love* me. In verse 16, Jesus also used *agape*. But in verse 17, he used Peter's vocabulary.

Contemporary theologians have overlooked the language of theology elsewhere in the world, particularly in the lives of non-Christians in the non-Western world. Christians have overlooked the cross-cultural aspects of Christian history, and the evidence of Christianity's global growth and expansion. There are new Christian developments in the non-Western world and Christian thinkers in the West would strengthen their faith and Christian identity if they paid more attention to them. What European Christians thought and intended has always been considered superior to the way Christians elsewhere have lived. Ironically, Christians in the non-Western world are the direct result of modern missionary movements. Yet little attention is paid to their emerging theological vocabularies. In the northern hemisphere, Christians do not often pay attention to these vocabularies of others, when these non-Western believers express the Christian faith and articulate its essential categories in indigenous idioms and with local realities. Perhaps Christians do not find it necessary to use the vocabularies of these *"Peters"* in the non-Western world. Perhaps it looks and sounds inferior to the pure language of love of the missionary-sending hemisphere. But how can we possibly continue to carry on our mission as ministers, totally unaffected by the unprecedented expansion of Christianity around the world? How can we possibly ignore the voices of the new "Peters" that are so clear in Asia, in Central and South America, and in Africa?

In the process of renewal of faith and identity, Christians in the Western world can no longer look at theological education and training of African Christians with the eyes of exclusiveness, but like Jesus, with the eyes of expansion and promise. There is growing evidence that the "heartlands" of Christianity now have extended beyond the Western geographical, cultural and linguistic borders. And Christians cannot afford to continue lagging behind in responding to the effects of the missionary movements.

The focus of this study has been that of diagnosis and prognosis rather than that of prescriptions and recommendations. The study maintains that the the Christian map of the world has been redrawn, incorporating Asian, African and Central and South American Christianity. Christians live in a unique time of challenge and opportunity. It seems as if this is the best time to be ministers of the Gospel of grace and healing. The inclination to exclude the vocabulary of *"Peters"* around the world (whether they are Christians or non-Christians) in articulating the categories of the Christian faith is untrue and antithetical to the genius of the Gospel of hope and reconciliation, and to the pressure of the world around us. In religious and political terms, the world is flat, and by excluding those who look differently, those who eat differently, and those who do not share our cultural values and political convictions, from participating in articulating the categories of the Christian faith, we make our wounds only ours, unable to be shared. The new global reality may require that we rethink our syllabus in theological education at seminaries and universities in the West. A new syllabus may be required that will include the language of love as Peter understood it and as Jesus used it.

Because the language of other *Peters* around the world represents a new challenge, it is going to be much easier for Christians to ignore it. It is going to be much easier for believers to carry on with the old intellectual Christian map. This is not only because a new language of theology is always difficult to learn but also because new discoveries are always intellectually threatening, requiring the abandonment of too many doctrinal certainties. But how do we respond to the new challenge of local Christian preachers, prophets and healers all over the Southern hemisphere today? They pay little attention to the traditional walls that have separated Christian denominations for more than a thousand and five hundred years.

Do we take care of this challenge simply by offering more elective courses in missions and World Christianity? That is, by making the breadbasket of course offerings at theological institution more generous? Do we scatter the seeds of new Christian consciousness in the new map through the entire range of theological education curriculum? Do we continue to hold on to the apron strings of our old intellectual wisdom? Or do we exchange them—and our theological cleverness—for new bewilderment?

Perhaps the way Jesus wanted Peter to respond to the call of renewal of his faith and identity was more than doing? It is being. For, by using Peter's language, Jesus demonstrated that he came to proclaim not the holiness of the few elect but the healing of the whole world.

Theological education can no longer ignore the fact that Christianity has become a genuinely multicultural world religion. Christianity is now expressed in the idioms of other languages and cultures, and it is marked by a lively cross-cultural and inter-religious sensibility.

In Africa fresh energy is being devoted to the production of new hymns, music, and artistic and liturgical materials, to the creation of fresh theological categories. The old charts of missionaries in Africa are now woefully inadequate in tracking new Christian directions, for we are now living in a new era in the life of the Church, and the habits of the old maps that have locked Christians into frozen positions will not sustain us.

Thus, Christians must allow new evidence of global Christianity to move believers to new directions so that Christians can go beyond the day one of the missionary landing in Africa, Asia, and Central and South America, and incorporate Peter's vocabulary and language of love into our Christian life and consciousness.

Therefore, Christians in our own generation must now take account of the global reality around them and dream a new dream. This is in part because the reality around us is now certainly taking account of us.

Christians must face the reality of what has always been, yet we must dream of what has never been that must now be. Amen.

Notes

[1] See Viggo Mortensen, ed. *Theology and the Religions: A Dialogue.* (Grand Rapid, Michigan: William B. Eerdmans Publishing Company, 2003), 475.

[2] Huston Smith, *The World's Religions* (New York: Harper Collin Publishers, 1991), 130.

[3] Viggo Mortensen, editor. *Theology and the Religions: A Dialogue* (Grand Rapids, Michigan: William B. Eerdmans Publishing company, 2003).

[4] Viggo Mortensen, editor, Theology and the Religions: A Dialogue (Grand Rapids, Michigan: William B. Eerdmans Publishing company, 2003), 467.

[5] Lamin Sanneh, *Translating the Message: The Missionary Impact on Culture* (Maryknoll, N.Y.: Orbis, 1989).

[6] Viggo Mortensen, 467.

[7] Ibid. 470.

[8] In compiling this column, I rely on the following works: (1) David J. Bosch, *Transforming Mission: Paradigm Shifts in Theology of Mission* (Maryknoll, New York: Orbis Books, 1991), 50 ff. (2) Viggo Mortensen, *Theology and the Religions: A Dialogue* (Grand Rapids, Michigan: William B. Eerdmans Publishing Company, 2003), 476ff.

[9] Viggo Mortensen, 470.

[10] Reinhold Niebuhr, *The Nature and Destiny of Man* (New York: Charles Scribner's Sons, 1964). In the first volume, Reinhold Niebuhr offered vigorous challenges to Western classical understanding of man based on widely accepted beliefs. He challenged the optimistic view of human nature that was prevalent in classical tradition. In the second volume, he offered a robust interpretation of the destiny of man. Consistent with the domain of Neo-orthodoxy, Niebuhr insisted that although human beings are sinners, they sinned inevitably, but not necessarily. Hence, they are responsible for their actions. Human beings are by the constitution of their nature both a part of the creature and a part of the spiritual entity at the same time.

[11] Genesis 1–2.

[12] Charles Nyamiti, a Tanzanian theologian, popularized this term to reflect the vision of the world in which God, humanity, and the world are united symbiotically. See Charles Nyamiti, "African Christologies Today" in Robert J. Schreiter, ed. *Faces of Jesus in Africa* (Maryknoll, New York: Orbis Books, 1991), 3–23.

[13] Efoé Julien Pénoukou, "Christology in the Village" in Robert J. Schreiter, ed. *Faces of Jesus in Africa* (Maryknoll, New York: Orbis Books, 1991), 34.

[14] Early Europeans were responsible for the nomenclature of Hinduism. They lumped together the vast uncoordinated, amorphous mass of new and old religious cults, customs and practices of India and called them Hinduism; its adherents know it only as Eternal Law (*sanathana dharma*). In the same manner, the term "Confucianism" is coined by joining "Kung," the true name of the founder, with "Fu-tzu" translated "the Master." Kung the Master (Kung Fu-tzu) became "Kungfu-tzu" and was later pronounced Confucianism.

[15] John Hick wrote the Foreword to Wilfred Cantwell Smith's book *The Meaning and End of Religion* in which he elaborated on the artificiality of our religion nomenclature. But not only this, Hick stated in the Foreword that even within Christianity, we have misunderstood the intentions and the meanings of the writings of the forefathers. See Wilfred Cantwell Smith, *The Meaning and End of Religion* (Minneapolis, Minnesota: Fortress Press, 1991), v–xii.

[16] Ibid.

[17] Paul F. Knitter, *One Earth Many Religions: Multifaith Dialogue and Global Responsibility* (Maryknoll, New York: Orbis Books, 1995), 22.

[18] Paul F. Knitter, *One Earth Many Religions: Multifaith Dialogue and Global Responsibility* (Maryknoll, New York: Orbis Books, 1995).

[19] Wilfred Cantwell Smith, *The Meaning and End of Religion* (Minneapolis, Minnesota: Fortress Press, 1991), 193–202.

[20] This is the major contribution that Wilfred Cantwell Smith made in his work, *The Meaning and End of Religion,* 1991.

THEOLOGICAL AND POLITICAL THEMES IN TIME

Before Written Records and the Arrival of Early European Settlers from antiquity to written record up till 1488

About 1.7 million years ago—

Modern cultural anthropologists believe that the earliest humans were Africans. Earliest human ancestors were believed to be found in South Africa's modern day Eastern Cape.

About 100,000 years ago—

Homo sapiens (anatomically modern humans) were present in South Africa.

About 30,000 years ago—

The origins of hunter-gatherer communities of the Khoisan peoples of South Africa started as well as the emergence of their cultures. It is believed that they were the earliest indigenous people of South Africa.

About 2000 year ago—

The emergence of metal-using farmers from the North (Central Africa and modern-day Cameroon region. They were the ancestors of the Bantu-speaking people in South Africa. The emergence of the pastoralists Khoikhoi cultures also occurred around this time.

Approximately 1488 C.E.—

Extensive Bantu-speaking settlement in most of the eastern half of South Africa including the highveld; Khoikhoi people in the western and southern cape; The arrival of the San people in the hinterland and mountains of much of South Africa.

Settlement of Early Europeans: Religions as weapons of Exploitation and Colonial Control 1488–1688

1488—

Bartholomew Dias landed on the Southern cape coast. He became the first known Western Christian to reach South Africa according to written record. The first Christian act was the raising of his cross at Kwaaihoek on the Southeastern coast.

1497—

Vasco Da Gama gave a Christian name to eastern coastal area, Tierra da Natal "Land of the Nativity" sighted on Christmas Day in 1497.

1560—

The Portuguese Jesuits began missionary activities in Southwestern and Southeastern Africa, with concentrations on Luanda and the Zambezi Valley.

1611—

The King James Version of the Bible was published in England on May 2nd and the Afrikaners translated it into Afrikaans language and exploited selected Old Testament passages to justify segregation by race in South Africa.

1652—

The arrival of the Dutch party to the Cape under the leadership of the legendary Jan van Riebeeck was in this year. The Dutch established a garrison at the Cape of Good Hope, halfway along the sea route from Europe to India.

1652-1665—

A period when the sole religious official at the Cape was the "sick-comforter."

1658—

The arrival of Mardyckers to South Africa. They were the first free Muslims at the Cape from Moluccan Islands.

1660—

A French Catholic Bishop, shipwrecked at the Cape, was denied permission to conduct Catholic mass.

1665—

Johan van Arckel, the first Dutch Reformed minister, arrived at the Cape; Consistory was formed.

1669—

The first record of Jewish presence at the Cape with records show that two youngJews converted to Christianity was in this year.

1688—

A party of Jesuit astronomers visited the Cape and ministered to the Catholics among the Dutch.

Beginning of Religious and Political Exploitation *1688–1805*

1688—

The Edict of Nantes was revoked in France; The French Huguenots began to arrive at the Cape.

1694—

The arrival of exiled Shaykh Yusuf at the Cape.

1737—

The arrival of the first Protestant Missionaries to the Cape. The leader was the Moravian missionary, George Schmidt.

1744—

George Schmidt established Genadendal Mission Station near Cape Town but left soon afterwards.

1750—

Three Dutch Reformed Church ministers established themselves in the Cape: (1) Cape Town, (2) Stellenbusch, and (3) Drakenstein.

1780—
The arrival of Tuang Guru, the second spiritual father of Islam at the Cape.
1787—
Shaka Zulu was born. He was the first indigenous leader to present a major military chal-
lenge to neighboring white colonists in South Africa.
1792—
The Moravian missionaries returned to Europe.
1795—
London Missionary Society (LMS) was founded. It had a decisive effect on African
Christianity, especially when the name changed to Church Missionary Society (CMS).
1795—
First Baptist occupation of the Cape.
1799—
LMS missionary, Johannes van der Kemp, arrived in Cape Town.
1803—
Resumption of the Dutch control of the Cape under the Batavian Republic.
1804—
De Mist's ordinance of religious tolerance was issued.
1804—
Fathers Lansink, Nelissen, and Prinsen arrived at the Cape. They were the first Catholic
Priests to arrive in South Africa.
1804?—
Approximate date of the building of the first Mosque on Dorp Street in Cape Town.

Intense Period of Colonial Control and the Beginning of Swart Gevaar (Black Threat) 1806–1910

1806—
General Baird expels the three Catholic Priests from the Cape. This signaled the beginning of second British occupation and Control in the Cape.
1806—
The Methodists and Congregational soldiers at the Cape built chapels in Cape Town.
1809—
Pass Law was introduced in the Cape Province by the British authorities, restricting the
movements of the indigenous black population. The pass law later became the cornerstone of repression with extensive harassment of the Blacks by the police and the courts.
1810—
Sara Baartman, a 20–year old Khoikhoi woman, was taken from Cape Town to London.
She became the icon of racial inferiority and an object of black female sexuality for over
100 years. In 1814 she was taken to France where she became an object of scientific and
medical research that formed the bedrock for European ideas about black female sexuality. When she died in 1815, her body was placed under the microscope and became an
object of scientific and anatomical investigations. Her sexual organs and brain were on
display in the Musée de l'Homme in Paris until 1985. Baartman was a stout woman with
steatopygia or excessive accumulation of fat tissue on her buttocks. This made her buttocks prominent. Her remains were returned to South Africa by the French authorities in
2002 and she finally received a dignified traditional burial in accordance with the local
customs of her people in Hankey, Eastern Cape, where she was born in 1790. The return
of her remains to South Africa was a victory over the early vestiges of colonialism and

gave all South Africans a sense of pride and victory over modern imperialism and associated mentality. Her burial was a cause for celebration in August 2002.

1813—

The Presbyterian Church was formed at the Cape.

1814—

Barnabas Shaw, a Methodist missionary, arrived from England

1817—

Robert Moffat, LMS missionary, arrived from England.

1820—

John Philip, LMS missionary, arrived from England.

1820—

William Shaw arrived at the Eastern Cape as chaplain to party of Methodist settlers.

1820—

English permanent settlement of the Eastern Cape began.

1821—

William Shaw built the first Church in Grahamstown.

1821—

John Philip established mission station across Orange River at Philippolis, a town that was named after him. Thus, John Philip became one of the first eponymous non-indigenous persons in South Africa.

1822—

Andrew Murray, Snr. commenced Dutch Reformed Church pastorate at Graaff-Reinet.

1822—

Father Scully built the first Catholic Church in Cape Town.

1823-30—

Rapid expansion of the Methodist Missions into the Eastern Cape and the Transkei.

1824—

John Bennie and John Scott, missionaries of the Church of Scotland founded the Lovedale Church in Eastern Cape. This Church became prominent under the leadership of influential Church leaders like the Rt. Rev. R. H. W. Shepherd.

1824—

First DRC commission on Missions at the Cape was formed.

1825—

Robert Moffat founded Kuruman Mission Station.

1828—

The publication of Dr. John Philip's book, Researches in South Africa.

1828—

Dingane assassinated Shaka Zulu, his elder (half) brother.

1832—

The First Anglican Church in Eastern Cape was founded at Bathurst.

1835—

Daniel Lindley, American Missionary, arrived and became the first regular minister to the Voortrekkers.

1836—

First Dutch Reformed Church mission to black people was established

1836—

The Great trek commenced. This is also the year when the Boers (Afrikaners who practice farming) severed their ties with Europe and they commemorated this year as the year that cemented their feet with South Africa.

1837—

The DRC in the Cape deplored the Great Trek formally.

1838—

First Roman Catholic Bishop, Patrick Griffith, arrived at the Cape.

1838—

Voortrekker vowed at the Blood River on 6th November.

1840—

First Catholic Mission Station was founded near Malmesbury in the Western Cape.

1840—

David Livingstone, one of the most celebrated British missionaries to Africa, of the London Missionary Society, arrived in Southern Africa.

1841—

The establishment of the Jewish Community in South Africa began with the founding of the First Congregation in Cape Town.

1844—

First recorded Jewish marriage solemnized in Cape Town.

1845—

First Jewish birth was recorded in South Africa.

1847—

First recorded Scroll of the Torah brought into South Africa.

1848—

Robert Gray was appointed the first Anglican Bishop of Cape Town.

1849—

First Jewish synagogue was built in Cape Town.

1853—

John William Colenso was appointed the first Anglican Bishop of Natal.

1853—

Nederduitsch Hervormde Kerk was formed in the Transvaal.

1856—

Transvaal Republican Constitution declared that no equality existed between blacks and whites in Church and State. Perhaps this was the beginning of a formalized segregation by race in South Africa.

1857—

NGK synod at the Cape permits separate worship because of the "weakness of some" (i.e. whites).

1857—

The Xhosa "cattle killing" ceremony was re-established.

1857—

DRC Theological Seminary was established at Stellenbosch.

1859—

Gereformeerde Kerk was formed in Transvaal.

1860—

Indian settlements in Natal began, marking the beginnings of Hinduism in South Africa and of Islam in Natal area.

1860—

The famous Andrew Murray, Jr., commenced his influential Christian ministry in the Cape.

1860—

Nederduitsch Hervormde Kerk (NHK) became the official Church of Transvaal Republic.

1861—

Bishop Colenso published his controversial commentary on the Epistle to the Romans.

1862—

The St. John's Street Synagogue or "Old Synagogue" in Cape Town was built. It was the first to be specifically designed as a synagogue.

1863—

Bishop Colenso tried and convicted of heresy by his Church; he was excommunicated and deposed. He then appealed successfully to the Privy Council in England.

1863—

Abubakr Effendi, a Turk of Kurdish decent, was sent to the Cape by the Ottoman Sultan at the request of the British Crown to serve the Muslims in South Africa.

1865—

The Privy Council in England ruled in favor of Colenso's reinstatement.

1867—

Diamond was discovered near Kimberley, South Africa. This would dramatically affect the economy of South Africa, moving the majority away from agrarian economic concerns to manufacturing industry.

1870—

Proposed union of DRC and Anglicans in the Cape.

1872—

First Black Indigenous Christian Church congregated in Lesotho.

1879—

Anglo-Zulu War erupted.

1881—

A large influx of East European Jews into South Africa (largely from Lithuania and Russia) began.

1882—

Roman Catholic Trappists founded the Mariannhill Monastery near Durban.

1882—

Muslims at the Cape protested the state vaccination measures on Religious grounds.

1883—

Bishop Colenso died.

1884—

Leader Nehemish Tile set up the Independent Tembu National Church.

1884—

The Grey Street Mosque in Durban was built. It was the first Mosque in Natal and it represented the beginning of a multi-religious dimension in the religious tapestry of South Africa.

1886—

The Cape Muslims resisted the authorities during a cemetery riots.

1886—

Gold was discovered at the Witwatersrand goldfields, changing the destiny of South Africans from traditional rural life and agrarian economy, to an urban society poised for industrial economy.

1887—

The Mosque in Central Pretoria, Guateng was built.

1892—

Elder Mangena Mokone, an indigenous leader of significance, founded the Ethiopian Church in the Transvaal. The Ethiopian Church represented an indigenous Christian aspiration and became a symbol of spiritual creativity in Southern Africa.

1893—

Mohandas Gandhi, a great political and spiritual leader, who merged European ideas with reformist Hindu teachings to lead India to independence, arrived in Durban from India in May. A month later, Gandhi was evicted from a train at Pietermaritzburg train station because of his skin color, marking the turning point in his life. In 2003, the 110th year anniversary was commemorated in Pietermaritzburg.

1894—

Natal Indian Congress was founded, and Gandhi served as its first secretary.

1894—

Ahmad Effendi stood for Cape Parliament, becoming the first non-white person to do so.

1895—

The first African Christian Zionist Congregation in Johannesburg was established.

1895—

A decision was made to establish the Roeland Street Synagogue in Cape Town, the first synagogue in the East European tradition and was later consecrated in 1902.

1896—

James Dwane became superintendent-general of the Ethiopian Church. The Order of the Ethiopian tradition developed from this Church.

1898—

South African Zionist Federation was formed.

1899—

Anglo-Boer war began, marking the beginning of political tension between the British and the Dutch settlers in South Africa. In this conflict, the political aspirations and the needs of the indigenous people were ignored.

The Foundations of Apartheid: Domination, Oppression and the Liberation Struggle 1902–1948

1902—

Peace of Vereeniging.

1902—

The enactment of the Cape Immigration Restriction Act occurred. This Act restricted the entry of Jews and Indians into South Africa.

1902—

Cecil Rhodes, the prime minister of Cape Colony and the most powerful man in the South African diamond-mining industry died.

1903—

Abdullah Abdurahman, a leading Muslim Cleric, made his entry into the civil affairs and Politics in South African body politics.

1903—

Mohandas K. Gandhi (1869–1948) started a newspaper in June, *Indian Opinion,* in Natal.

1903—

Transvaal Jewish Board of Deputies was formed. This orthodox Jewish body was the first of its kind and later played a pivotal political role in the South African Jewish identity.

1904—

Cape Jewish Board of Deputies was formed.

1904—

South African General Missionary Council was formed.

1904—

Gandhi and his close friends established the Phoenix Settlement near Durban.

1905—

The Hindu Young Men's Association in Natal was established.

1906—

Bambata Rebellion in which four thousand native Africans were murdered. This was a watershed in the thought of young Gandhi and he organized an Ambulance Corps to nurse the wounded Zulus and those who needed medical care but were denied by the British settlers.

1907—

Gandhi and his friends launched a passive resistance movement in South Africa.

1908—

The Apostolic Faith Mission (AFM) was formed. This was the precursor of Pentecostal Movements in South Africa.

1910—

The Union of South Africa was formed following the end of Anglo-Boer war with British granting political Independence to South Africa. Little was done, however, to protect the civil and religious rights of South African black majority population.

1911—

Isaiah Shembe, somewhat of a black Messiah in South Africa, started the Nazareth Baptist Church in Kwa-Mashu, near Durban.

1911—

Census indicated that more than 25 percent of the indigenous population in South Africa professed to be Christians.

1911—

The end of Indian immigration to South Africa.

1912—

South African Native National Congress (SANNC) was formed in Bloemfontein. The name later changed to African National Congress (ANC) in 1923.

1912—

South African Jewish Board of Deputies was established.

1912—

The South African Hindu Maha Sabha was formed.

1913—

The Native Land Act limited the black population (over 70 percent of total population) to only 7 percent of the land in South Africa.

1914—

After spending 21 years in South Africa, Gandhi left South Africa and returned to his native country of India.

1914—

National Party was formed. The party would later legalize segregation by race and apartheid would be formalized as a law in 1948 when the National Party came to power.

1914—

The Assemblies of God in South Africa was formed.

1915—

Judah Leo Landau appointed first Chief Rabbi.

1915—

Beyerd Naudé was born on May 10. He became a member of the Broederbond in 1964. More than any other person in the modern history of South Africa, Naudé was a persistent voice of protest against apartheid and he rose to international fame in the 1970s by establishing the Christian Institute as a non-racial ecumenical body that became the organ of theological resistance against apartheid. By responding to his criticism of the government, the authority indirectly enhanced his international reputation.

1917—

The Overport Sakya Buddhist Society was founded in Durban.

1918—

The Afrikaner Broederbond was formed. Its membership was limited to Afrikaner males who were members of the Dutch Reformed Church. D. F. Malan, a Dutch Reformed Church minister and a member of the Broederbond, rose to become Prime minister in 1948 and was instrumental in the formalization of apartheid.

1920—

The Full Gospel Church was established.

1921—

The Government troops massacred the "Israelite" Millenarian group at Bulhoek in the Eastern Cape.

1922—

First Apostolic Delegate was appointed to South Africa.

1922—

The Jamiat al 'Ulama (the Islamic Association of the Learned) in the Transvaal was founded.

1923—

South African Native National Congress (SANNC) was renamed the African National Congress (ANC).

1923—

The Bantu Presbyterian Church was founded.

1923—

Cape Malay Association (CMA) was founded.

1924—

The apartheid government passed the Industrial Conciliation Act. The legislation excluded the blacks from being designated as "employees." They were designated as "native labor" to protect unskilled whites from black competition in the labor market.

1925—

The Arya Pratinidhi Sabha, the national umbrella body of the Hindu Arya Samaj in South Africa was established.

1929—

The Cape United Council of Orthodox Hebrew Congregations was inaugurated.

1930—

The Immigration Quotas Act severely limited the immigration of Jews from Eastern Europe (especially from Lithuania) to South Africa.

1930—

Riotous Assemblies Act.

1931—

Methodist Church of South Africa was formed through a union of three branches of Methodism.

1932—

The Baptist Union of South Africa publicly condemned the government policy towards the "Native Peoples" of South Africa.

1933—

The formation of the Federation of Synagogues in Johannesburg.

1933—

The establishment of the Reformed Judaism in South Africa.

1934—

First visit to South Africa by an official representative of the Ramakrishna Mission in India, Swami Adhyanand.

1934—

The Congregational Church became the First Christian denomination to ordain a woman to the Christian Ministry in South Africa.

1936—
   Christian Council was founded.
1937—
   The Aliens Acts effectively halted Jewish immigration from Germany to South Africa.
1937—
   Emilie Solomon was elected Chair of the Congregational Union, the first woman to hold a leadership position in a South African Church.
1941—
   Nederduitsch Gereformeerde Kerk participation in Christian Council ended.
1942—
   Formation of Muslim Progressive Society.
1943—
   Militant Younger Members of the ANC was formed, and called the Congress Youth League. Most of the leaders of ANC belonged to the Youth League and were trained by the organization in exile in the 1940s and 1950s.
1945—
   The formation of the Muslim Judicial Council.
1946—
   Founding of the Ramakrishna Center of South Africa in Durban.
1947—
   Southern African Catholic Bishops' Conference (SACBC) was formed.
1947—
   Ecumenical Faculty of Divinity was established at Rhodes University.

Establishing Indigenous Credibility and Embracing A New Identity 1948–1975

1948—
   The World Council of Churches was founded in Amsterdam.
1948—
   The Modern State of Israel came into being.
1948—
   First Jewish day school was established in Johannesburg.
1948—
   The National Party came to power in South Africa and the formalization of apartheid and the struggle for black freedom started.
1949—
   Christian Council convened a conference at Rosettenville on "The Christian Citizen in a Multi-racial Society."
1949—
   First branch of the Divine Life Society started.
1949—
   Prohibition of Mixed Marriages became official.
1950—
   The Arabic Study Circle was formed in Durban.
1950—
   The population Registration Act divided South African population by race and categorized them as: Whites, Coloureds, Indians and Blacks. The concept of race was so narrowly defined that one can say that the population can only be seen as either white or black.

1950—

The Group Area Act determined where each "race" could live. The Coloured communities were deported in large numbers from District Six in Cape Town and their Churches were left empty. The government authorities removed more than 58,000 Africans by force from the City of Johannesburg by the end of 1950. Black people then flooded Soweto, a suburb South West of Johannesburg. The first two letters of three words—South West Town—coin Soweto.

1950—

Immorality Act was legislated. The measure restricted sexual relations between white and non-white South Africans, (not just blacks).

1950—

Unlawful Organization Act, prohibiting political and social assemblies against the government.

1950—

Suppression of Communism Act (also called Internal Security Act). Communism was defined so broadly that any opponent of the regime was a communist. The detention of black opposition leaders became rampant.

1951—

Roman Catholic Church set up a hierarchy of four archbishoprics and numerous bishoprics in South Africa.

1951—

The Bantu Authorities Act. It was legislated to abolish the Native representative council.

1953—

The Bantu Education Act effectively ended missionary education for black people. Nationalizing missionary schools by this Act effectively strengthened the revolutionary movement among Black South Africans. The Act was a signal to the black majority in South Africa that white South Africans knew that if blacks had access to education as the whites did, it would undermine the white strategy to keep black people down in perpetual servitude. Beginning in 1953, the slogan among revolutionary leaders in South Africa became: "Revolution first, then Education."

1953—

The Reservation of Separate Amenities Act. Also called Public Safety Act. The legislation was to restrict blacks from swimming in the same facilities with whites.

1953—

The Criminal Law Amendment Act.

1953—

Alan Paton, the author of *Cry the Beloved Country* (1958) formed the Liberal Party of South Africa in May along with Margaret Ballinger and Leo Marquard.

1954—

Annual Methodist Conference narrowly defeated an attempt to segregate the Methodist Church in South Africa.

1955—

The Congress of the People at Kliptown adopted the Freedom Charter.

1955—

Second Assembly of the World Council of Churches at Evanston, Illinois, condemned racism (with specific reference to apartheid in South Africa). It is significant to note that as African-Americans were fighting for Freedom in the United States, black South Africans intensified their own efforts for political freedom in South Africa and both struggles mutually depended upon each other.

1955—

Founding of Natal Jamiat al-'Ulama.

1956—
Riotous Assemblies Act.
1956—
The Native Administration Act.
1956—
Industrial Conciliation Act. The measure put job restriction on black people and what they could and could not do in the labor force.
1956—
The Official Secrets Acts. The legislation censor books and films.
1957—
"The Church Clause" in Native Laws Amendment Act, which would obstruct black people wishing to worship in white groups areas was passed.
1957—
The Anglican Archbishop Geoffrey Clayton died and was succeeded by Joost de Blank.
1957—
Roman Catholic Archbishop Whelan of Bloemfontein declared that apartheid was nothing less than a heresy.
1957—
Formation of the District Six-based Muslim Youth Movement.
1958—
The Claremont Muslim Association was founded by Imam Abdullah Haron.
1958—
Henrik Verwoerd, the supreme architect of the ideology of apartheid, came to power as South African Prime Minister.
1959—
Robert Sobukwe, Witwatersrand University Professor, formed the Pan Africanist Congress (PAC) in March.
1959—
University Education Act. It was a measure to restrict black South Africans from receiving advanced University education.
1960—
The Sharpeville Massacre (March 21). The world attention was drawn to the plight of the black majority in South Africa and the massacre constituted a turning point in the struggle for freedom for black South Africans. 20,000 people (majority of them were high school students) protested and surrendered their passes at the Sharpeville Police Station. They were willing to be arrested. The police opened fired, killing 67 and injuring more than 186 unarmed high school students.
1960—
The apartheid government banned the ANC and the PAC.
1960—
Consultation of Churches at Cottesloe, Johannesburg condemned apartheid.
1960—
Federal Theological Seminary was established at Alice in the Eastern Cape.
1960—
Alphaeus Zulu became the suffragan Bishop of Zululand.
1960—
Chief Albert Luthuli, the ANC president, was awarded the most coveted international Nobel Peace Prize.
1960—
The Unlawful Organization Act.

1961—

Cape and Transvaal Synods of Dutch Reformed Church formerly withdrew from the World Council of Churches.

1962—

Nelson Mandela was arrested and suspected of treasonable offence.

1962—

The General Laws Amendment Act.

1963—

Beyers Naudé, along with others, founded the Christian Institute and Naudé became its first Director. The Christian Institute was a non-racial ecumenical body and became the organ of theological protest against apartheid.

1963—

The Rivonia Trial, the trial of Nelson Mandela, lasted from December 1963 through June 1964.

1964—

Nelson Mandela made the famous statement on April 20: "During my life time I have dedicated myself to this struggle of the African people. I have fought against white domination, and I have fought against black domination. I have cherished the ideal of a democratic and free society in which all persons live together in harmony and with equal opportunities. It is an ideal, which I hope to live for and to achieve. But if needs be, it is an ideal for which I am prepared to die."

1964—

Seth Mokitimi became the first black President of the Conference of the Methodist Church.

1966—

The Federation of Evangelical Lutheran Churches of Southern Africa was formed.

1966—

Demetrio Tsafendas assassinated Hendrik Verwoerd on September 6. Verwoerd is notorious as the architect of apartheid and its structures.

1967—

Christian Council (CC) was renamed the South African Council of Churches (SACC).

1967—

In July, Chief Albert Luthuli was knocked down and killed by a train on a narrow bridge near his home of Groutvill on the Natal Coast, north of Durban.

1967—

Formation of the United Congregational Church of South Africa.

1967—

Church Unity Commission was formed.

1967—

University Christian Movement (UCM) was formed.

1967—

The Terrorism Act.

1968—

The joint publication of "The Message to the People of South Africa" by the SACC and the Christian Institute.

1969—

Imam Abdullah Haron died in detention in Cape Town.

1969—

First known Sai Baba (Hindu) group was formed in Durban.

1970—

The formation of Muslim Youth Movement of South Africa, in Durban.

1970—
Homeland Citizenship Act.
1970—
Arthur Nortje, a Coloured poet and a brilliant student at Oxford committed suicide in England rather than return to his native South Africa where his education would have meant nothing while the color of his skin would have meant everything.
1971—
World Council of Churches launched its program to combat racism.
1972—
Roman Catholic hierarchy issued its "Call to Conscience."
1973—
Congress on Mission and Evangelism in Durban, under the auspices of SACC and African Enterprise.
1974—
The Dutch Reformed Church General synod issued "Human Relations in the Light of the Scriptures," providing a way for the government policy on the racial question.
1975—
Evangelical Lutheran Church of Southern Africa was formed.
1975—
The formation of Islamic Council of South Africa.

Crisis, Sanctions, Struggle and Collapse of apartheid 1976–1990

1976—
The Roman Catholic Church decided to integrate its schools throughout South Africa.
1976—
The Soweto Uprising started leading to the massacre of High School children on June 16, and this created a state of emergency and nationwide unrest. June 16 is now a public holiday and designated "Youth Day" in South Africa.
1977—
The apartheid government banned the Christian Institute along with certain anti-apartheid organizations and publications.
1977—
The launching of Odyssey Magazine, a vehicle for "new age" ideas.
1977—
Anti-apartheid South African Student Organization leader, Steve B. Biko, died in police custody, sending a signal that brutality was sponsored by the state.
1978—
Desmond Tutu became the first non-white General Secretary of the SACC.
1978—
The Dutch Reformed Church in South Africa severed ties with the historical "parent" Reformed Church in the Netherlands over its support for the liberation movement in South Africa.
1978—
The formation of the Sunni Jamiat al-'Ulama of South Africa.
1978—
Robert Sobukwe, the PAC leader, died.

1979—
South African Christian Leadership Assembly (SACLA) was organized by the African Enterprise.
1979—
Islamic Revolution in Iran.
1980—
The formation of Qiblah Mass Movement in South Africa, which identified with the revolutionary (Iranian) Islam.
1980—
The Buddhist Retreat Center near Ixopo was open.
1981—
Alliance of Black Reformed Christians in South Africa (ABRECSA) was formed.
1982—
Allan Boesak, the anti-apartheid South African theologian, was elected Moderator of the World Alliance of Reformed Churches (WARC) in Ottawa, Canada.
1982—
NG Sendingkerk issued the Belhar Confession, stressing the unity of the Church over against apartheid.
1983—
Tricameral Constitution was adopted by the white parliament, with freedom of religion for all but still favoring Christianity over other religions.
1983—
Allan Boesak, along with other leaders, especially Trevor Manuel, launched the United Democratic Front against apartheid.
1983—
Eloff Commission of Enquiry into SACC.
1984—
Call of Islam (COI) severed ties with MYMSA on the issue of political alliances with United Democratic Front.
1984-
Archbishop Desmond Tutu was awarded the most coveted International Nobel Peace Prize.
1985—
Jewish Board of Deputies condemns apartheid at its 33rd National Congress.
1985—
Jews for Justice and Jews for Social Justice were formed in Cape Town and Johannes-burg, respectively.
1985—
National Initiative for Reconciliation in Pietermaritzburg was launched.
1985—
The Kairos Document was published, drawing attention of Church leaders to the incon-sistencies of apartheid with Christianity worldwide.
1985—
Hare Krishna Temple in Chatsworth, near Durban, was open.
1986—
NHK resolved to remain white.
1986—
Desmond Tutu was elected the Anglican Archbishop of Cape Town in April.
1986—
NGK General Synod issued Kerk en Samelewing, rejecting theological justifications of apartheid.

1986—
   Formation of the Union of Orthodox Synagogues of South Africa.
1986—
   Formation of the short-lived Hindu Alliance of South Africa.
1987—
   Frank Chikane became the General Secretary of SACC.
1987—
   SACC National Conference discusses Christianity and violence in South Africa.
1990—
   National Conference of Church leaders at Rustenburg issued the Rustenburg Declaration, completely rejecting apartheid.
1990—
   The apartheid government unbanned the ANC and PAC and released many political prisoners some that have been incarcerated for more than two decades.
1990—
   Nelson Mandela was released from Prison on February 11 after 27 years of incarceration, mostly in Robben Island. He also made his first public appearance in front of a large enthusiastic crowd on the Green Parade in Cape Town.

Negotiations, End of apartheid and the Beginning of Constitutional Full Democracy 1991–2004

1991—
   Convention for a Democratic South Africa (CODESA) was launched.
1991—
   National Peace Accord (NPA) was launched to counter the climate of violence that was rapidly engulfing South Africa.
1992—
   The massacre of 43 ANC supporters in Boipatong on June 17.
1993—
   The Inkatha Freedom Party (IFP) and Conservative Party (CP) withdrew from political negotiations led by African National Congress (ANC) in July.
1993—
   Chris Hani was assassinated and the ANC demanded full democratic election no later than a year after his assassination.
1994—
   Full Democratic Elections were held from April 26-29 for the first time in South African history. Nelson Mandela, the anti-apartheid ANC leader, was elected President.
1995—
   Truth and Reconciliation Commission was formed and Nelson Mandela appointed Archbishop Desmond Tutu to be the chair of the commission.
1996—
   Archbishop Desmond Tutu retired in June but was named Archbishop Emeritus in July.
2003—
   Archbishop Desmond Tutu gave the final report of the Truth and Reconciliation Commission (TRC) to President Thabo Mbeki.
2003—
   One hundred and tenth year anniversary of Mohandas K. Gandhi (1869–1948) arriving in Durban, South Africa was commemorated in Pietermaritzburg.

2003—

Nelson Mandela, the African statesman who led South African to freedom celebrated his 85th birthday with dignitaries around the world, including the former President of the United States, Bill Clinton and his wife, Senator (D-New York) and former first lady, Hillary Rodham Clinton.

2004—

Thabo Mbeki was re-elected to the second term as President of South Africa. He succeeded Nelson Mandela, the First full Democracy President, in 1999. The African National Congress (ANC) strengthened its majority stance in the South African Parliament.

2004—

Beyers Naudé, the great Dutch Reformed theologian and anti-aparthed pastor, died and was accorded a state funeral with Archbishop Desmond Tutu preaching at his funeral.

2004—

South Africa bid successfully for soccer World Cup 2010, becoming the first successful Sub-Saharan African country that will host the respected international soccer (football) competition.

❋ BIBLIOGRAPHY

Abraham, Willie. *The Mind of Africa* Chicago: University of Chicago Press, 1962.

Achtemeier, Paul J. *Harper's Bible Dictionary* HarperSanFrancisco, 1985.

Adedeji, Adebayo, "The Shaping of African Economics," paper delivered at the Africa 40 conference in London, (October, 1997).

Albright, W. F. "The Song of Deborah in the light of Archaeology" in *Bulletin of the American School of Oriental Research.* 62 (1936).

Anderson, Gerald H. and Thomas F. Stransky, C.S.P. eds. *Mission Trends No. 3: Third World Theologies,* New York: Paulist Press and Grand Rapids: Eerdmans, 1976.

Armstrong, J., and N. Borden, "The Slaves 1652-1834" in *The Shaping of South African Society: 1620–1840,* ed. R. Elphick and H. Giliomee, (Cape Town, 1989).

Arkin, Marcus, ed. *South African Jewry: A Contemporary Survey.* Cape Town: Oxford University Press, 1984.

Arkin, A. J., K. P. Magyar and G. J. Pillay, eds. *The Indian South Africans: A Contemporary Profile.* Durban: Owen Burgess, 1989.

Asmal, K. "Apartheid and Terrorism: The Case of Southern Africa" in *Terrorism and National Liberation,* ed. H. Kochler and P. Lang. Frankfurt, Bonn, New York, 1987.

Ayegboyin, Deji and S. Ademola Ishola. *African Indigenous Churches.* Lagos, Nigeria: Greater Heights, 1997.

Balia, Daryl M. *Black Methodists and White Supremacy in South Africa.* Madiba Publications, 1991.

Barclay, William. *The Gospel of Mark* revised edition. Philadelphia: The Westminster Press, 1975.

Barrett, David B. et al. *World Christianity Encyclopedia.* 2nd ed. New York: Oxford University Press, 2001.

Bediako, Kwame, *Christianity in Africa: The Renewal of a Non-Western Religion,* Edinburgh: Edinburgh University Press, 1995.

Benson, M. *South Africa: The Struggle for a Birthright.* London, 1966.

Biko, Steve. "Black Consciousness and the Quest for a True Humanity" in ed. B. Moore. *Black Theology.* London, 1973.

Boesak, Allan A. *If this is Treason, I am Guilty.* Grand Rapids: William B. Eerdmans, 1987.

———. "Your Days are Over!" in *Crucible of Fire: The Church Confronts Apartheid.* Jim Wallis and Joyce Hollyday, eds. Grand Rapids: William Eerdmans, 1986.

Boesak, Willa, *God's Wrathful Children: Political Oppression and Christian Ethics,* Grand Rapids, Michigan: William B. Eerdmans Publishing Company, 1995.

————. "The Significance of June 16" in *Dunamis: Witness for the Struggle for a Relevant Church,* (4th quart. 1987).

Bohannan, Paul and Philip Curtin, *Africa & Africans,* Prospect Heights, Illinois: Waveland Press, Inc., 1995.

Borer, Tristan Anne. *Challenging the State: Churches as Political Actors in South Africa 1980–1994.* Notre Dame, Indiana: University of Notre Dame Press, 1998.

Bosch, David J. "Nothing But a Heresy" in *Apartheid is a Heresy,* ed. John de Gruchy and Charles Villa-Vicencio. Claremont, Surrey, 1983.

————. *Transforming Mission: Paradigm Shifts in Theology of Mission* Maryknoll, New York: Orbis Books, 1991.

Botman, H. Russell. "The Offender and the Church" in eds. James Cochrane, John de Gruchy, and Stephen Martin, *Facing the Truth: South African Faith Communities and the Truth and Reconciliation Commission* Cape Town: David Philip Publishers, 1999.

Bozzoli, B. and P. Delius. "Radical History and South African Society" in *Radical History Review: History from South Africa 46/7,* ed. J. Brown et al. New York, 1960.

Bradlow, Frank R. and Margaret Cairns. *The Early Cape Muslims.* Cape Town: A. A. Balkema, 1978.

Bredekamp, H. "The Origin of the Southern African Khoisan Communities" in *An Illustrated History of South Africa,* T. Cameron and S. Spies, eds. Johannesburg, 1986.

————. "From Fragile Independence to Permanent Subservience: 1488–1713" in *An Illustrated History of South Africa,* T. Cameron and S. Spies, eds. Johannesburg, 1986.

Brown, W. E. *The Catholic Church in South Africa, from its Origins to the Present Day.* London: Burns & Oates, 1960.

Brueggemann, Walter. *The Prophetic Imagination.* Philadelphia: Fortress Press, 1978.

Buhlmann, Walbert. *The Coming of the Third Church.* Slough, U.K: St. Paul, 1976.

Bultman, Rudolf. *Jesus Christ and Mythology.* New York: Charles Scribner's Sons Publishing, 1958.

Buthelezi, M. "Violence and the Cross in South Africa." *Journal of Theology for Southern Africa* no. 29 (December, 1979).

Buttrick, David. *Homiletic: Moves and Structures* Philadelphia: Fortress Press, 1987.

Cahill, Thomas. *The Gifts of the Jews: How a Tribe of Desert Nomads Changed the Way Everyone Thinks and Feels.* New York: Nan A. Talese Publishing Group, Inc., 1998.

Castellio, Sebastian. *Conseil à la France Désolée* (1562, reprint in 1967).

Colson, Charles W. *Loving God* Grand Rapid, Michigan: Zondervan Publishing House, 1983.

Comaroff, Jean and John. *Of Revelation and Revolution: Christianity, Colonialism, and Consciousness in South Africa* Chicago: University of Chicago Press, 1991.

————. *Of Revelation and Revolution: the Dialectics of Modernity on a South African Frontier* Chicago: University of Chicago Press, 1997.

Coward, Harold. *Plurality: Challenge to World Religions.* Maryknoll, New York: Orbis Books, 1985.

Chazan, Naomi et. al. *Politics and Society in Contemporary Africa,* 3rd ed. Boulder, Colorado: Lynne Rienner Publishers, Inc., 1999.

Chidester, David. *Religions in South Africa.* London and New York: Routledge, 1992.

————. "Stories, Fragments and Monuments" in James Cochrane, John de Gruchy and Stephen Martin, eds. *Facing the Truth: South African Faith Communities and the Truth and Reconciliation Commission.* Cape Town: David Philip Publishers, 1999.

Cochrane, James. *Servants of Power: The Roles of English-Speaking Churches in South Africa 1903–1930.* Johannesburg: Ravan Press, 1987.

Cochrane, James, John de Gruchy, and Stephen Martin, eds. *Facing the Truth: South African Faith Communities and the Truth and Reconciliation Commission.* Cape Town: David Philip Publishers, 1999.

Cochrane, J. "Nation Building: A Socio-theological View" in W. Vorster, ed. *Building a New Nation: The Quest for a New South Africa,* The Business Section of UNISA, Pretoria, 1991.

Cochrane, James R. "Religion in Civil Society: Readings from South African Case" in James R. Cochrane and Bestienne Klein, eds. *Sameness and Difference: Problems and Potentials in South African Civil Society.* South African Philosophical Studies, I: The Cultural Heritage and Contemporary Change Series II, Africa, Vol. 6. Washington, D.C.: The Council for Research in Values and Philosophy, 2000.

Colvin, Tom. *Ghana Folk Song CHEREPONI* with harmony by Charles H. Webb in 1988 Hope Publishing Co., 1989.

Cox, Harvey. *Fire from Heaven: The Rise of Pentecostal Spirituality and the Reshaping of Religion in the Twenty-First Century.* New York: Addison-Wesley Publishing Company, 1995.

Creel, Margaret Washington. "Gullah Attitudes toward Life and Death" in Joseph E. Holloway, ed. *Africanisms in American Culture.* Bloomington, Indiana: Indiana University Press, 1990.

Cronje, J. M. *Born to Witness: A Concise History of the Churches Born out of the Mission Work of the Dutch Reformed Church of South Africa.* Pretoria, 1982.

Curtin, Philip D. *The Image of Africa: British Ideas and Actions, 1780–1850* Madison, Wisconsin: University of Wisconsin Press, 1964.

———. *The Atlantic Slave Trade: A Census* Madison: University of Wisconsin Press, 1969.

Davids, Archmat. *Mosques of the Bo-Kaap.* Cape Town: South African Institute of Arabic and Islamic Research, 1980.

Davidson, Basil. *The African Slave Trade.* Atlantic-Little Brown, 1961.

D'Costa, Gavin. *Theology and Religious Pluralism,* New York: Basil Blackwell Inc., 1986.

De Gruchy, John W. *The Church Struggle in South Africa.* Grand Rapids: Eerdmans and Cape Town: David Philip, 1986.

De Gruchy, eds. *Living Faiths in South Africa.* Cape Town and Johannesburg: David Philip, 1995.

De Gruchy, John W. and Martin Prozesky, eds. *A Southern African Guide to World Religions.* Cape Town: David Philip, 1991.

De Gruchy, John W. *Christianity and Democracy.* Cape Town and Johannesburg: David Philip, Cambridge University Press, 1995.

———. "The Revitalization of Calvinism in South Africa: Some Reflections on Christian Belief, Theology and Social Transformation." *Journal of Religious Ethics* 14, no. 1, (Spring, 1986).

———. The London Missionary Society in Southern Africa, 1799–1999 Athens: Ohio University Press, 2000.

Dickson, Kwesi, A. and Paul Ellingworth, eds. *Biblical Revelation and African Beliefs,* Maryknoll, New York: Orbis Books, 1969.

Dubow, S. *Racial Segregation and the Origins of Apartheid in South Africa: 1919–1936.* Oxford, 1989.

Duncan, S. "The Right to Land: An Unresolved Dispute" in *Challenge: Church and People,* no. 5. (April, 1992).

Du Toit, Cornel. "Blessed are the Powerful: Christian Righteousness and the Retribution of Power" in *Religion and the Reconstruction of Civil Society,* John W. de Gruchy and S. Martin, eds. Pretoria: University of South Africa, 1995.

Echeruo, Michael J. C. "An African Diaspora: The Ontological Project" in Isidore Okpewho, Carol Boyce Davis and Ali A. Mazrui, eds. *African Diaspora: African Origins and New World Identities* Bloomington, Indiana: Indiana University Press, 1999.

Ellis, Marc H. *Unholy Alliance: Religion and Atrocity in our Time* Minneapolis, Minnesota: Fortress Press, 1997.

————. *Revolutionary Forgiveness: Essays on Judaism, Christianity, and the Future of Religious Life* Waco, Texas: Baylor University Press, 2000.

————. *Out of the Ashes: The Search for Jewish Identity in the Twenty-First Century* London: Pluto Press, 2002.

————. *O, Jerusalem! The Contested Future of the Jewish Covenant* Minneapolis, Minnesota: Fortress Press, 1999.

————. *Practicing Exile: The Religious Odyssey of an American Jew* Minneapolis, Minnesota: Fortress Press, 2002.

Esposito, John L. Darrell J. Fasching, and Todd Lewis. *World Religions Today* New York: Oxford University Press, 2002.

Everett, Susanne. *History of Slavery* Secaucus, New Jersey: Chartwell Books, Inc., 1991.

Fage, J. D. *A History of Africa.* (4th ed.) London: Routledge, 2002.

Foster, John. *Beginning From Jerusalem: Christian Expansion through Seventeen Centuries.* New York: Association Press, 1956.

Frawley, David. "The Missionary Position, BPJ: News Reports" online at http:www.bjp.org/news/feb1799.htm.

Frazier, E. Franklin. *The Negro Church in America.* Boston: 1963.

Gifford, Paul, *African Christianity: Its Public Role,* Bloomington: Indiana University Press, 1998.

Goba, Bonganjalo. "The Role of the Black Church in the Process of Healing Human Brokenness" in *Journal of Theology for Southern Afric,* no 28 (September, 1979).

————. "Doing Theology in South Africa" in *Journal of Theology for Southern Africa,* no 31 (June, 1980).

————. "The Role of Religion in Promoting Democratic Values in a Post-apartheid Era" in John De Gruchy and S. Martin, eds. *Religion and the Reconstruction of Civil Society.* Pretoria: University of South Africa, 1995.

Gonzáles, Justo L. *Out of Every Tribe and Nation: Christian Theology at the Ethnic Roundtable* Nashville, Tennessee: Abingdon Press, 1992.

Graybill, Lyn S. *Truth and Reconciliation in South Africa: Miracle of Model?* Boulder, Colorado: Lynne Rienner Publishers, 2001.

Gutiérrez, Gustavo. *A Theology of Liberation* Maryknoll, New York: Orbis Books, 1973.

Hankins, Barry. *Uneasy in Babylon: Southern Baptist Conservatives and American Culture.* Tuscaloosa, Alabama: The University of Alabama Press, 2002.

Hartshorne, Charles. *The Divine Relativity: A Social Conception of God* New Haven: Yale University Press, 1948.

Heim, S. Mark. *The Depth of the Riches: A Trinitarian Theology of Religions Ends,* Grand Rapids, Michigan: Eerdmans Publishing Company, 2001.

Hellig, Jocelyn. "The Jewish Community in South Africa" in De Gruchy, John W. and Martin Prozesky, eds. *A Southern African Guide to World Religions.* Cape Town: David Philip, 1991.

Hendriks, Jurgens and Johannes Erasmus. "Religious Population in South Africa" in *Journal of Theology for Southern Africa.* Vol. 109. (March, 2001).

Herrman, Louis. *A History of the Jews in South Africa.* London: Gollancz, 1935.

Herskovits, Melville J. *The Myth of the Negro Past* Boston: Beacon Press, 1958.

Hewitt, G. *The Problems of Success: A History of the Church Missionary Society, 1910–1942.* London, 1971.

Heyns, J. "The Religious-Ethical Foundation for a New South Africa" in *The Southern African Policy Forum: Third Conference of The Aspen Institute,* ed. D. Clarke, (April, 12-15, 1990).

Hick, John. *An Interpretation of Religion,* New Haven: Yale University Press, 1989.

————. *Problems of Religious Pluralism* London: McMillan Press,1985.

————. "Religious Pluralism and Salvation" in *Faith and Philosophy* Vol. 5 no. 4 (October, 1988).

————. *God and the Universe of Faith* London: McMillan Press, 1973.

Hinchliff, Peter. *The Church in South Africa*. London: SPCK, 1968.

Hoedemaker, Bert. *Secularization and Mission: A Theological Essay*. Harrisburg, PA: Trinity Press International, 1998.

Hoffmann, Gerhard, "The Crisis in World Mission: An Issue of Death or of Life," trans. W. J. Hollenweger, Berlin, Germany: German Evangelical Missionary Council, 1970.

Holloway, Joseph E. "The Origins of African-American Culture" in Joseph E. Holloway, ed. *Africanisms in American Culture* Bloomington, Indiana: Indiana University Press, 1990.

Huckaby, P. "The Black Identity Crisis." Theology Today 24, no 4 (January, 1968).

Idowu, E. Bolaji. *Olodumare: God in Yoruba Beliefs*. London: Oxford University Press, 1969.

Isichei, Elizabeth. *A History of Christianity in Africa*. Grand Rapids, MI: Eerdmans, 1995.

Jacottet, E. "Paper on the Native Churches and Their Organization." *Report of the Proceedings of the First General Missionary Conference Held in Johannesburg, 13-20 July, 1904*. (Johannesburg, 1905).

Jenkins, Philip. *Hidden Gospels: How the Search for Jesus Lost its Ways,* Oxford: Oxford University Press, 2001.

————. *The Next Christendom: The Coming of Global Christianity* Oxford: Oxford University Press, 2002.

Johnson, Paul. *A History of the Jews* New York: Haper & Row Publishers, 1987.

Kastfelt, Niels. Religion and Politics in Nigeria: A Study in Middle Belt Christianity. London: British Academic Press, 1994.

Kato, Byang H. *Theological Pitfalls in Africa,* Nairobi, Kenya: Evangel Publishing House, 1974.

Keck, Leander E. *The Church Confident: Christianity Can Repent, but It Must Not Whimper* Nashville, Tennessee: Abingdon Press, 1993.

Kerr, Hugh T. ed. *Reading in Christian Thought,* Nashville, Tennessee: Abingdon, 1966.

Kerson, R. "The Emergence of Powerful Black Unions" in *The Anti-apartheid Reader: The Struggle against White Racist Rule in South Africa,* D. Mermelstein, ed. New York, 1987.

Kinghorn, J. "Modernization and Apartheid: The Afrikaner Churches" in R. Elphick and R. Davenport, ed. *Christianity in South Africa.* (no dates): 135–154.

Kirwen, Michael. *The Missionary and the Diviner* Maryknoll, New York: Orbis Books, 1986.

Kitshoff, M. C. *African Independent Churches Today* Lewiston, N.Y: Edwin Mellen, 1996.

Knitter, Paul. *One Earth Many Religions: Multifaith Dialogue and Global Responsibility* Maryknoll, New York: Orbis Books, 1995.

Kraemer, Hendrik. *The Christian Message in a non-Christian World* New York: Harper and Brothers, 1938.

Kretzschmar, Louise. *Privatization of the Christian Faith: Mission, Social Ethics and the South African Baptists.* Legon, Ghana: Theological Studies Series, 1998.

Kriegger, David. "Conversion: On the Possibility of Global Thinking in an age of Particularism" in *Journal of the American Academy of Religion* 58 (1990).

Kuhn, Thomas S. *The Copernican Revolution: Planetary Astronomy in the Development of Western Thought* Cambridge, Massachusetts: Harvard University Press, 1985.

Kunnie, J. "Christianity, Black Theology, and Liberating Faith" in *The Unquestionable Right to be Free: Essays in Black Theology,* I. Mosala and B. Tlhagale, eds. (Johannnesburg, 1986).

Kuper, L. *Passive Resistance in South Africa.* London, 1956.

Lapide, Pinchus. *The Resurrection of Jesus: A Jewish Perspective* S.P.C.K., 1984.

Legum, Colin, *Africa Since Independence,* Bloomington: Indiana University Press, 1999.

Lincoln, C. Eric and Lawrence H. Mamiya. *The Black Church in the African American Experience.* Durham: Duke University Press, 1990.

Lincoln, C. Eric ed. *The Black Experience in Religion: A Book of Readings.* Garden City, New York: Anchor Books, 1974.

Macquarrie, John. "The Keystone of Christian Faith" in *If Christ Be not Risen: Essays in Resurrection and Survival,* John Greenhalgh and Elizabeth Russell eds. San Francisco, California: Collins Liturgical, 1986.

Maggs, T. "Towards a Theology of Humanization." *Journal of Theology for Southern Africa,* no. 41, (December, 1982.

Majeke, Nosipho. *The Role of the Missionaries in Conquest.* Johannesburg: Society of Young Africa, 1952.

Makhubu, Paul, *Who are the Independent Churches?* Johannesburg: Skotaville Publishers, 1988.

Malherbe, V. "The Khoi Captains in the Third Frontier War" in *The KhoiKhoi Rebellion in the Eastern Cape 1799–1803)* S. Newton-King and V. Malherbe, eds. Centre for African Studies, Communications no. 5 (Cape Town, 1984).

Mark, S. "Khoisan Resistance to the Dutch in the Seventeenth and Eighteenth Centuries" *Journal of African History* 13, no. 1, (Cambridge, 1972).

Maxwell, David. "Historicizing Christian Independency: The Southern African Pentecostal Movement (1908–1960)" in *The Journal of African History.* Vol. 40 No. 2 (1999): 243–264.

Maylam, Paul. *A History of the African People of South Africa: From the Early Iron Age to the 1970s.* Cape Town: David Philip, 1986.

Mays, James L. *Harper's Bible Commentary* HarperSanFrancisco, 1988.

Mazrui, Ali A. *Cultural Forces in World Politics,* London: James Currey and Nairobi, Kenya: Heinemann, 1990.

————.*The Africans: A Triple Heritage,* Boston: Little Brown and Company, 1986.

Mbali, Zolile. *The Churches and Racism: A Black South African Perspective.* London: SCM Press, 1987.

Mbiti, John S. *Introduction to African Religion.* 2nd rev. ed. Portsmouth, NH: Heinemann Educational, 1991.

————. *Bible and Theology in African Christianity.* Nairobi, Kenya: Oxford University Press, 1986.

————. *African Religions and Philosophy.* London: Heinemann, 1969

————. "Christianity and East African Culture and Religion." *Dini na Mila* 3, no. 1 (May, 1968).

————. "Theological Impotence and the Universality of the Church" in *Lutheran World*: Vol. 21 no. 3. (1974).

McGeary, Johanna. "Death Stalks a Continent" in *Time Magazine* (February 12, 2001).

Mill, John Stuart. *On Liberty.* Garden City, NY: Dolphin Books, 1961.

Mofokeng, T. "The Cross in Search of Humanity." *Journal of Black Theology in South Africa* 3, no. 2, (November 1989).

Moosa, Ebrahim. "Islam in South Africa" in Martin Prozesky and John deGruchy, eds. *Living Faiths in South Africa.* Cape Town: David Philip, 1995.

Mortensen, Viggo ed. *Theology and the Religious: A Dialogue* Grand Rapids, Michigan: William B. Eerdmans Publishing Company, 2003.

Mosala, I. "The Relevance of African Independent Churches and Their Challenge to Black Theology" in *The Unquestionable Right to be Free: Essays in Black Theology,* I. Mosala and B. Tlhagale, eds. (Johannesburg, 1986).

————. "The Meaning of Reconciliation." *Journal of Theology for Southern Africa,* no. 59, (June 1987).

Mosoma, D. "Black Power and Justice" in *Journal of Black Theology in South Africa,* Vol. 6, no. 1 (May, 1992).

————. "Restitution/Reparation: A Commitment to Justice and Peace." Journal of Black Theology in South Africa 5, no 1 (May, 1991).

M'Passou, Denis Basil. *History of African Independent Churches in Southern Africa.* 1892–1992 Mulanje, Malawi: Spot, 1994.

Mudimbe, V. Y. *The Invention of Africa: Gnosis, Philosophy, and the Order of Knowledge* Bloomington & Indianapolis: Indiana University Press, 1988.

Mugambi, J. N. Kanyua, ed. *Critiques of Christianity in African Literature* Nairobi, Kenya: East African Educational Publishers, 1992.

Musopole, A. C. "Needed: A Theology Cooked in an African Pot" in K. Fiedler, K. P. Gundani, and H. Mijoga, eds. *Theology Cooked in an African Pot.* Malawi: Assemblies of God Press, 1998 (7. ATISCA Bulletin 5/6, 1996/7).

Mussner, Franz. *Tractate on the Jews: The Significance of Judaism for Christian Faith* (trans. Philadelphis, 1984).

Neusner, Jacob. *Self-Fulfilling Prophesy: Exile and Return in the History of Judaism* Beacon Press, 1987.

Ngubane, J. "Theological Roots of the African Independent Churches" in *The Unquestionable Right to be Free: Essays in Black Theology,* I. Mosala and B. Tlhagale, eds. (Johannesburg, 1986).

Niebuhr, Reinhold. *The Nature and Destiny of Man* New York: Charles Scribner's Sons, 1964.

Nyamiti, Charles. *Christ as Our Ancestor: Christology from an African Perspective,* Gweru, Zimbabwe: Mambo Press, 1984.

————. "African Christologies Today" in *Faces of Jesus in Africa.* Robert J. Schreiter, ed. Maryknoll, New York: Orbis Books, 1991.

Okorocha, Cyril C. *The Meaning of Religious Conversion in Africa* London: Avebury, 1987.

Okpewho, Isidore, Carole Boyce Davies and Ali A. Mazrui, eds. *The African Diaspora: African Origins and New World Identities.* Bloomington & Indianapolis: Indiana University Press, 1999.

Oladipo, Caleb Oluremi. *The Development of the Doctrine of the Holy Spirit in the Yoruba (African) Indigenous Christian Movement.* New York: Peter Lang Publishing Company, 1996.

————. "Piety and Politics in African Christianity: The Roles of the Church and the Democratization Process." *Journal of Church and State* Vol. 45 No. 2 (Spring, 2003): 325–348.

————. "An Epistemological Defense of Religious Tolerance: Faith, Citizenship, and Crises of Religious and Cultural Identities in Post-Western Missionary Africa." *Philosophia Africana* Vol. 8 No. 1 (March, 2005): 21–35

Orlinsky, H. M. "The Tribal System of Israel and Related Groups in the Period of Judges," in *Oriens Antiquus,* 1 (1962).

Parrinder, Geoffrey. *Religion in Africa* Middlesex, England: Penguin, 1969.

Parsons, Robert T. *Religion in an African Society* Leiden: E. J. Brill, 1964.

Pascal, Blaise. *Pensees* translated by A. J. Krailsheimer New York: Penguin Classic, 1966.

Pelikan, Jaroslav. *The Vindication of Tradition.* The 1983 Jefferson Lecture in the Humanities. New Haven and London: Yale University Press, 1984.

Pénoukou, Efoé Julien. "Christology in the Village" in *Faces of Jesus in Africa,* Robert J. Schreiter, ed. Maryknoll, New York: Orbis Books, 1991.

Petersen, Robin. "The AICs and the TRC: Resistance Redefined" in eds. James Cochrane, John de Gruchy and Stephen Martin. *Facing the Truth: South African Faith Communities and the Truth and Reconciliation Commission.* Cape Town: David Philip Publishers, 1999.

Prozesky, Martin (ed.) *Christianity in South Africa.* London: Macmillan, 1990.

Prozesky, Martin and John de Gruchy, eds. *Living Faiths in South Africa.* Cape Town and Johannesburg: David Philip, 1995.

Quarles, Benjamin. *The Negro in the Making of America.* New York: Collier Books, 1969.

Race, Alan. *Christian and Religious Pluralism: Patterns in the Christian Theology of Religions,* London: SCM Press, 1993.

Radin, Paul. "Status, Phantasy, and the Christian Dogma" in *God Struck Me Dead: Religious Conversion Experience and Autobiographies of Negro Ex-Slaves.* Nashville, Tenn: Social Science Institute, Fisk University, 1945.

Reat, N. Ross and Edmund F. Perry. *A World Theology: The Central Spirituality of Humankind.* Cambridge: Cambridge University Press, 1991.

Regehr, Ernie. *Perceptions of Apartheid: The Churches and Political Change in South Africa.* Herald: Scottdale, 1979.

Sanders, E. P. *The Historical Figure of Jesus* Middlesex, England: Allen Lane-The Penguin Press, 1993.

Sanneh, Lamin. *West Africa Christianity: The Religious Impact.* London: C. Hurst, 1983.

———. *Translating the Message: the Missionary impact on Culture* Maryknoll, N.Y.: Orbis Books, 1989.

———. *Encountering the West, Christianity and the Global Cultural Process: The African Dimension,* Maryknoll, New York: Orbis Books, 1993.

———. *Abolitionists Abroad: American Blacks and the Making of Modern West Africa.* Cambridge, Massachusetts: Harvard University Press, 1999.

Saron, Gustav and Louis Hotz, eds. *The Jews in South Africa: A History.* Cape Town: Oxford University Press, 1955.

Schärf, W. "The Resurgence of Urban Street Gangs and Community Responses in Cape Town During the Late Eighties" in *Towards Justice?: Crime and State Control in South Africa,* D. Hansson and D. Van Zyl Smit, eds. (Cape Town, 1990).

Schreiter, Robert J. ed. *Faces of Jesus in Africa,* Maryknoll, New York: Orbis Books, 1991.

Sebidi, L. "Towards an Understanding of the Current Unrest of South Africa" in *Hammering Swords into Ploughshares: Essays in Honour of Archbishop Desmond Mpilo Tutu,* B. Tlhagale and I. Mosala, eds. (Johannesburg, 1986).

Shell, Ellen Ruppel. "Resurgence of a Deadly Disease" in *The Atlantic Monthly* (August, 1997).

Shimoni, Gideon. *Jews and Zionism: The South African Experience, 1910–1967.* Cape Town: Oxford University Press, 1980.

Sibley, James L. and D. Westermann. *Liberia Old and New* London: James Clark, 1928.

Soskice, Janet Martin. *Metaphor and Religious Language.* Oxford: Clarendon Press, 1985.

Smith, Huston. *The World's Religions.* New York: Harper Collins Publishers, 1991.

Smith, Mark S. *The Early History of God: Yahweh and the Other Deities in Ancient Israel* New York: Harper Collins Publishers, 1990.

Smith, Wilfred Cantwell. *The Meaning and End of Religion* Minneapolis, Minnesota: Fortress Press, 1991.

Spong, John Shelby. *Resurrection Myth or Reality? A Bishop's Search for the Origins of Christianity.* San Francisco: Harper Collins Publishers, 1994.

Stanley, Brian. "Conversion to Christianity: The Colonization of the Mind" A paper presented at the Yale-Edinburgh Conference on the History of Missions and Christianity in the non-Western world" At the University of Edinburgh, Scotland, 2002.

Stendahl, Krister. "Notes for Three Bible Studies." in G. H. Anderson and T. F. Stransky, eds. *Christ's Lordship and religious Pluralism.* Maryknoll, New York: Orbis Books, 1985.

Stock, E. ed. *The History of the Church Missionary Society: Its Environment, Its Men and Its Works.* Vol. I. London, 1899.

Stutley, Margaret. *Shamanism: An Introduction.* New York: Routledge Taylor and Francis Group, 2003.

Sundkler, B. G. M. *Bantu Prophets in South Africa.* Cape Town: Oxford University Press, 1961.

Sundkler, Bengt and Christopher Steed, *A History of the Church in Africa.* Cambridge University Press, 2000.

Temples, Placinde. *Bantu Philosophy,* translated from French by Colin King. Paris: Presence Africaine, 1959.

Thangaraj, M. Thomas. *The Common Task: A Theology of Christian Mission.* Nashville, Tennessee: Abingdon Press, 1999.

Thiong'o, Ngugi wa. *The River Between* London: Heinemann, 1965.

Thomas, David. *Christ Divided: Liberalism, Ecumenism and Race in South Africa.* Pretoria: University of South Africa, 2002.

Thompson, Leonard, *A History of South Africa.* New Haven: Yale University Press, 1995.

Thornton, John K. *The Kongolese Saint Anthony.* New York: Cambridge University Press, 1998.

Troeger, Thomas H. *Borrowed Light: Hymn Texts, Prayers, and Poems.* New York: Oxford University Press, 1994.

———. "Solid Meanings Fold: The Terror of Resurrection" *Keynote address at the 2004 Worship and Preaching Conference.* Baptist Theological Seminary at Richmond, 2004.

Tutu, Desmond Mpilo, *No Future Without Forgiveness.* New York: Doubleday, 1999.

———. *The Rainbow People of God: South Africa's Victory Over Apartheid.* New York: Doubleday, 1994.

———. *Crying in the Wilderness: The Struggle for Justice in South Africa.* London: Mowbray, 1990.

Usry, Glenn and Craig S. Keener. *Black Man's Religion: Can Christianity be Afrocentric?* Downers Grove, Illinois: InterVarsity Press, 1996.

Villa-Vicencio, Charles. *Trapped in Apartheid: A Socio-Theological History of the English-Speaking Churches.* New York: Orbis Books and Cape Town: David Philip, 1988.

———. *A Theology of Reconstruction: A Nation Building and Human Rights.* Cambridge: CUP, 1992.

———. ed. *On Reading Karl Barth in South Africa.* Grand Rapids, Michigan: William B. Eerdmans Publishing Company, 1988.

———. "Mission Christianity" in Martin Prozesky and John de Gruchy, eds. *Living Faiths in South Africa.* Cape Town and Johannesburg: David Philip, 1995.

———. "Some Refused to Pray: The Moral Impasse of the English-Speaking Churches" in *When Prayer Makes News.* Allan A. Bocsak and Charles Villa-Vicencio, eds. Philadelphia: Westminster Press, 1986.

Viswanathan, Gauri. *Outside the Fold: Conversion, Modernity, and Belief.* Princeton, New Jersey: Princeton University Press, 1998.

Walls, Andrew F. *The Significance of Christianity in Africa.* Edinburgh, Scotland: The Church of Scotland, St. Colm's Education Centre and College, 1989.

———. *The Missionary Movement in Christian History: Studies in the Transmission of Faith.* New York: Orbis Books, 1996.

Walshe, P. "The Rise of African Nationalism in South Africa" in *The African National Congress, 1912–1952.* London, 1970.

Ward, Keith. "Truth and Diversity of Religions" *Religious Studies* Vol. 26 no. 1 (March, 1990).

Warner-Lewis, Maureen. "Cultural Reconfigurations in the African Caribbean" in Isidore Okpewho, Carole Boyce Davies, and Ali Mazrui, eds. *The African Diaspora: African Origins and New World Identities.* Bloomington, Indiana: Indiana University press, 1999.

Waruta, Douglass W. "Who is Jesus Christ for Africa Today? Prophet, Priest, Potentate" in Robert J. Schreiter, ed. *Faces of Jesus in Africa.* New York: Orbis Books, 1991.

———. "Celebrating Christ: The Hope of Africa" in *All Africa Baptist Theological Educators' Conference: African Baptist Theology and Identity* (Ibadan, Nigeria: Oritamefa Baptist Church and Africa Exchange Resource Center).

Wheatcroft, Andrew. *Infidels: The Conflict Between Christendom and Islam 638–2002.* London: Viking Penguin Books, 2002.

Wuthnow, Robert. *Christianity in the Twenty-First Century.* New York: Oxford University Press, 1993.

Young, Henry J. *Major Black Religious Leaders: 1755–1940.* Nashville, Tenn: Abingdon Press, 1977.

❇ INDEX